To Anne and Bob,

Best wishes always to two good friends, and with special appreciation for all that you did and still do for me, Anne.

Richard P. deis Brien
University of Notre Dame
May 13, 1992

Report on the Church

Other Books by Richard P. McBrien

Caesar's Coin: Religion and Politics in America
Catholicism, Volumes I and II
Catholicism: Study Edition
Church: The Continuing Quest
Do We Need the Church?
Ministry: A Theological, Pastoral Handbook
The Remaking of the Church

REPORT ON THE CHURCH

Catholicism After Vatican II

Richard P. McBrien

HarperSanFrancisco
A Division of HarperCollins*Publishers*

FIRST EDITION

Library of Congress Cataloging-in-Publication Data

McBrien, Richard P.
    Report on the Church : Catholicism after Vatican II / Richard P. McBrien.
        p.   cm.
    Includes bibliographical references.
    ISBN 0–06–065336–1 (alk. paper.)
    1. Catholic Church—History—1965–I. Title.
BX1390.M48   1992
282'.09'045—dc20   91–50498
                                                                                      CIP

92 93 94 95 96 RRD(H) 10 9 8 7 6 5 4 3 2 1

This edition is printed on acid-free paper that meets the American National Standards Institute Z39.48 Standard.

In grateful memory of

John Francis Whealon
Archbishop of Hartford (1969–1991)

for his steadfast support

Contents

Foreword

By Martin E. Marty

Parents of today's high schoolers, not merely the students themselves, do not have memories of the Catholic ways of life pre–Vatican II. A great divide exists between those who had an adult experience of Catholicism before 1958, when Pope John XXIII acceded, and those who came to realize the world around themselves during and after the council he opened in 1962.

The older generation includes at least three sorts of people. First, there are those who live with what I call the "Phil Donahue syndrome" (after the television host). They were children in a Church whose legalistic side alone reached them (or which they conveniently find having done so). They had not yet grown to see the more tender mercies of priests, nuns, laity. They spend their subsequent lives in a perpetual tantrum of rejection based on caricature.

On the other hand are the nostalgics who yearn for a Church that never was in a world they now invent. A Golden Age (which was really yellow). They adopt Muggeridgean and Waughian curmudgeonly postures and grump their way faithlessly through the end of the millennium.

Richard McBrien seems called to address them both, while most of the people in these two camps prefer to huddle together and do their whingeing with their backs turned to each other and the future. But McBrien's real calling is to the third sort: the majority of the survivors of mid-century Catholicism and their children. These are people who are and want to be called Catholic, who love Christ the Head and would love the Church that is Christ's Body— even when the custodians of that Church make it hard. These communicants have lives to live, problems to solve, hopes to realize, decisions to make, occasions to celebrate. They are often patient when the Church mishears them but refuse to be silent when they believe that its leadership, and, for that matter, the followership, mishears the Gospel and the best of the tradition.

Not that McBrien, who has a life to live, problems to solve, hopes to realize, decisions to make, and occasions to celebrate, is above their struggle, carrying credentials with which he can condescend to them. He is part of the leadership and followership who does his own mishearing and misrepresenting. Infallibility, alas, has not yet reached the hierarchy of weekly columnists. Instead, as this book shows, we get to partake of McBrien's own pathmaking through the mazeways of postconciliar life. Some of his clearings work for us readers, and others only suggest how clearings are to be made.

I have some confidence commending Richard McBrien to a book readership. First, for several years we were the "M & M" team who did the Catholic-Protestant editing for the jillion-word *Encyclopedia of Religion*. Earning seven or eight cents per hour—encyclopedia work being the only job paying less than weekly column writing—we consoled ourselves by learning a good deal about the subjects and each other's approach to them. One can intimately appraise someone who is appraising topics and authors on the vast subject of Christianity.

McBrien wore and wears well. I decided then that he is not a "theologians' theologian." The Church has many of them, including several very good ones. He respects the highly technical practitioners and learns from them, but while fashioning his own theology, he chooses to mediate their work to the larger Church and world. He also capably carries report from those spheres back to the generating centers, such as the theology department at the University of Notre Dame, which for some years he has headed.

The other McBrien for whom I feel empathy and whom I can size up is the columnist, whose columnar work you will find in this book. Having been in the weekly column business for a third of a century, I have watched with and talked to many colleagues. If one is assigned the task of bringing a lighter touch, of allowing for some irony, or even for that most hopeful form of literature (because it assumes the world can be changed), satire, a strange thing happens. The columnist creates a double who seems to sit a foot away from the real person. This creation uses the word *I* more than is appropriate in academic discourse. He or she has to be vulnerable, both emotionally and because in short column space it is impossible to protect all fronts, or one's own rear. Thus one survives.

Richard McBrien has not learned how to do that creating. The same priest and theologian and department head and sinner and celebrant that you get in class or pulpit or on a walk is the one who writes these columns. There is no zone of protection, no shield, no alter ego to take the darts while the author takes the bows. That is why I think this book of columns should be taken so seriously as a coherent whole.

The excitement of this "whole" results in part from the fact that the columns were written over a 25-year period. McBrien displays the Irish equivalent of chutzpah in presenting, unrevised, some writings dated from 1966 to the present. What could seem to be a liability of the book turns into its asset. Here there is no chance for revision or revisionism: the vision of 1966, 1976, and 1986, born of participation in events that were occurring at white-heat temperatures, is the one we here revisit.

This means that the senior generation of readers and the younger ones as well can get a sense of closeness, of being involved with the unfolding of the post–Vatican II Church. I especially enjoyed McBrien's sizing up of personalities, both in the columns devoted to doing just that and in the ones where such personalities just show up as instigators or interpreters of events and trends.

One rule about forewording of books is that the foreword writer not spill the contents in advance. Here, dusted off from diocesan papers, out of old files and archives and library depositories, are samplings of comment through the years. Here is Catholic history in the making in the form of "Essays in Theology" essayed while that theology is developing before our eyes. Here is a path, pitted and pocked, but still a path, through the maze. And a wide and clear one it is.

Introduction

The period covered by this "Report on the Church" represents only a thin slice of Catholic history. What is 25 years against Catholicism's nearly 2,000 years of existence?

To be sure, many sectarian Protestants would "protest" that latter figure. For them, Catholicism did not begin until after the so-called Edict of Milan in 313 when the Emperor Constantine granted favored status to the Church; the Catholic Church, in sectarian eyes, is a post-Constantinian phenomenon. For some mainline Protestants, on the other hand, Catholicism didn't begin until after the Reformation; it is essentially a Counter-Reformation phenomenon.

But even a theologian as "liberal" as Hans Küng has disputed these assumptions (see, for example, his *Structures of the Church* [New York: Crossroad, 1982]). He and many other scholars—Catholic and Protestant alike— have argued with some force that so-called early Catholicism existed already in the New Testament, as attested especially by Matthew's Gospel and the Pastoral Epistles (1 and 2 Timothy, and Titus).

Catholicism has been extraordinarily dynamic over the course of its 2,000-year history. The first mistake people (including Catholics themselves) tend to make about it is to identify the whole of the Catholic reality with one of its particular, historically contingent moments; for example, to confuse a form of medieval Catholicism with Catholicism itself or to equate the neo-Scholastic Catholicism of the 19th and early 20th centuries with the essence of the Catholic tradition.

On the other hand, these past 25 years have not been an ordinary slice of Catholic history. The Second Vatican Council (1962–65) is, by any reasonable standard of measurement, one of the most significant events in the entire history of the Church, and perhaps the most important single religious event of this century. One should expect, therefore, that the quarter-century immediately following the council would have been a time of profound and far-reaching change.

It has been. And this book provides a critical glimpse into it, through the medium of one theologian's chronicled reflections on that process of change. The reflections were initially published in a syndicated column of theological essays, which appear weekly in various Catholic newspapers and parish bulletins across the United States and Canada. The column is syndicated by the

Catholic Transcript, the weekly newspaper of the archdiocese of Hartford, Connecticut, which is also my home diocese.

Less than a year before the first column appeared (July 8, 1966), I had completed my doctoral studies at the Pontifical Gregorian University in Rome, having lived and worked in the Eternal City during the second and third sessions of Vatican II. It was an extraordinary opportunity, which relatively few theologians in the entire history of the Church have had—to be studying theology in the same city and at the same time that an ecumenical council was being held. Not surprisingly, the council has influenced and shaped my own theological perspective and agenda more than any other single force. To understand the council is to understand something of the content and evolution of my own thought. These columns, organized according to key topic areas, provide a record of that development.

Each chapter begins with a brief introductory comment that sets the chronologically arranged columns in some wider context. For example, how has the issue of ecclesiastical authority evolved over the past 25 years? What have been the principal points of contention? Where is the discussion leading?

The chapter headings themselves tell something of the story of postconciliar Catholicism. It has been a time of ongoing reflection on the council itself (chapter 1), on church authority (chapter 2), on tensions and conflict in the Church (chapter 3), on changes in the ministries of bishops, priests, and deacons (chapter 4), on the reemergence of the laity (chapter 5), on the role of women in the Church (chapter 6), on the relationship between the Church and society (chapter 7), politics (chapter 8), and other churches and religions (chapter 9), on major personalities who have shaped and transformed the life of the Church (chapter 10), and on recent and current expressions of papal leadership (chapter 11). The final chapter provides an exercise in extrapolation. It looks beyond this 25-year period to the next century and to the beginning of the third Christian millennium.

In the end, the book offers a mixed "Report on the Church." The postconciliar Church shows signs of vibrancy and malaise alike. It is marked at the same time by uncertainty, demoralization, conflict, and alienation, on the one hand, and by a remarkable liturgical, ministerial, and spiritual renewal, on the other. As Charles Dickens put it at the beginning of *A Tale of Two Cities,* it is for the Church the best of times and the worst of times.

I am indebted to several people for the making of this book, especially to Msgr. John Sexton Kennedy. It was Monsignor Kennedy who, as editor of the *Catholic Transcript,* first encouraged me to write a weekly column. I am also grateful to his successors, the late Donald Foskett, Vivian Stephenson, and the current editor, David Fortier, and to all of the *Transcript* staff who have assisted in the preparation and distribution of the essays.

I am indebted in a special way to br. Donal Leader, my former graduate assistant, for reviewing almost 1,300 columns and for his advice and computerized assistance in selecting and topically arranging a representative sample of them. My friend and colleague, Thomas F. O'Meara, O.P., provided the initial encouragement to do this book. I would add a warm word of thanks to my secretary, Donna Shearer, for retyping many of the earlier columns, which were done before the invention of the personal computer, and for her other help in preparing the manuscript for publication. A final expression of gratitude goes to Prof. Martin E. Marty, of the University of Chicago, for graciously accepting my invitation to write the Foreword.

Richard P. McBrien
University of Notre Dame

October 28, 1958   Card. Angelo Giuseppe Roncalli, Patriarch of Venice, is elected pope and takes the name John XXIII.

January 25, 1959   Pope John XXIII announces his intention to call an ecumenical council.

May 15, 1961   Pope John XXIII publishes his first major social encyclical, *Mater et Magistra*.

December 25, 1961   Pope John XXIII formally convokes the council via an apostolic constitution entitled *Humanae Salutis*.

October 11, 1962   Official opening of the Second Vatican Council.

November 21, 1962   Pope John XXIII intervenes in the council's deliberations to rule that the traditional schema on revelation, which had been rejected by more than half but not the necessary two-thirds of the council fathers, should be redrafted by a new committee.

April 11, 1963   Pope John XXIII publishes his second major social encyclical, *Pacem in Terris*.

June 3, 1963   Pope John XXIII dies.

June 21, 1963   Card. Giovanni Battista Montini, archbishop of Milan, is elected pope and takes the name Paul VI.

December 4, 1963   The Second Vatican Council's Constitution on the Sacred Liturgy, *Sacrosanctum Concilium*, is promulgated by Pope Paul VI.

November 21, 1964   The Second Vatican Council's Dogmatic Consti- tution on the Church, *Lumen Gentium*, and the Decree on Ecumenism, *Unitatis Redintegratio*, are promulgated by Pope Paul VI.

December 7, 1965   The Second Vatican Council's Pastoral Constitution on the Church in the Modern

	World, *Gaudium et Spes,* and the Declaration on Religious Freedom, *Dignitatis Humanae,* are promulgated by Pope Paul VI.
December 21, 1966	Fr. Charles Davis, a prominent English theologian, announces his decision to leave the Catholic Church and the priesthood and to marry.
March 26, 1967	Pope Paul VI publishes his major social encyclical, *Populorum Progressio.*
August 16, 1967	John Courtney Murray, S.J., dies.
December 2, 1967	Card. Francis Spellman dies.
July 25, 1968	Pope Paul VI publishes his encyclical on birth control, *Humanae Vitae.*
January 22, 1973	The U.S. Supreme Court hands down its *Roe v. Wade* decision on abortion.
July 29, 1974	Eleven women are ordained to the Episcopal priesthood in Philadelphia by four bishops acting without the authorization of their Church.
October 21–23, 1976	The Call to Action Conference meets in Detroit.
August 6, 1978	Pope Paul VI dies.
August 26, 1978	Card. Albino Luciani, patriarch of Venice, is elected pope and takes the name John Paul I.
September 3, 1978	Pope John Paul I is inaugurated without the traditional crowning ceremony.
September 28, 1978	Pope John Paul I dies.
October 16, 1978	Card. Karol Wojtyla, archbishop of Kraków, is elected pope and takes the name John Paul II.
March 4, 1979	Pope John Paul II publishes his first major encyclical, *Redemptor Hominis.*
October 7, 1979	Sr. Theresa Kane delivers an address in the National Shrine, Washington, D.C., in the presence of Pope John Paul II.
December 18, 1979	Fr. Hans Küng has his canonical mission to teach Catholic theology revoked.
January 14, 1980	The papally convoked Synod of Dutch Bishops meets in the Vatican.
May 13, 1981	Pope John Paul II is shot and wounded in St. Peter's Square during a public audience.

September 14, 1981	Pope John Paul II publishes a major social encyclical, *Laborem Exercens,* on human work.
May 3, 1983	The U.S. Catholic bishops publish a pastoral letter on war and peace entitled "The Challenge of Peace: God's Promise and Our Response."
March 31, 1984	Karl Rahner, S.J., dies.
September 13, 1984	Gov. Mario M. Cuomo of New York delivers a major speech on religion and politics, with special reference to the abortion issue, at the University of Notre Dame.
August 18, 1986	Fr. Charles Curran, professor of moral theology at The Catholic University of America, is officially informed by Archbp. James Hickey of Washington, D.C., that the Vatican has declared Fr. Curran neither suitable nor eligible to teach Catholic theology.
November 13, 1986	The U.S. Catholic bishops publish a pastoral letter entitled "Economic Justice for All: Catholic Social Teaching and the U.S. Economy."
June 1, 1987	Fr. Theodore M. Hesburgh, C.S.C., retires as president of the University of Notre Dame after 35 years in office.
December 30, 1987	Pope John Paul II publishes another major encyclical, *Sollicitudo Rei Socialis,* on the social concerns of the Church.
May 15, 1991	Pope John Paul II publishes yet another major social encyclical on the occasion of the centenary of Pope Leo XIII's *Rerum Novarum.* The new encyclical is entitled *Centesimus Annus.*

Vatican II

Introduction

The Second Vatican Council may have been the most significant religious event of the 20th century. It was certainly the most significant event of the century for the Catholic Church. For Catholics, the council has become the line that divides one kind of Catholicism from another.

To be "preconciliar" is to favor a type of Catholicism that lays stress on authority and obedience, on individual morality, on devotion to Mary and the saints, on fear of hell and the devil, on the set-apartness of priests and nuns, on the Catholic Church as the "one, true Church of Christ," on the primacy and infallibility of the pope, and so forth.

To be "postconciliar" (or simply "conciliar") is to favor a type of Catholicism that lays stress on freedom and responsibility, on social as well as personal morality, on the historical Jesus as the model of the Christian life, on the gospel as the "good news" of salvation, on ministry as service, on the role of the laity and especially of women in the Church, on ecumenism, on collegiality, and so forth.

The temptation is to see these two types of Catholicism as radically opposed to each other. To be sure, there are important and undeniable differences between them, but there is also a substantial measure of continuity as well.

The essays in this first chapter (including the inaugural column of July 8, 1966) all have to do, in one way or another, with the connection between preconciliar Catholicism and postconciliar Catholicism. To what extent did the council introduce something really new into the Church? To what extent did the council preserve and carry forward key elements from the past?

"As usual," I wrote in the column of January 19, 1990, "the truly Catholic position is one that takes a both/and, not an either/or, approach."

"Theological Gap" Painfully Clear

(July 8, 1966)

In the classical meaning of the term, theology is "faith seeking understanding" (St. Anselm). Theology is the scientific and systematic reflection of the Church upon her faith. Its chief aim is understanding, not certitude. Theology is there to give us a greater understanding of what we already believe. Apart from faith, theology has no meaning. It is subordinate to faith and remains under the control of faith.

Theology is, in a real sense, a "paradoxical enterprise" (to borrow an expression from Fr. Charles Davis). Thinking and believing, reason and faith, are not born to harmony. Their reconciliation is achieved only with effort. Consequently, theology must be methodical and scientific. It must be prepared to examine each aspect of the Christian faith in the light of its own historical development.

That is, theology must always have its starting point in Sacred Scripture, in the writings of the early Fathers of the Church, in the official teachings of the councils, and so forth. Theological understanding will grow also when elements of the faith are viewed in relation to other elements. Thus, a more profound understanding of the person and work of Christ will enlighten our understanding of the nature and mission of the Church, which is his Body.

If theology exists for the sake of the Christian faith, then the *theologian* exists for the sake of the Church, as a servant of faith. No theologian can work apart from the Church. Karl Barth, perhaps the most significant Protestant theologian in this century, begins his multivolume *Church Dogmatics* in this fashion: "Dogmatics is a theological discipline. But theology is a function of the Church." And the late Paul Tillich, probably the most outstanding American Protestant theologian (although born in Germany), begins his three-volume *Systematic Theology* with this sentence: "Theology, as a function of the Church, must serve the needs of the Church."

The appearance of the "death-of-God theologians" is doubly curious because these men, Thomas Altizer and William Hamilton in particular, have made a declaration of independence from the Church. But a theology that does not serve the Christian community is no theology at all. It might be a philosophy of religion, religious sociology, comparative religion, history of religions—and these are all legitimate academic pursuits—but it is *not* theology. Theology is faith seeking understanding, done in the context of the Church. Apart from the Church (and I am speaking of the Church in its widest connotation, as employed, for example, in the Decree on Ecumenism of the Second Vatican Council), theology has neither meaning nor existence.

Vatican II has been adjourned just a few months, and it is already painfully obvious that there exists a wide gap between the theological advances of this council and the theological understanding of many Catholic people—clergy included. This does not mean that no attempts have been made to close the "theological gap." Some efforts have been very successful: Fr. Charles Davis's "Theological Asides" in *America* magazine is a case in point. But others, with far less competence (indeed, with no discernible competence at all in the area of theology), have not hesitated to write on issues of theological import, and with disheartening results.

Recently there appeared in the diocesan press an article by a nationally syndicated Austrian columnist with a theologically naive attack on Harvey Cox's *The Secular City.* And another regular columnist, whose original charter called for essays in the area of social reform, turned his attention briefly to matters of ecclesiology, and specifically the question of the teaching authority of the Church. His comments were frankly discouraging in the light of the council's Constitution on the Church.

But the temptation for the professional theologian is simply to scoff at such efforts and dismiss them from the mind as quickly as possible. However, if the theologian is to be a servant of the Church, then he must be willing to make his findings—or better still, his tentative reflections—available to others within the same Christian community. Failing this responsibility, others with no theological qualifications will fill the vacuum by default. And the theologian has no one to blame but himself.

It is in the light of these reflections that this column has been born. A Church cannot long endure without theological understanding that is at a level comparable to the maturity of her members in related areas of thought and knowledge. The American Church has long since passed beyond the time when it could dispense with the need for serious theological reflection. Theology is not the preserve of the clergy—or, worse still, of a minute portion of the clergy. The Second Vatican Council is meant for the whole Church. The "theological gap" must be closed. This series of essays is a modest attempt to bring this hope to fruition.

Subsequent columns will contain discussions of various conciliar decrees, of "death-of-God theology," of changing concepts of the Church's mission, and other questions of a similar nature. It is the hope that these theological reflections will enlighten rather than confuse, that they will be stimulating rather than deadening, that they will—to some perceptible degree—contribute to the theological awareness and maturity of the reader, to bring him abreast of the Church of Vatican II and to prepare him in some measure for the Church of the 1970s.

If Pope Has Final Say, Why Fuss with Councils?

(July 15, 1966)

The Second Vatican Council must have been a puzzling phenomenon for the Catholic who had always regarded the Church as an absolute monarchy. After all, in 1870 the *First* Vatican Council defined the infallibility of the pope. Presumably that should have been the council to end all councils. What further need of such assemblies of bishops when, in the final analysis, it is the pope, and the pope alone, who holds the supreme authority in the Church: as teacher, ruler, and sanctifier?

But presumption must always yield to fact, and the fact of the matter is that Pope John XXIII *did* summon another ecumenical council and it actually conducted business for four sessions. Therefore, what must be called into question is not the existence of the *Second* Vatican Council but the theological interpretation that some people (including theologians) have given to the teaching of the *First* Vatican Council.

One of the most important principles of theology is that the official teachings of the Church, whether they be promulgated in conciliar decrees, papal encyclicals, or some other form, are to be regarded as *accurate* expressions of the Christian faith but not necessarily (in fact, never) as *adequate* expressions of that faith. Thus, what may be proclaimed most solemnly in one council may require elaboration or development in another council.

The Council of Trent, for example, insisted that the Crucifixion of our Lord was a true sacrifice and that it truly redeemed us. It said nothing about the redemptive value of the Resurrection. Why not? Because it was not an issue of controversy at the time. Recent theological investigations have emphasized the essential place of the Resurrection in the mystery of our redemption by Christ. This does not represent a repudiation of Trent. It is simply a matter of theological development.

Theology is faith seeking understanding, done in the context of the Church. The Church is a living organism, and we should not be surprised if her understanding of the gospel is subject to growth. The teaching of Trent, therefore, was *accurate* (i.e., the Crucifixion was a true redemptive sacrifice), but *inadequate* (i.e., the council considered only a part of the redemptive work of Christ).

We have further illustration of this principle in the case of the First Vatican Council's teaching with regard to the place of the pope in the Church. What the First Vatican Council proposed regarding papal authority and infallibility is an *accurate* and authentic interpretation of the gospel, but that council did not offer a complete, that is, an *adequate,* theology of the Church. Vatican I was forced to adjourn before it had an opportunity to consider the problem of the episcopacy in relation to papal primacy. This became the unfinished business of Vatican II.

The Second Vatican Council's doctrinal position is contained in the third chapter of its Dogmatic Constitution on the Church (*Lumen Gentium*). The apparent conflict between papal and episcopal authority is resolved in the concept of collegiality. Our Lord bestowed the supreme authority upon the entire group of apostles and set Peter apart as the head and center of unity in this college. Peter has supreme authority in the Church insofar as he acts as head of the Apostolic College; and the Apostolic College has supreme authority in the Church insofar as it acts in unity with its head (par. 22). Thus, the founding of the Apostolic College preceded the naming of Peter as its head.

Peter is named the head of the College "in order that the episcopate itself might be one and undivided" and in order that he (Peter) might be "a permanent and visible source and foundation of unity of faith and communion" (par. 18). "Just as in the Gospel," the document continues, "St. Peter and the other apostles constitute one apostolic college, so in a similar way the Roman Pontiff, the successor of Peter, and the bishops, the successors of the apostles, are joined together" (par. 22).

There are not two *supreme* authorities in the Church (i.e., pope and the college of bishops). This would be a contradiction. Supreme authority in the

Church resides in one subject, the college of bishops with the pope as its head. The primacy of the pope, therefore, is a primacy *within* and not *over against* the college of bishops.

Catholics will encounter real theological difficulty if they attempt to translate these facts into juridical and legal concepts, in terms of certain preexisting categories: monarchy, quasimonarchy, oligarchy, democracy, and so on. This is theologically futile. The fact is that, as Karl Rahner put it, the Church "is ruled by a *college*, without its head thereby becoming the mere elected representative of the college; the head truly rules the college, without the college thereby becoming his mere executive organs. . . . The structure of the Church rests essentially on something suprainstitutional, on the Nomos [law] of the Spirit, which cannot and will not adequately be translated into institutional terms" (*The Episcopate and the Primacy,* pp. 79–81).

An ecumenical council, therefore, can never be regarded as a superfluous event in the life of the Church. The assembled bishops are not merely the advisers of the pope, having been delegated—on a temporary basis—authority that the pope, and the pope alone, possesses. An ecumenical council is the highest expression of the unity of the Church. The basis of that unity is the college of bishops with the pope at its head. The essential structure of the Church is collegial, not monarchical.

Did Council Change Anything?

(December 23, 1966)

The strongest and, in the long run, the most effective opposition to the Second Vatican Council comes not from the vocal detractors of the council's spirit and orientation but rather from those who insist that the council really changed nothing at all.

We have perhaps automatically assumed that all the negative reaction to the conciliar Church has its source on the far right of the ecclesiastical spectrum. It would seem, however, that there is a much larger group, closer to the center does not voice the same angry discontent and yet that is no less disturbed by the recent turn of events in the Church. The approach is more sophisticated, but the intent is the same: to sidestep the Second Vatican Council and to try and forget that it ever happened.

Those who would prefer to believe that the changes initiated by Vatican II were exclusively in the area of style and language are hard-pressed to explain, for example, the sharp differences that exist between the theological antecedents of the Dogmatic Constitution on the Church (*Lumen Gentium*) and the document itself. The differences are more than superficial. There is a fundamental change in orientation and perspective.

This is not to suggest that Vatican II's idea of the Church is a repudiation of the biblical, patristic, and classical theological concepts of the Church. Far from it. The authors of this document and the overwhelming majority of bishops who voted in favor of it (only six voted no) would insist rather that the council has restored the traditional view of the Church and has sought to make it relevant and meaningful for the world of the 1960s.

But isn't this precisely the point? The council changed nothing. It is just a matter of style and language, of updating and trimming. Not at all.

What fails here is a sense of history. Too often we measure the best (or the worst) of the present against the best (or the worst) of the past. For example, when placed alongside the Pauline notion of the Church as the Body of Christ, of course the Second Vatican Council is not charting new territory or breaking with the past. But when measured against the ecclesiology (theology of the Church) of the Counter-Reformation period or that of the first half of the 20th century, the council has changed much indeed.

And that really is the crux of the difficulty many Catholics are having with the Second Vatican Council. They see things changing: not only the language of the Mass but even, it seems to them, the substance of doctrines as well. But what many Catholics are doing is measuring these changes not against the authentic tradition of the Church (as found in the Bible, the great Fathers and theologians of the Church, and ecumenical councils of the past) but rather against the relatively narrow theology of the first half of this century.

Much of the childhood theology of our adult Catholics was not good theology at all. This is the theology that referred to the eucharistic Lord as the "prisoner of the tabernacle" and coined other similar theological barbarisms. This is the theology that taught, implicitly at the very least, that the Catholic Church has a monopoly on truth, that there is nothing of Christian value in non-Catholic churches, that there is no possibility of real development in our understanding of the gospel.

This is the theology that looked upon the Church primarily as a hierarchically structured organization that exists to serve the religious needs of religiously-minded people, to make and keep them religious. (The so-called filling-station concept of parish life flows from this view.) This is the theology that made the Christian life a matter of following rules and obeying laws, which offered too little incentive to the people to read and meditate upon Sacred Scripture. This is the theology that, in its laudable efforts to preserve the divinity of Christ, ran the risk of dehumanizing him and the parallel risk of dehumanizing the Church as well.

This is the theology that made the pope the only person who really mattered in the hierarchy of the Church and that regarded bishops, at best, as the pope's vicars and delegates. This is the theology that assumed, therefore, that the essential structure of the Church was monarchical and that every level of the Church—diocese, parish, seminary, college, university—should reflect this monarchical character.

I have drawn something of a caricature of early 20th-century theology, to be sure. This same period produced men of singular brilliance in the area of theology, Sacred Scripture, spirituality, and so forth. (Karl Adam, M. J. Lagrange, Abbot Marmion come readily to mind.) Nor are these comments intended as a reflection on the Catholic *life* of the period. The gospel is, indeed, ever new, but there were others before us who knew it and lived it. Any suggestion to the contrary would be spiritually arrogant and totally irresponsible. The Catholic social action movement alone is proof of the vitality of the gospel in the Church of the first half of the 20th century. This was the Servant Church at work.

The point is simply this: When opponents of Vatican II insist that the council really changed nothing at all, they are right if they mean that it brought to a fuller flowering the authentic tradition of the Church. But one may seriously question if this *is* what they mean. For the council does, in fact, pose a challenge to change. It has changed much that was once considered a part of the authentic tradition of the Church: some of the theology of our catechisms and seminary manuals and pulpit oratory.

What the council has shown is that this theology, so long assumed to be "traditional," was not traditional at all, that it was too sharply divorced from its biblical roots, from the rich insights of the great Fathers of the Church, and from the truly catholic perspective of greater theologians such as St. Thomas Aquinas.

What's New? Understanding the Council Texts

(February 18, 1972)

This week's column raises three questions and prepares the way for a fourth: (1) Did the Second Vatican Council say anything really new about the Church? (2) If so, what is the documentary evidence? (3) Is there any documentary evidence on the other side of the argument? (4) How are we to resolve the textual conflicts?

My regular readers will already be familiar with the content of the first two responses. It is summarized in the first chapter of *Who Is a Catholic?* (Dimension Books, 1971).

The word *new,* of course, is a relative term. I do not mean to suggest that Vatican II somehow changed the historic faith of the Christian community, as proclaimed in the New Testament and as handed down by the Church through the centuries.

Rather, I mean "new" in relation to the common understanding of Christian faith and mission in the thinking of many 20th-century Catholics, an understanding communicated to a large portion of the Church's membership through catechisms, theology textbooks, sermons, inquiry classes, and religious education programs of various types.

It was something "new" for many Catholics to start thinking about the Church primarily as a community or as the People of God rather than as a visible society, hierarchically structured, to which they simply belonged and from which they were entitled to receive certain spiritual benefits. (See chapters I and II of the Dogmatic Constitution on the Church.)

It was something "new" for many Catholics to start thinking about the Church as a collegial rather than a monarchical entity. (See n. 22ff., of the Constitution on the Church.)

It was something "new" for many Catholics to start thinking of themselves as having direct responsibility for the mission of the Church rather than as simply participating in the mission of the hierarchy by an act of delegation ("Catholic Action"). (See chapter IV, and especially n. 33, of the same Dogmatic Constitution.)

It was something "new" for many Catholics to start thinking that every baptized Christian is called to perfect holiness and that there are no spiritual elites (priests and sisters, for example) who alone are called to the fullness of Christian sanctity. (See chapter V of the Constitution on the Church.)

It was something "new" for many Catholics to start thinking of Protestants as sharing directly in the life of the Body of Christ and indeed to start thinking of the Body of Christ itself as something larger than the Catholic Church alone. (See the Decree on Ecumenism, nn. 20–23, and the Constitution on the Church, n. 15.)

It was something "new" for many Catholics to start thinking of the "social apostolate" as an integral part of the mission of the Church rather than as something Christians could engage in as an activity merely preliminary to the real work of the Church. (See the Pastoral Constitution on the Church in the Modern World, e.g., n. 43.)

Some Catholics point out, however, that these passages must be read in the light of the corrective material that abounds throughout the various documents.

The Church may now be called the People of God, but nothing more than the terminology has really changed. Christ rules the Church through the supreme pontiff and the bishops, and full incorporation into the Church requires the acceptance of the "entire system" and union with "her visible structure" (Constitution on the Church, n. 14).

Collegiality means only that the pope ought to consult the bishops when it is convenient, but meanwhile he retains the full and supreme governing authority over the whole Church. (See n. 25 of the Constitution on the Church and also the explanatory note at the end of the same document.)

These same passages remind us, too, that the apostolate of the laity, and indeed of the religious and so-called lower clergy, is always subject to, and is carried on at the pleasure of, the hierarchy and ultimately the pope himself.

While the council does remind the laity of the obligation to strive for holiness, the council devotes four separate documents to the question of the apostolate and call to sanctity of bishops, priests, and religious.

The council may have cast a kinder eye upon non-Catholics, but it continued to insist that those who know that the Catholic Church was made necessary by God through Jesus Christ and yet who would refuse to join her or to remain in her cannot be saved (n. 14 again).

The council acknowledged that the Church has no proper mission in the political, economic, or social order. Her purpose, rather, is a religious one (Pastoral Constitution, n. 42).

Awareness Is Its Main Character

(February 25, 1972)

There are several points of conflict in the documents of the Second Vatican Council. I cited some examples in last week's column.

How are we to resolve thesse apparent inconsistencies? Did the council intend to take away with the right hand what it had already given with its left?

Was the council even aware at the time that what it was saying in one document tended to differ from what it had already said in another document, or indeed that what it was saying in one part of a document tended to differ from what it had already said in another part of the same document?

Or, finally, did the council intend to adhere as closely as possible to the traditional teaching while, at the same time, not try to claim more for that traditional teaching than contemporary scholarship and pastoral experience would allow?

There is probably some truth in every one of these three hypotheses.

1. The council did make some major advances on the question of coresponsibility in the Church, particularly with its teaching on collegiality in the third chapter of the Dogmatic Constitutuion of the Church and in its discussion of the laity in the fourth chapter of the same document. But then it hastened to add that none of this material could be regarded as prejudicial to the primacy and jurisdiction of the pope.

The council also expanded our notion of the Body of Christ to include, it would seem, Protestants and other non-Catholic Christians. But the council also continued to insist on the special place of the Catholic Church and on the intrinsic obligation of all mankind to join it.

Those who have accepted this first hypothesis have been able to make their theory work in the post-conciliar Church. In many places throughout the Catholic world, diocesan pastoral councils and parish councils, to cite but two means of implementing the doctrine of collegiality, do not even exist, and where they exist they are often weak and ineffective.

Futhermore, the various directives that have been issued on ecumenism since Vatican II tend to reflect the view that the only conciliar texts that really count are those which reaffirm the traditional theology operative before the council. Thus, intercommunion occurs only outside the official limits of ecclesiastical law and the striking conclusions of the various bilateral conversations, as have occurred in the United States since 1965, are generally disregarded.

2. It is also possible that some of the apparant inconsistency in the documents of Vatican II arises from the complexity of the drafting process. There were sixteen documents. These were developed over a period of four annual sessions by many different committees. The Dogmatic Constitution on the Church, for example, went through four major drafts.

Sometimes changes were made at the last minute (e.g., the addition of the material in n. 5 of the Dogmatic Constitution on the Church) without adequate time or inclination to rewrite other portions of the document that were at least indirectly affected by the new material.

Doctrinal fundamentalists are not really concerned about the process itself, only with the hard results. But those who agree that doctrinal formulations must be subjected to the same kind of critical inquiry that we apply to the Bible will find indispensable guidance in the five-volume collection, *Commentary on the Documents of Vatican II*, edited by H. Vorgrimler and published by Herder and Herder, 1967–1969.

3. While I find some truth in each of the previous hypotheses, I should be prepared to argue that the third view is the strongest of all; namely, that the council was keenly aware of theological pluralism and did not wish to close discussion prematurely. Condemnation was simply not the style of Vatican II.

On the other hand, the council was not prepared to give its official endorsement to the various newer views, at least not without some qualification. Thus, collegiality could be accepted, but not with prejudice to the papacy. Ecumenism could be approved, but not with prejudice to Catholic identity. The lay apostolate could be promoted, but not with prejudice to the hierarchical nature of the Church. And so on.

If we accept Vatican II as a beginning rather than as an end, these apparent inconsistencies assume a much different character. The council was not closing a discussion so much as opening one.

Few positions (apart from faith in the reality of God, the Lordship of Jesus, or the redemptive power of the Holy Spirit) can claim total support in the council documents. But for many of these so-called newer views, "the seeds are there, like unopened buds awaiting the sun" (Card. Suenens).

In a very real sense, we are still too near the council to judge how high or how sturdy these plants will be. Cultivation is a task that requires patience. In the meantime, can we at least agree that all of us ought to have the good of the whole garden at heart?

Vatican II in Retrospect

(October 29, 1982)

October 11 was the 20th anniversary of the opening of the Second Vatican Council. The anniversary occasioned a number of articles and symposia designed to put the council in some larger perspective.

There are Catholics who become anxious in the face of such assessments. In their minds, every positive word said about Vatican II implies a negative word about the pre–Vatican II Church. That is not the case, but it's the perception many seem to have.

One can say a word of profound appreciation for the Second Vatican Council without repudiating preconciliar Catholicism. Indeed, that is precisely what Pope John Paul II did in his *Sources of Renewal,* published before his election to the papacy.

There are many things about preconciliar Catholicism that remain at the center of Catholic faith and practice: all of the great mysteries (Trinity, the redemption, the Holy Spirit, eternal life, the Kingdom of God), the sacraments, our commitments to charity, justice, and the other theological and cardinal virtues, and on and on.

But just as it would be a grave error to assume that the council substantially altered the Catholic faith, so it would be a grand delusion to believe that the council did no more than change some terminology, while leaving all basic thought patterns and practices untouched.

Because of the council the Catholic Church *is* very different today from what it was in 1940 or 1950 or even 1960.

We are less inclined today to see the Church primarily as a hierarchical institution. The Church understands itself now as the whole People of God, with laity as much a part of the Church as clergy and members of religious orders and congregations.

To be part of the People of God is to share responsibility for the Church's life and mission. Since the council, therefore, we have seen the development of parish councils, diocesan pastoral councils, and other organizations composed largely of laity.

We are less inclined today to think only of the Roman Catholic Church when we say "Church," for the Body of Christ embraces all baptized Christians.

Even though intercommunion and the mutual recognition of ministries have not been officially approved, we have made extraordinary progress in areas such as common prayer, common theological study, and collaboration in works of charity and social justice.

Although we Catholics have not embraced religious indifferentism, we recognize today more than in the preconciliar period that we have much to learn from other Christian churches and from non-Christian religions as well.

God works outside the Catholic Church and even outside the Body of Christ. We have to be prepared to discern the divine presence "out there" and to respond to it. And we have to respect the outsider and to defend his or her right to worship God in accordance with the dictates of conscience.

Thus, we are called less to the way of apology and polemics and more to the way of listening and dialogue. Pope Paul VI, in fact, made this the central theme of his first encyclical letter, *Ecclesiam Suam.*

We are less inclined today to see the Church only as an instrument of salvation achieved through the celebration of the sacraments and the teaching of saving truths and more as a sacrament in itself.

To be sure, the Church is still very much a means of salvation, but the Church mediates God's saving grace not only in preaching, teaching, and sacraments but in a whole range of activities on behalf of the needy, the oppressed, the dispossessed, the outcast, and so forth. And it demonstrates the presence of saving grace by the way it acts toward its own members and toward those in its employ.

As the Third International Synod of Bishops would put it some six years after Vatican II, the mission of the Church includes in its essence the struggle for justice and the transformation of the world. The social apostolate, as it was once called, is as much a part of the Church's mission as its liturgy and its catechesis.

The same document declared that a Church that proclaims justice outside can only be credible if it practices justice inside.

This principle is the same as the one articulated by Pope John XXIII at the opening of the council: "The substance of the ancient doctrine of the deposit of faith is one thing, and the way in which it is presented is another."

The Second Vatican Council's great achievement was in recognizing this connection between internal reality and external sign. The Church must not only *be* what it signifies, but it must also *signify* what it is.

Spirit of Pope John XXIII and Council
(November 5, 1982)

It was a good and useful simile that Pope John XXIII employed in speaking of the need for opening windows to let some fresh air into the Church, and obviously it "took."

But there was another simile in his opening address to the council on October 11, 1962, that was no less compelling and that helps us to evaluate the Second Vatican Council some twenty years later.

"The council now beginning rises in the Church like daybreak, a forerunner of most splendid light," he declared. "It is now only dawn."

If the council happened at dawn, the Church is still somewhere in that sleepy-eyed period before breakfast, with the aroma of coffee sending wake-up calls from kitchen to bedrooms.

In other words, it's still relatively early to assess the impact of Vatican II. Nevertheless, one can at least review what has actually happened in the Church these past twenty years in light of the council's stated purposes and its teachings.

Nowhere is the council's purpose articulated more clearly or more directly than in that opening address of Pope John XXIII.

The council was *not* held to condemn errors in the Church or in the world at large, as Pope Pius IX had done in his Syllabus of Errors in 1864, as Pope

Pius X had done in his anti-Modernist decree of 1907, and as Pope Pius XII had done in his encyclical *Humani Generis* in 1950.

The post–French Revolution Pian Church had reached the end of its line. The Church was now summoned by a new, positive, hope-filled voice of leadership to correlate the Church's "sacred patrimony of truth," as Pope John XXIII called it, with "the new conditions and new forms of life introduced into the modern world which have opened new avenues to the Catholic apostolate."

"The substance of the ancient doctrine . . . is one thing," he insisted, "and the way in which it is presented is another."

This was not the time for negativism and condemnations, even though the pope acknowledged publicly that he was surrounded by "prophets of gloom, who are always forecasting disaster, as though the end of the world were at hand."

The pope was not speaking of his housekeeping staff nor of his secretaries and immediate aides nor of the Swiss Guard. He was speaking of the Roma Curia—of those who opposed not only the council but also his new, more Christian way of handling problems and of exercising papal authority.

"Though burning with zeal," he continued, "[they] are not endowed with much sense of discretion or measure. In these modern times they can see nothing but prevarication and ruin."

But in John XXIII's vision, "Divine Providence is leading us to a new order of human relations." The Church can counteract errors now "by demonstrating the validity of its teaching rather than by condemnations."

And so the positive program of the council: a renewal and reform of the Church so that the Church's message will be embodied in its life, in everything that it is and does. No wonder that the sacramentality of the Church became so important an element of the council's ecclesiology.

Pope John XXIII called upon the Church to open "the fountain of its life-giving doctrine which allows everyone, enlightened by the light of Christ, to understand well who they really are, what their lofty dignity and their purpose are, and, finally, through its children, it spreads everywhere in fullness of Christian charity, than which nothing is more effective in eradicating the seeds of discord, nothing more efficacious in promoting concord, just peace, and the human solidarity of all."

That grand Johannine vision still lives in the Church in the hearts and minds of most of its active members, but the negative, condemnatory spirit also perdures among those Catholics who devote books, articles, lectures, and letters to attacking their fellow Catholics by name, calling their faith into question.

Such Catholics continue to believe that the most effective way for the Church to deal with "error" (real or imagined) is by the suppression of "erroneous" ideas and the silencing of those who promote them.

We'll know that the midmorning sun has burned away the fog and the mists and has begun to warm the flesh and stir the world to action when Catholics learn how to disagree without being disagreeable, when there is "unity in what is necessary, freedom in what is unsettled, and charity in any case" (Pastoral Constitution on the Church in the Modern World, n. 92).

What Went Wrong with Church?
(May 13, 1983)

Occasionally a letter to an editor effectively encapsulates a whole network of dubious assumptions about the recent history of the Catholic Church. Such a letter appeared last month in *Newsweek* in response to a story on the shortage of priests.

First of all, the letter offers a textbook example of the *post hoc, ergo propter hoc* fallacy, that is, because B follows A, A is the cause of B.

"Before Vatican II: crowded seminaries, monasteries and convents," the writer begins. "After Vatican II: a worsening shortage of priests, nuns and seminarians."

The only scientific studies that, to my knowledge, have been done on the connection between Vatican II and postconciliar disruptions and reversals in the Catholic Church establish a different conclusion. There were other factors at work, including the birth-control encyclical, *Humanae Vitae*.

Furthermore, Pope John Paul II, who is usually at the top of the anti–Vatican II Catholic's "most admired" list, has also had a completely different estimation of the council's effect on the Church.

As archbishop of Kraków, Pope John Paul II wrote a book on the council as an expression of gratitude for its achievements. The book, entitled *Sources of Renewal: The Implementation of Vatican II* (Harper & Row, 1980), was originally published in 1972, then revised and translated into Italian in 1979. The American edition is taken from the updated Italian version.

"Through the whole experience of the Council," he writes in the introduction, "we have contracted a debt towards the Holy Spirit, the Spirit of Christ which speaks to the churches. During the Council and by way of it, the word of the Spirit became particularly expressive and decisive for the Church" (pp. 9–10).

These are hardly the words of a man who feels that Vatican II was a disaster, the cause of the present shortage of priests and of other assorted woes.

The letter writer identifies some of these other woes. "An antiseptic liturgy replaced majesty and mystery with banality."

Either the man is too young to remember the pre–Vatican II liturgy or his memory has selectively failed him.

There was indeed much "majesty and mystery" (although the latter word is incorrectly used) in the preconciliar liturgy, but there was also much that was wrong with it.

At funerals, for example, no one, including the family of the bereaved, was expected to receive Holy Communion.

At the late Masses, with the fasting-from-midnight rule in force, about 5 percent of the congregation at most would receive the sacrament.

At Sunday Mass, a tiny minority followed along with their missals, some recited the rosary, and most simply remained lost in their own personal thoughts, bestirred now and then by the ringing of the bells.

Catholics who charge that today's liturgy is "antiseptic" or filled with "banality" ought to think of switching churches for weekly Mass. Literally millions of U.S. Catholics would attest to the very opposite experience in their own parishes.

The extraordinary rise in the percentage of those who receive Communion at Mass is one example of an undeniable gain achieved by the so-called modern Church. No spiritually serious Catholic can deny that as an inestimable blessing: unless, of course, they think most of the communicants are in mortal sin because they haven't been to confession recently.

It is curious, too, that today's clergy should be criticized for "acting out new roles as social workers and psychological counsellors" when, before Vatican II, so many parish priests spent much of their time counseling people in the rectory parlor, coaching the parish baseball team, driving young people to amusement parks, helping parishioners get jobs or through the bureaucratic maze at city hall, and so forth.

The recent history of pre–Vatican II Catholicism is redrafted by our *Newsweek* letter writer in such a way that sermons before the council are assumed to have been always theologically meaty, ethically demanding, and rich in biblical evidence. Indeed, one would have been lucky in many a parish to get a sermon at all, so often was pulpit time taken up with commentaries on the printed bulletin or appeals for money.

Yet another assumption is that there was complete discipline and obedience to clerical authority in the pre–Vatican II Church, as if such obedience was always a good thing and, in any case, always practiced.

There are a few retired bishops who could recount stories of pastors they couldn't control in the 1930s, 1940s, and 1950s. Vatican II brought no innovation on that score.

In a word, it is wrong to romanticize the pre–Vatican II Church, just as it is wrong to exaggerate its failings. Pre–Vatican II Catholics were good and bad people just like us. In fact, many of them were us!

Like all living things, we continue to grow. And the Church grows with us and in us.

An Ecumenical Council Is Announced

(February 3, 1984)

We just passed the 25th anniversary of Pope John XXIII's announcement, at the Basilica of St. Paul's Outside the Walls in Rome, of his intention to summon an ecumenical council. The date was January 25, 1959.

A year and a half later, on June 5, 1960, the Holy Father established the preparatory commissions and secretariats, and on Christmas Day of the same year he formally convoked the council.

The council opened on October 11, 1962, and the rest, as they say, is history.

I was in my first of four years of seminary theology when Pope John XXIII caught the world—and the Church—by surprise at St. Paul's. It may be instructive to recall some of the initial reactions.

One of my professors, who had little confidence in the theological acumen of bishops, feared that the council would deteriorate into an ecclesiastical free-for-all and urged us to pray that it would never be held.

Some were confused by the term *ecumenical*. Was the Holy Father going to call the heads of all Christian denominations together to try and restore Christian unity?

More just didn't know what to make of it. After all, didn't Vatican I's definition of papal primacy and infallibility render future councils unnecessary?

By the following year a few thought they had a clearer idea of the pope's intentions. The council would be a kind of theological and canonical clearing-house, affording the Church an opportunity to correct minor defects in the system.

Thus, another professor—a philosopher doing double duty as a moral theologian (a common occurrence in pre–Vatican II seminaries)—informed us one morning that he had submitted just one recommendation to the preparatory commission: the council should clarify the Church's teaching on the servile work.

For those of you too young to know what "servile work" means, it had to do with the amount of "heavy lifting" that any one of us could morally do on Sunday.

Among the great moral issues of the time was deciding whether sewing was work or a form of recreation. If work, it was a sin to sew on Sunday; if recreation, it was acceptable.

The point is that many, if not most, Catholics—even those who would have been regarded in those days as "informed"—expected relatively little from the council. Their attitudes covered the spectrum from confusion through guarded optimism to anxiety.

Some would later insist that the pope himself wasn't sure about what he was doing. The less pleased one happened to be with the results of Vatican II, the stronger the hypothesis.

But how could one reasonably disagree with this view? How could Pope John XXIII have foreseen all that the council accomplished, much less its impact on the Catholic Church these past two decades?

For those who are fundamentally happy about, and grateful toward, the Second Vatican Council (beginning with Pope John Paul II, whose book, *Sources of Renewal: The Implementation of Vatican II,* was written to pay "a debt to the Holy Spirit"), there is a lesson to be learned about human hopes and expectations, on the one hand, and divine fulfillment, on the other.

It is a lesson that is especially pertinent today, some 18 years after the final adjournment of the council, when so many Catholics look to the immediate future with some measure of uneasiness, even despondency.

Well beyond the hopes and expectations of the boldest progressives of the 1950s and early 1960s, the Second Vatican Council:

- Renewed the liturgy of the Church, increasing congregational participation and insuring a much fuller understanding of the rites.

- Expanded our understanding of what it means to *be* Church, not simply to "belong to" the Church, with its concept of the Church as People of God.

- Recognized that every baptized Christian, lay, cleric, and religious alike, shares directly in the mission Christ gave the Church: to teach, to worship, and to transform the world.

- Acknowledged the bonds of faith, hope, and charity we Catholics share with all other Christians, as well as our common brotherhood and sisterhood under God with the other religious bodies of the world.

- Summoned us to assume, with renewed vigor and dedication, our duty to evangelize the world, not only through preaching and catechesis but also through the struggle for social justice, human rights, and peace.

- Reminded us that the Church itself is always in need of repentance and purification and that the strongest argument for the truth of the gospel is the Church's own living of it.

- Reaffirmed the importance of the local church and, therefore, the right and duty of each local church to incarnate the gospel in ways that are consistent with local cultures.

- Declared the radical equality of all human beings before God and their right to worship God according to the dictates of their own consciences.

And these are only some of the highlights.

Hopes and expectations were exceeded in their fulfillment. Servile work, indeed!

Bishops Praise Vatican II Unanimously

(January 3, 1986)

Negativists of left and right can pick through the remains of the Extraordinary Synod and find "evidence" to justify their presynodal fears and expectations.

On the left: Someone said something terribly nasty about liberation theology. The bishops agreed to the preparation of a universal catechism. The pope was so much in control of the proceedings that the bishops had to work in an atmosphere of tension and uncertainty.

On the right: The legitimacy of national episcopal conferences has yet to be studied. A universal catechism will put an end to dissent. The bishops have acknowledged that there have been false interpretations of Vatican II.

But neither side can deny the only evidence that really counts: the bishops' own final report of their discussions and suggestions. The report contradicts the brooding fears of the left and the bellicose expectations of the right.

"Unanimously," the bishops declared, "we celebrate the Second Vatican Council as a grace of God and a gift of the Holy Spirit from which there have been many spiritual fruits in the universal Church, in the particular churches, and among all people."

The synod, therefore, urged a renewed effort to acquaint Catholics with the documents of Vatican II, particularly candidates for ministry and religious life.

The synod praised theologians for their contributions to Vatican II and for their efforts to interpret the council for the general faithful.

Even as the synod expressed concern about theological discussions that have confused some members of the Church, the bishops called for "a greater, closer mutual communication and dialogue . . . between bishops and theologians for the building up of a more profound understanding of faith."

In the minds of individual bishops, perhaps, the idea of a universal catechism is appealing because it has possibilities of separating the orthodox wheat from the heretical chaff. But not so with the synod as a whole.

The catechism or compendium is to serve as a guide for the production of national catechisms. All of these catechisms are to be biblical and liturgical in content, accommodated to the daily life of Christians.

Indeed, the synod identified liturgical renewal as "the greatest visible fruit of the council." In spite of some difficulties, the liturgical changes "have been accepted happily and with great profit by the faithful."

The principal enemy of the Church and of the gospel are not fellow Catholics. The enemy is secularism, that ideology that denies and then seeks to drive out every trace of the sacred from daily life.

Therefore, the Church, which is first and foremost a mystery, must allow the hidden presence of God to shine through. The Church, which is holy, must also appear to be holy.

The Church is not just the hierarchy; it is a community. A spirit of collaboration must exist at all levels of the Church.

The synod insisted, for example, that pastors should welcome women as collaborators in the work of the Church "with a grateful spirit" and expressed special concern for the young.

The Church is at the same time universal and local. It is not just the Church centered in the Vatican. The Church is a communion of local churches.

Regarding national episcopal conferences: "There is no one who doubts their pastoral usefulness, indeed even their necessity in modern times."

Moreover, the Church is at the same time Catholic and ecumenical. The dialogue is to continue at both theological and spiritual levels so that the Church might be seen more clearly as the sacrament of unity.

Finally, the Church is a sacrament for the salvation of the world. Its mission is at the same time spiritual and temporal.

In fidelity to the council document *Gaudium et Spes,* the synod underscored the need to incarnate the faith in diverse cultures, to dialogue and collaborate with non-Christian religions and with nonbelievers, and to stand with the poor and the oppressed.

The Second Vatican Council, the synod concluded, is "the *magna carta* [of the Church] and will remain so for the future."

A positive, hopeful note on which to begin a new year.

Taking a Stand on Second Vatican Council

(January 19, 1990)

It's becoming clearer now. Conservative Catholics are in the process of reinforcing certain defenses against some of the major discomforts of the postconciliar Church.

Unhappy with the increasingly critical spirit of Catholic scholars and with the growing openness of clergy, religious, and laity alike, conservatives are beginning to challenge the commonly accepted view that the Second Vatican Council introduced something really new into the life and practice of the Church.

Not so, they reply. The council was fine. We have no problem with it. We're even prepared to say that it was a great event.

But Vatican II didn't say or do anything new. It reaffirmed, in different words perhaps, what the Church has always believed, taught, and practiced.

Accordingly, there is nothing in pre–Vatican II Catholicism that isn't still valid today. The council neither repudiated nor substantially modified any of it.

The argument of these conservatives is fashioned in terms of a false either/or dichotomy between continuity and discontinuity.

The correct view of the council (their own) has it that the council was wholly a work of continuity, and not at all one of discontinuity.

The erroneous view of the council (that of their liberal opponents) holds that the council essentially repealed pre–Vatican II Catholicism and replaced it with something totally discontinuous with it.

One finds traces of this continuity-versus-discontinuity dichotomy in a recent review in *America* of a book entitled *Educating in Faith* (Harper & Row) by Sister Mary Boys, S.N.J.M., an associate professor of religious education at Boston College.

The reviewer chastises the author for propagating "the myth of radical discontinuity between the pre– and post–Vatican II church."

He asserts that this "myth of radical discontinuity" has been "an important reason for the polarization of contemporary Catholicism."

Although a gifted and experienced religious educator himself, the reviewer implies that religious educators have no mandate to challenge or to correct outdated notions of Catholic belief and practice—because the category of "out-datedness" is meaningless.

Moreover, in challenging or in seeking to correct certain postconciliar beliefs and practices, religious educators contribute to the polarization of the Church. They make "traditional" Catholics uncomfortable, angry, and upset, and that's why these Catholics have no choice except to strike back in defense of their own version and vision of the Church. A state of war ensues.

The continuity-versus-discontinuity dichotomy also surfaces at higher levels of Catholic theological scholarship.

In his excellent overview of Catholic ecclesiology in the past 50 years (*Theological Studies,* September 1989 issue), Avery Dulles, S.J., identifies as "progressives" those who have "interpreted the Council on the principle that its innovations were more central than its reaffirmations of previously official positions."

He calls this "the hermeneutics of discontinuity." (I should point out that Dulles identifies me with this view, along with Edward Schillebeeckx, O.P., and Lutheran theologian George Lindbeck, of Yale University.)

On the other side he places Card. Joseph Ratzinger and another German theologian, Hermann Josef Pottmeyer, who interpret Vatican II as "continuous with previous Catholic teaching."

Given Father Dulles's extraordinary sense of balance and fairness, I would have expected him to state explicitly that no dichotomy exists between the one and the other.

It's not *either* continuity *or* discontinuity; it's *both* continuity and discontinuity.

The problem with the extreme left is that it acknowledges only discontinuity. But the no-less-serious problem with the extreme right is that it acknowledges only continuity.

Indeed, Father Dulles himself has walked on both sides of the line.

For example, in his fine little commentary on the Dogmatic Constitution on the Church (*Lumen Gentium*) in the Abbott edition of *The Documents of Vatican II,* Dulles wrote: "When the Council Fathers came together, they immediately saw the need of setting forth a *radically different* vision of the Church, more biblical, more historical, more vital and dynamic" (my emphasis).

In recent years, however, Father Dulles seems to be more insistent on the principle of continuity and more skeptical of the principle of discontinuity.

Did Vatican II reaffirm and carry forward many, many elements of Catholic belief and practice? Of course it did. And therein lies a challenge to the left.

Did Vatican II also modify and even change certain other elements of Catholic belief and practice? Indeed it did. And therein lies a challenge to the right.

As usual, the truly Catholic position is one that takes a both/and, not an either/or, approach.

Vatican II Amended Church Elements Significantly

(April 27, 1990)

Few disgruntled Catholics ever attack the Second Vatican Council head-on. Even the schismatic and excommunicated Archbp. Marcel Lefebvre once insisted that he accepted the council—properly interpreted, of course.

That has been a common tactic of those in sympathy with the defeated minority at Vatican II. Instead of rejecting the council outright, they reinterpret it.

The council, they claim, didn't say anything new. Everything is as it was before.

While it is true that the vast majority of doctrines remained firmly in place following the council, the Second Vatican Council did amend or surpass some significant elements of traditional Catholic theology and official Catholic teachings.

I mention 10 by way of example.

1. Before the council, theology, catechesis, preaching, and official teaching did not speak of the Church as a sacrament. There were only seven sacraments, and the Church was not one of them. The council, however, called the Church itself a sacrament (Dogmatic Constitution on the Church, n. 1), thereby laying the groundwork for the whole movement of postconciliar renewal and reform.

2. Before the council, the Church and the Kingdom of God were regarded as one and the same. The council changed that equation. At most the Church is "the initial budding forth" of the Kingdom (Constitution on the Church, n. 5).

3. Before Vatican II the Catholic Church and the Church of Christ were also regarded as "one and the same" (the exact wording of Pope Pius XII's 1950 encyclical *Humani Generis*). Vatican II changed that equation as well. At most the Church of Christ "subsists in" rather than "is" the Catholic Church (Constitution on the Church, n. 8).

4. Before the council, sin was never attributed to the Church as such but only to individuals within the Church. The council changed that, insisting that the Church is at the same time holy and sinful, always in need of being purified and of incessantly pursuing the path of penance and renewal (Constitution on the Church, n. 8).

5. Before Vatican II it was taken for granted that salvation was available only in and through the Church. The council taught instead that salvation is available outside the Church (Constitution on the Church, n. 16), and that non-Christian religions may serve as instruments of salvation (Declaration on the Relationship of the Church to Non-Christian Religions, n. 2).

6. Before the council it was assumed that bishops are creatures of the pope and as such his vicars or delegates. Vatican II taught that bishops are *not* vicars of the Roman pontiff (Constitution on the Church, n. 17). They are constituted as members of the college of bishops not by an act of papal jurisdiction but by sacramental consecration (n. 22).

7. Before the council it was also simply assumed in Catholic theology, catechesis, preaching, and teaching that the Church was an absolute monarchy under the pope. Over against this view, the council taught that the governance of the universal Church devolves upon the whole college of bishops and that their pastoral authority is exercised in regional councils and in national episcopal conferences as well as in ecumenical councils (Constitution on the Church, nn. 22–23).

8. Before Vatican II the role of the laity in the Church was understood in the mode of helpmates to the hierarchy and the clergy. But the Council taught that the laity participate directly in the mission of the Church by reason of their baptism and confirmation and not by episcopal delegation (Constitution on the Church, n. 33). All—laity as well as clergy and religious—share in the threefold mission of Jesus as prophet, priest, and king (n. 30).

9. Before the council it was taken for granted that the Body of Christ was composed of Catholics alone. Vatican II included non-Catholic Christians as well (Decree on Ecumenism, n. 3).

10. Before the council it was assumed that "error has no rights." Religious freedom could not be accorded to non-Catholic forms of worship so long as the power of the state could prevent it (as in Franco Spain). Vatican II taught that religious freedom is for all, including non-Catholics, because of our common human dignity and the freedom of the act of faith (Declaration on Religious Freedom, nn. 2ff. and 9ff.).

Before the council, Fr. John Courtney Murray, S.J., was forbidden to write and speak on the subject of religious freedom because his views were regarded as those of a dissenter from official Catholic teaching.

At Vatican II the "dissenter's" theology became official Catholic teaching. There's a lesson there that still has to be learned in today's Church.

2

Authority

Introduction

One of the most pointed questions ever put to Jesus had to do with his claim
to authority: "On what authority are you doing these things? Who has given
you the power to do them?" (Mark 11:28).

It is also the question put most often to the Catholic Church. In the
pre–Vatican II period, many people "converted" to Catholicism precisely because of the authority issue (many others, of course, came into the Church
through marriage). The Catholic Church alone seemed to have a legitimate
claim to the authority of Christ himself: "He who hears you hears me" (Luke
10:16).

The Second Vatican Council reaffirmed the authority of Christ in his
Church, but at the same time gave this authority a new and richer meaning.
Authority is not for domination and control but for service. Authority is to be
exercised by many in the Church, not just the ordained few and certainly not
just the pope. And authority is something to be earned, not simply received
through the conferral of an office.

The authority issue flared anew in 1968 with the publication of Pope
Paul VI's encyclical on birth control, *Humanae Vitae*. According to scientific
surveys undertaken by the National Opinion Research Center in Chicago, it
was the encyclical, not the council, that radically altered the way Catholics
understand and respond to authority in the Church.

The columns in this chapter touch upon the birth-control controversy as
well as some of the other topics that have been central to the debate about
authority in the Catholic Church: the papacy, collegiality, the problem of authoritarianism, academic freedom, and democracy in the Church.

As psychologist Eugene Kennedy pointed out in a brief but remarkably
incisive article in *America* magazine, "The Problem with No Name" (April 23,
1988), the turning-away from authority in its preconciliar forms "represents a
search for authority rather than a rejection of it."

And that is also the case with the columns reproduced in this chapter. They
do not reject the authority of the Church; they are part of the ongoing search
effort.

The Pope and Birth Control
(August 9, 1968)

A year ago I wrote in this column that "it is one of the great theological and pastoral tragedies of our time that the average Christian's attitude toward the papacy and papal authority should be formed exclusively within the context of the birth control issue." The recent encyclical letter of Pope Paul VI (*Humanae Vitae*) provides an occasion for reaffirming this judgment with an even deeper sense of urgency.

Various opinions within the Church had already become dangerously hardened prior to the encyclical's appearance last week. Now that the pope has chosen to endorse the minority point of view, there may be a tendency on the part of some Catholics to begin reading one another out of the Church or for some to leave the Church on their own initiative, in sadness and disillusionment. (The editor of a right-of-center Catholic magazine has already called for such an exodus on the left.)

Either course of action would reflect an implicit acceptance of the post–Vatican I ecclesiology that exalted the pope to the status of a supertheologian and clothed his every pronouncement with the aura of impeccable and incontrovertible accuracy.

But the theology that has developed over the past several decades and that emerged so unexpectedly (for many Catholics) at the Second Vatican Council has produced in the Church today a more critical attitude toward papal authority—an attitude that eschews both cynicism and rigidity. It portrays the pope for what he is: the leading moral authority in the Church, who nevertheless shares our human condition in all things, including sin and error. His authority, though supreme, is never divorced from that of the rest of the college of bishops, nor indeed can it be independent of the Spirit that has been given to the whole Church.

Furthermore, as Msgr. Ferdinando Lambruschini made clear when releasing the document in Rome, this encyclical is not infallible. It is subject, therefore, to error and later correction, and that is why he made it a point to invite theologians and other specialists in the Church to discuss and debate this declaration.

One should not conclude, however, that a Catholic may adopt a casual or indifferent attitude to major pronouncements such as this one. The pope is the chief spokesman for the entire Christian community. He is the heart and center of the college of bishops and as such is a symbol of unity for the whole Church. In the formation of one's conscience, the Catholic must pay serious heed to the pastoral and theological directives of his Church's principal bishop.

Accordingly it would be irresponsible for a Catholic to dismiss this latest encyclical without study, consultation, and prayer. It is not a light matter to adopt a moral position at odds with the pope's. However, those who so decide must be spared the pharisaical abuse that issues such as this so often provoke.

But why should a Catholic respond with some measure of enthusiasm to the call of the pope on issues of war and peace or social justice (where infallibility is similarly not at stake) when this same Catholic may seem cool, if not in open opposition, on other matters, such as the recent "Credo" of Pope Paul VI or his birth-control encyclical? Is there a radical inconsistency here? Have we reverted once again to the pick-and-choose polemics of the 1940s and the 1950s when Catholics would quote fragments of papal statements against one another?

Inconsistency is a problem only for those who uncritically accept the ecclesiology of the early 20th century: the pope is the one theologian who ultimately matters, and what he says goes.

Yet it has become exceedingly awkward today for many Catholics to support this rigid view of papal authority. For example, we have some of them saying that the pope has spoken authoritatively on contraception, but he is "naive" about nuclear disarmament or the Vietnam War. They say there is to be no compromise or discussion about the clear strictures of his birth-control statement (indeed, Catholics who don't like it should leave the Church), but we can imagine all sorts of "factors" to mitigate and effectively nullify the force of his social encyclical, *Populorum Progressio,* or Pope John XXIII's *Mater et Magistra* (we recall the flippancy of the right: "Mater, si; magistra, no!").

The far right wing must somehow resolve its own inner contradictions. My concern here is for those who may have grown cynical about the papacy, particularly in view of this recent pronouncement, but who may still recognize the call of the gospel in so many papal utterances and gestures (e.g., his appearance in 1965 before the United Nations). For it is precisely in proclaiming the gospel that the pope fulfills his role as chief shepherd and holy father. If the proclamation is genuinely evangelical, the Holy Spirit will see to the echo throughout the whole Church; if it is not, he will see to the static.

On the birth-control issue the pope's present position does not seem to reflect the consensus of the Church, and static fills the air. The encyclical is at odds with the conclusions of the overwhelming majority of the pope's own commission of experts, the public resolutions of the Third World Lay Congress in Rome, the majority of Catholic moral theologians, the consciences of many Catholic married couples, and the pastoral and theological judgments of the large majority of non-Catholic Christian churches that participate in the life of the Body of Christ and in his spirit. (For a fuller critique, see the statement of the 87 Catholic theologians, the *New York Times,* July 31.)

If the teaching of *Humanae Vitae* is faithful to the authentic tradition of the gospel, it will eventually produce a consensus of approval throughout the whole Church. If not, it will take its place with past authoritative statements on religious liberty, interest taking, the right to silence, and the ends of marriage. I should expect that this will happen.

Meanwhile the debate enters yet another major phase with this important new ingredient. Confusion will be compounded if this interim period is not marked by clarity of argument and charity of manner. Ridicule and re-crimination, flippancies and fulminations will only serve to compromise the Church's enduring mission to be the sign and principal instrument of God's Kingdom on earth and the community of hope for the future of man-kind. This is hardly the time for closing doors, particularly in one another's faces.

Pope Essential to Catholicism

(September 20, 1968)

What is it that distinguishes the Roman Catholic communion for all other communities within the Church? The simplest possible response is to direct the reader to the third chapter of the Second Vatican Council's Dogmatic Con-stitution on the Church. Therein we can find, in conveniently synthetic form, the heart of the distinctively Roman Catholic conception of the Church. Whereas the specific difference between Christian and non-Christian lies in the fact of baptism and the explicit confession of faith in the Lordship of Jesus Christ, the basic difference between Roman Catholicism and every other form of Christianity is its understanding of ecclesiastical office, and, more specifi-cally, the office of the pope.

Article 18 begins with the observation that Christ instituted a variety of ministries in the Church for the nurturing and constant growth of the People of God and that these ministers, who are endowed with sacred power, are "servants of their brethren." Most non-Catholic churches could accept this without much difficulty.

The council proceeds, however, to specify these ministries. Jesus estab-lished his Church by sending forth the apostles as he himself had been sent by the Father (John 20:21): "He willed that their successors, namely the bishops, should be shepherds in his Church even to the consummation of the world." With the affirmation of an episcopal structure, many lower-church Protestant denominations depart from the consensus.

The final stage of disengagement is reached when the council insists: "In order that the episcopate itself might be one and undivided, he placed blessed Peter over the other apostles, and instituted in him a permanent and visible source and foundation of unity and fellowship. And all this teaching about the institution, the perpetuity, the force and reason for the sacred primacy of the Roman Pontiff and of his infallible teaching authority, this sacred synod again proposes to be firmly believed by all the faithful."

The Catholic, therefore, is one who, while recognizing the bond of unity he has with all other Christians inside the Body of Christ, is convinced that the heart and center of this Body resides in the Roman Catholic communion. The Catholic believes that the source of unity in the Church is the Eucharist and that the ministerial or hierarchical foundation of the Eucharist is the college of bishops with the pope at its head. There are degrees of incorporation in the

Church, but the norm of incorporation is one's proximity to these sacramental and collegial realities.

There may, indeed, be areas for discussion, such as the precise meaning of infallibility or the proper relationship between pope and bishops or the theological understanding of the presence of Christ in the Eucharist. But for the Catholic, a Church without the college of bishops, without the chief bishop as the successor of Peter, or without the Eucharist would be no Church at all.

The Catholic is convinced, therefore, that the Church was never meant to be a totally unstructured "movement" or "happening." He would share the view of the Anglican New Testament scholar Bp. John Robinson that "it is impossible to be a biblical theologian without being a high Churchman."

The question that confronts the Catholic Church in our time, however, is not whether we should have a pope or bishops or stylized sacraments but whether the historical development of each of these central realities does, in fact, conform to the biblical pattern and whether there may now be room for a different kind of development.

How Do Teachers Know Content of Faith?

(December 6, 1968)

Few conciliar statements have been so popular with the defenders of *Humanae Vitae* as the second paragraph of article 25 in the Dogmatic Constitution on the Church. Herein we are reminded that the teaching of the bishops on matters of faith and morals is to be accepted with "a religious assent of soul," while a "religious submission of mind and will must be shown in a special way to the authentic teaching authority of the Roman Pontiff, even when he is not speaking *ex cathedra.*" But this text raises some questions.

Why do we insist that the college of bishops, when it includes the pope, is the supreme teaching authority in the Church, to the extent that its teaching has a solemn claim upon our minds and wills? Surely it isn't enough to say that this authority is supreme because Christ conferred it upon the Church and intended it to be accepted as such. That does not really answer the fundamental question: *How* do these official teachers come to know the content of faith that they are commissioned to pass on to the rest of the Church?

Is there a special channel of communication that God has opened between himself and the pope and the bishops? Are the principal office-holders in the Church the recipients of special private revelation, involving either visions or direct infusion of knowledge? Certainly no one in the Catholic Church believed this, and least of all the pope and the bishops.

How, then, do we know if what the pope and the bishops are teaching on a given occasion is true or false? Must we assume that they are always right? Is blind obedience the expected response? Not even the most rigidly juridical theology of the past has ever made such a claim. On the contrary, the *First* Vatican Council condemned such an attitude as "Fideism."

Is it enough to say that the magisterium (teaching authority) of the Church is endowed with the enlightenment of the Holy Spirit? The council document indicates that the pope and the bishops do, in fact, operate "under the guiding light of the Spirit of truth" when they are involved in the transmission of revelation to the whole Church (art. 25, par. 7). But does the Spirit guarantee 100 percent accuracy? Again, not even the most rigidly juridical theologies of the past made such a claim.

The council reminds us here, as it did in the Constitution on Divine Revelation (art. 10, par. 2), that the teaching office is not above the Word of God but serves it. The magisterium must teach not its own truth but the truth of God's Word. But the question remains, How does the magisterium apprehend this truth? What criteria does it use, and what criteria do the Church use, in evaluating the success or failure of this quest for truth?

Article 25, paragraph 7, insists that the pope and the bishops must "strive painstakingly and by appropriate means to inquire properly into that revelation and to give apt expression to its contents." And this is to be understood as a moral duty incumbent upon all who share in the teaching authority of the Church.

The "appropriate means" consist of constant recourse to Sacred Scripture, the work of biblical scholars, historians, dogmatic theologians, anthropologists, sociologists, and so forth. A consistent effort must be made to overcome the tendency to rely exclusively on one school of theology and thereby to identify the Word of God with the opinions of that one school of thought. There must be a free and open exchange of views, living contact with the faith and "public opinion" of the whole community—institutional and charismatic, Catholic and non-Catholic, Christian and non-Christian.

Consequently it is not enough to say that because such-and-such a doctrine has been proposed by the magisterium of the Church, every Catholic must accept it as true, with a "religious submission of mind and will." The magisterium, too, has a learning responsibility. It must always "strive painstakingly and by appropriate means to inquire properly into that revelation and to give apt expression to its contents."

When there is evidence that this has not been done adequately, the "submission of mind and will" cannot be engaged. There "human" criteria do not exclude the "guiding light of the Spirit of truth," but in their absence, the appeal to the Spirit is both unwarranted and meaningless.

Problems of Authority Related to How Guidance Is Offered
(December 13, 1968)

A survey conducted soon after the release of Pope Paul VI's encyclical on the regulation of births disclosed that *Humanae Vitae* changed the minds of only 2 percent of the American Catholic clergy. That is, among the group that had earlier favored contraception as a viable moral option, only two priests in a hundred were persuaded to return to the more "traditional" position by the papal encyclical.

I have no intention to reopen the birth-control controversy in this week's essay. The deeper issue is the credibility and effectiveness of the magisterium of the Church, and the deeper question: How many minds are actually formed or changed by official documents of the Church?

How many Catholics, particularly among the affluent, have in fact changed their opinions about the stewardship of wealth in response to the social encyclicals of Pope Leo XIII, Pope Pius XI, Pope John XXIII, and Pope Paul VI?

How many Catholics, rich and poor, have actually changed their attitudes toward black people because of the American bishops' statement in 1958?

How many American Catholics have altered their political ideas about nuclear disarmament in the light of Vatican II's clear strictures against the continuation of the arms race?

How many Catholics have actually modified their understanding of the papacy because of the council's teaching on collegiality? How many, despite this teaching, still look upon the pope as a kind of absolute monarch?

How many Catholics abandoned their fundamentalist attitude in the interpretation of Sacred Scripture precisely because of Pope Pius XII's encyclical *Divino Afflante Spiritu* (1943) or the decree of the Pontifical Biblical Commission (1964) or the Constitution on Divine Revelation of the Second Vatican Council (1965)?

How many Catholic institutions (parishes, hospitals, schools, etc.) have raised salaries, extended fringe benefits, or encouraged the formation of unions in specific response to one of the many documents containing the social teachings of the Church?

How many Catholics changed their emotional and political attitudes toward war and violence as a solution to social and economic problems just because of Pope Paul VI's dramatic speech before the United Nations in 1965?

Indeed, how many Catholics have actually read (in whole or in substantial part) any of the social encyclicals, any of the council documents, any of the pastoral letters of the American bishops, any of the speeches of the incumbent pope or his immediate predecessors?

One has only to attempt such a reading to see why the official and quasi-official teachings of the Church receive little more than casual attention (and much of the attention they do receive seems to spring from the curiosity of the secular press about the human power struggles that often surround the publication of such documents). Written in a style that is often a pale imitation of diplomatic rhetoric or court prose, magisterial texts are so florid, cumbersome, and strategically subtle as to become practically unintelligible for the average reader. The confusion and diversity of interpretation following the recent American bishops' statement on the birth-control question (even among some of the bishops themselves) is a case in point.

In this time of rapid change and sharp, open debate in the Catholic Church, several of its members have come rushing forward to the defense of the magisterium, insisting all the while that a Church without an infallible and binding doctrinal authority is a Church without moorings, without certainty, without security. But one has a right to wonder which world such Catholics are describing—the abstract world of early 20th-century, Catholic textbooks, or the factual world of mid-20th-century human experience?

There is, indeed, a crisis of authority in the Church. But the crisis does not arise primarily from the failure of Catholics to listen to and obey legitimate ecclesiastical authority. The more radical problem is how to make the office-holders themselves study, reflect, consult, speak, and act in such a way that their individual and collective doctrinal utterances are understandable, believable, and practical.

All those who care for the future of the Church must put themselves at the disposal of these office-holders in a spirit of fraternal cooperation and mutual concern for the realization of God's Kingdom. The office-holder must, in turn, seek out this help—but from the widest possible spectrum of competence and opinion that he can find. Consultation with those for whom there are no questions, only answers, will not dissolve the crisis that is upon us all.

Authority and the Generation Gap
(July 6, 1973)

Some over-45 Catholics find it hard to understand younger people's apparently diffident, even disrespectful, attitude toward established authority.

These Catholics, it should be remembered, were already in their 30s, and beyond, when the precedent-shattering 1960s began. They had come to adulthood under the strong and all-pervasive presidency of Franklin D. Roosevelt or during the father-grandfather-image incumbency of Dwight D. Eisenhower.

J. Edgar Hoover, with an unchallenged reputation for moral probity and bulldog tenacity, served during most of their lifetimes as the national symbol of fearless and efficient law enforcement.

In those years a "Support Your Local Police" bumper sticker would have been as superfluous as a shill at a giveaway sale.

In the Catholic Church, meanwhile, the papal office had steadily risen to perhaps the highest level of magisterial activism in modern ecclesiastical history. Few questioned the trend privately; none publicly.

Catholics wondered only about the time lapse between the inevitable death of Pope Pius XII and his equally "inevitable" canonization.

But there are, of course, many other Catholics who were not yet in their 30s when John F. Kennedy was elected president of the United States.

- These Catholics were coming into young adulthood when the Bay of Pigs fiasco exploded in the faces of our newly ascendant political leadership. It would prove to be one of the earliest indications that those in power do not always know best.

- The civil rights movement, with its marches and demonstrations throughout the South, tore off the mask of respectability from the corporate face of our law enforcement agencies.

  Peaceful protests on behalf of an undeniably legitimate cause provoked cattle proddings, clubbings, and high-powered hosings. Younger people began wondering about the axioms of their elders. Are the police always on the side of right and justice?

- The ineptitude, bad judgment, and outright deception on the part of our political leaders in the genesis and conduct of the Vietnam War are only now being pieced together in such widely circulating books as David Halberstam's *The Best and the Brightest.*

  But many younger Americans, having grown increasingly skeptical, even cynical, about the manipulation of political power had, almost from the beginning, rejected and deplored the direction and rationale of our war policy.

  "Hell, No, We Won't Go" was a slogan many light-years removed from the patriotic rhetoric of those William Bendix and Lloyd Nolan World War II movies wherein wars were fought for Uncle Sam, Mom's apple pie, the girl next door, and the dream of another World Series at Ebbets Field.

- The disturbances in Chicago during the summer of 1968 were, according to the Walker Report, a Selma-north outrage, "a police riot." A United States senator excoriated the mayor for his use of "Gestapo" tactics to suppress and control the demonstrators.

- And finally there is Watergate. An administration that surged into office on the crest of a law-and-order mandate is exposed as probably the most scandal-ridden political operation in the history of the American republic.

The Bay of Pigs, Selma, Vietnam, Chicago '68, Watergate—only a dozen years separate the first from the last. There are many Americans, now at age 33 or thereabouts, whose entire adult lives have run exactly parallel to these events.

Is there really any wonder why some of these younger Americans should be disposed to challenge the all-knowing wisdom and trustworthiness of established authority?

They have come to adulthood during a decade when those in authority have flagrantly betrayed their oath of office or have manifested a measure of incompetence sufficient to shake the confidence of the naive.

To be sure, this is not justification for antinomianism, a systematic rejection of every claim of law and office, but it may explain at least partially the great generation gap that perdures, both in America and in the Catholic Church, on this gnawing problem of authority.

What Is Collegial Principle?

(February 22, 1974)

Even at this relatively late date, "collegiality" remains one of the least understood concepts among contemporary Catholics.

Many continue to think that collegiality refers only to the spirit of cooperation that should exist between pope and bishops, with the pope always reserving the right to initiate the process.

Thus, an ecumenical council is an act of collegiality because the pope willingly and openly seeks the advice of the bishops in the difficult task of governing the universal Church.

An international synod (three of which have been held since Vatican II; a fourth will meet this October) is similarly collegial in nature, because, once again, the pope freely and deliberately chooses to share his decision-making problems with ecclesiastical officials beneath him in authority.

Collegiality, according to this particular view, is something that applies directly, if not exclusively, to the pope. It is a "something" that gives the pope the right (perhaps even a mild obligation) to consult the bishops on matters of far-reaching church policy.

After the council, when many priests (and later, many parishioners) sought to apply the collegial principle to pastor-curate (and pastor-parishioner) relationships, they were politely advised that collegiality referred only to the relationship between pope and bishops, nothing more.

A second common misunderstanding of collegiality, coming this time from the left side of the spectrum, makes of it such a broad concept that it applies to just about any exercise of cooperation between otherwise competing or conflicting parties.

I have even heard the term used by a history department chairman at the university level. He spoke highly of one of his colleagues, at the time under consideration for tenure, on the basis of that colleague's spirit of collegiality in department affairs.

The chairman meant, of course, that the junior professor was a cooperative and conciliatory person, one not given to academic petulance or arrogance.

Seminary students, for several years after Vatican II, appealed to the collegial principle in demanding a fuller participation in the policy-making process. Collegiality means not only cooperation among diverse parties but also a lifting-up of a lower group to a higher level of responsibility and authority.

Thus, collegiality would mean giving priests' senates some authority previously reserved to the pastor, and so forth.

This, too, is a misreading of the theology of collegiality. It is neither restricted to the papal-episcopal relationship nor is it so broad that it applies to every instance of cooperation or power sharing.

Collegiality, in its first and deepest meaning, refers to the unique manner in which the Body of Christ exists. The Church is not a single, uniform entity subdivided into dioceses and parishes for the sake of administrative efficiency.

Rather, the Church is a communion of churches. It is a community of communities.

The question may seem purely academic. It is not.

· The reason for many of our most serious disagreements in the Catholic Church today over such issues as the election of bishops, the tenure of the pope, the power of parish councils, and reform of marriage courts is the continued, and often unacknowledged, division of opinion on the very makeup of the Church.

Many Catholics, some of whom occupy positions of real influence in the Church, persist in the view that the Church is, for all practical purposes, a single parish with a single pastor, the pope.

They think that dioceses exist (and bishops, too) because the pope cannot govern such a Church without help; and that parishes (and pastors) exist because bishops have the same problem in relationship to their own dioceses.

In other words, according to this view, the local church is but a division of the universal Church. The bishop is a kind of division manager, the pastor a subdivision manager. Supreme and absolute authority remains at the top, distributed solely at the will of the chief officer, the pope.

Over against this view we have one of Vatican II's most important, and least appreciated, teachings on the theology of the local church: "This Church of Christ is truly present in all legitimate local congregations of the faithful which, united with their pastors, are themselves called churches in the New Testament. For in their own locality these are the new people called by God, in the Holy Spirit" (Dogmatic Constitution on the Church, n. 26).

A proper understanding of collegiality will inevitably enhance the place of the local Christian community in the life of the Church universal. And many, if not most, proposals for Church reform today are geared precisely to this end.

The Pope and the Synod of Bishops
(November 22, 1974)

I don't suppose that the majority of my readers followed the synod very closely. If they had, there was a lesson to be learned from it, particularly in the way it ended.

One of the conventional assumptions abroad in the Catholic Church today—shared by as many progressives as conservatives—is that the pope and the bishops stand together as a solid bloc over against some liberal laity, younger religious, activist clergy, and the all pervasive "fifth columnist" theologians.

But anyone tracing the course of the Fourth International Synod of Bishops would have to reach a different conclusion about the state of the contemporary Catholic Church.

The pope's final message had a mildly scolding tone to it. It contained some of the warnings he has issued frequently in the past about respect for his

authority and against confusing political struggles for justice with the spiritually liberating mission of the Church.

But this time his words were not directed at the restless lower clergy nor
independent-minded religious.

On certain key issues, the pope rejected the majority thinking of the synod
itself—and the synod, we ought not to forget, is a body of bishops representing
the entire Roman Catholic world.

"We would not be able to remain silent," he noted on the final day. "We
could not allow false directions to be followed."

What were some of the "false directions" that provoked the pope into
breaking his silence?

Many of the bishops, especially those from the developing countries in
Africa, had called for a change in the relationship between the particular
churches and the Apostolic See.

These bishops had pressed for greater freedom to decide important pastoral cases at the local level without recourse to the centralized offices in Rome.

The pope perceived this as an undermining of his "full, supreme, and
universal power" over the whole Church. It was observed, however, that in
quoting from the Vatican II text on the Church that supports papal supremacy,
he passed over a balancing statement in the same section that concedes that the
same full and supreme authority is also vested in the bishops acting in union
with the pope.

Second, the pope warned the bishops about the dangers of their speaking
of diversified theologies according to continents and cultures.

At the same time he seemed to be forgetting that the process of theological
adaptation has been going on in the Church since the faith was first proclaimed
and reflected upon in the context of the Middle Eastern culture of Pales-
tine, then readapted theologically to the Roman and Hellenic cultures of the
apostolic and postapostolic periods and then again to the Western European
culture of the High Middle Ages.

Finally, Latin American bishops had urged a greater commitment to social
and political liberation, but the pope warned against an undue emphasis on the
temporal sphere "to the detriment of the essential meaning [of] evangelization."

Significantly, the pope made no mention of the role of women in the
Church, even though the subject had occupied several hours of discussion in
the synod itself. Neither did he make more than a glancing reference to the lay
apostolate to which the bishops had also given substantial attention.

It is known that the pope had personally rejected the original topic suggested for this synod: the family. This would have led inevitably to discussions
of such delicate issues as birth control, world population, and abortion. The
pope may have feared the impact of press accounts of episcopal disagreements,
particularly on the first and second issues.

Ironically this synod on evangelization—a safe topic on the surface—
provoked enough controversy of its own.

The final scene, with the pope placing himself at some distance from the large numbers of the bishops on key issues of ecclesiastical reform, should serve to shatter the illusion that progressives have little or no significant support within the episcopal college itself.

The division of theological opinion between the pope and many of the bishops is nothing to exult over. On the other hand, we ought not to ignore its meaning and pastoral implications.

Dutch Synod Raises Questions

(March 14, 1980)

The recent synod of Dutch bishops held in the Vatican evokes a series of theological questions:

1. Given the principle that the Church is the whole People of God and that the Church in a particular country is the whole People of God in that country, on what basis is the discussion of such a central issue as unity reserved to bishops alone? Why were not laity, religious, and other clergy part of the synodal process?

2. Given the principle that local (parochial, diocesan, national) churches are not simply administrative subdivisions of the Church universal but are churches in their own right (Dogmatic Constitution on the Church, n. 26, not to mention the New Testament in general), and given the related principle that local churches together constitute the Church universal by their relationship one with another and by their *common* relationship with the Church of Rome, why should a synod of a single local church be presided over by the pope?

The question suggests no impropriety in the pope's presiding over an international synod or indeed over an ecumenical council. On the contrary, this is precisely one of the pope's most important responsibilities as a sign and instrument of Church unity (Dogmatic Constitution on the Church, n. 23).

3. Even granting the possibility that a serious threat to the unity of a local church might be addressed by bishops alone or that they might even call upon the pope to facilitate their deliberations regarding such a threat, on what basis is a bishop of still another local church (the new archbishop of Brussels, Belgium), invited to co-preside over the synod? And on what basis are heads of various Vatican Congregations brought in as (apparently) fully active, voting members of the synod?

If there are theologically disturbing aspects to the Dutch synod, those disturbing aspects are not so much related to the resolutions that emerged from the synod as they are to the process through which those resolutions were formulated at all.

It may be the case that the Dutch Church needs to tighten its pastoral policies regarding intercommunion, married clergy, seminary education, and whatever else.

One could not disparage the recent synod, in other words, simply because it adopted positions that many other Catholics would find unduly restrictive and even regressive.

Indeed, the questions I have raised at the beginning of this essay would be just as valid had the synod encouraged more intercommunion, closed down the one remaining traditional seminary in the Netherlands, supported optional celibacy for priests, and reaffirmed the right of the laity, religious, and other clergy to participate directly in the governance of the Church.

Catholics who want to applaud the actions of the recent Dutch synod and to say an extra prayer of gratitude for such a good pope should try to imagine how they would feel today if the presiding pope had been John XXIII, or someone even more progressive than he, and if the resolutions had been decidedly to the left of Vatican II.

Conservative Catholics in particular ought never forget the pain and confusion—and even the sense of betrayal—many felt when Vatican II reforms were imposed on unprepared parishes and dioceses. The reforms themselves may have been exactly correct, but the process was too often inept, insensitive, and educationally naive. One always looks a bit silly, for example, *mandating* participation without any prior participation in the decision to mandate.

Unless one looks upon the Catholic Church in primarily hierarchical terms, and unless one believes that the Catholic Church is, by the will of God, an absolute monarchy and that bishops are only the vicars or delegates of the pope, and unless one thinks that laity, religious, and other clergy have only as much responsibility and power as they are allotted by the hierarchy ("Catholic Action"), then one can only be troubled by this recent synod and by the inexplicable acquiescence of Cardinal Willebrands and his fellow bishops to the proceedings and to their results.

Looking Back at Humanae Vitae

(September 9, 1983)

On July 25, 1968, just over 15 years ago, Pope Paul VI released his encyclical "On the Regulation of Birth," known by its Latin title as *Humanae Vitae*. The Catholic Church hasn't been the same since.

Anyone over 35 years of age can easily recall the storm of controversy that that long-awaited document precipitated. For the first time in modern history, wide-ranging dissent greeted an official church teaching, dissent not from skeptical non-Catholics but from Catholics themselves.

Having grown accustomed to viewing theologians as conservative scholars who explain and defend papal teachings, many Catholics were astonished to see so many theologians attaching their names to public letters of opposition to the new encyclical.

The postencyclical period was a very confusing and tormented one for the Church. Since some of the dissenters had teaching positions in seminaries, for example, efforts were made to remove them from the staff. Sides formed quickly—and firmly. The word *polarization* entered the ecclesiastical vocabulary.

No one was more distressed than the Holy Father himself. He had acted in good conscience, convinced that he had no alternative. Although he expected some measure of disappointment and even disagreement, he was not prepared for the reaction it did evoke, nor were very many others.

Now, some 15 years later, the press has been asking several of those who were active in Church affairs at the time if they have had any second thoughts about it. Not surprisingly, few have. Minds were long since made up, and lines boldly drawn.

In the spirit of dialogue, however, and in fidelity to the truth, it might serve the cause of reconciliation within the Church if Catholics on both sides of the controversy were prepared to reevaluate the encyclical now from the other side's point of view.

How might a critic or dissenter look at it today, from the other side? Would he or she find nothing at all worth affirming? Or could one even go so far as to say there are prophetic strains in the document?

One is struck, first of all, by the pope's healthy, positive attitude toward conjugal love. It must be "fully human, that is to say, of the senses and of the spirit at the same time." Second, it must be an expression of "a very special form of personal friendship, in which husband and wife generously share everything, without undue reservation of selfish calculations." And third, it must be marked by complete fidelity.

One is also impressed with the pope's concerns about some of the likely consequences of the new contraceptive mentality: conjugal infidelity, a general lowering of moral standards among the young, a loss of respect for women in casual, newly "safe" relationships, and particularly the imposition of birth control by authoritarian states. Has none of that happened?

Despite the hard-line moral position it adopts, the encyclical shows an underlying pastoral sensitivity. The pope acknowledges in the section directed explicitly to married couples that this teaching will pose serious difficulties for many of them, but he urges them to continue to draw strength from the Eucharist and never to be discouraged or feel themselves cut off from the Church.

He urges priests to exercise "patience and goodness," following the example of Christ himself, who came not to condemn but to save. "He was intransigent with evil, but merciful toward individuals."

Finally, in his admonition to bishops, Pope Paul VI implored them to work "ardently and incessantly for the safeguarding and the holiness of marriage." But then he noted that such a mission "implies concerted pastoral action in all the fields of human activity, economic, cultural and social."

The teaching on contraception, therefore, is to be received within the wider framework of the Church's social doctrine.

Let critics of the encyclical reread it now with a more sympathetic heart, even if they continue to disagree with its central point, and let its strongest defenders reread it in light of the same Holy Father's *Populorum Progressio* (1967), *Octagesima Adveniens* (1971), and *Evangelii Nuntiandi* (1974), and indeed the whole of the Church's recent teachings on justice, human rights, and peace.

One suspects that history will treat Pope Paul VI much more kindly than his critics, both of the left and of the right, did in his lifetime.

If the Church Isn't a Democracy, What Is It?

(November 6, 1987)

When Catholics get into arguments (as they occasionally do) about the policies of the pope, the Curia, their bishop, or their pastor, someone always feels compelled to remind the others that the Church is not a democracy.

That may be true, but if the Church isn't a democracy, what is it? A monarchy? A dictatorship?

Such an understanding of the Church is simply wrong—historically, theologically, doctrinally, and canonically.

Those who believe the Church to be a monarchy (with the pope as the sole ruler) are innocent, first, of the most basic elements of Church history.

Indeed, if Jesus intended the Church to be monarchical in structure, he would have made that clear to his closest disciples, and especially the apostles.

But, in fact, when the Council of Jerusalem was held in A.D. 49 or 50, it was James, not Peter, who presided. It was James, not Peter, who executed the council's decisions.

For literally hundreds of years the bishops of Rome did not exercise even the quasi-monarchical authority over the universal Church that modern canon law cedes to them.

Theologically the Church is neither a monarchy nor a democracy; it is a collegial reality. This means that the Church is a college of local churches that together constitute the universal Church.

In each local church the unity of the faithful is rooted not only in the presence of the Holy Spirit, in the Eucharist, in the other sacraments, and in the Word of God but also in the ministerial office of the bishop.

The unity of the bishops is a manifestation and representation of the unity of the whole Church. Their unity finds expression in ecumenical councils, in world synods, in regional councils, and in national episcopal conferences.

The diocese of Rome and its bishop hold a unique place in this college of local churches and of their bishops because, by tradition, Rome is where Peter's ministry and life ended in martyrdom.

Moreover, according to Catholic doctrine, the bishop of Rome functions as the center of unity within the college of bishops. He is, in the words of the Second Vatican Council, "the perpetual and visible source and foundation of the unity of the bishops and of the multitude of the faithful" (Dogmatic Constitution on the Church, n. 23).

But the bishops' ministry and authority do not depend on the pope. Bishops are not vicars of the pope, Vatican II also declared.

"Their power, therefore, is not destroyed by the supreme and universal power. On the contrary it is affirmed, strengthened, and vindicated thereby, since the Holy Spirit unfailingly preserves the form of government established by Christ the Lord in His Church" (Dogmatic Constitution on the Church, n. 27).

That "government" includes bishops, not just Peter and his successors.

Consequently if one wants to talk about the government of the Church in modern political terms, it would be far more accurate (though still misleading) to call it an oligarchy rather than a monarchy.

Indeed, it wouldn't be at all accurate to call it a monarchy, even though many Catholics regard it as such.

What is clear from history, theology, and doctrine is also clear, finally, in canon law as well.

The code acknowledges that the college of bishops is "also the subject of supreme and full power over the universal Church" (canon 336). So it is not the pope alone who exercises "supreme and full power."

But this is putting everything in a kind of legalistic framework. There is much more to the Church than its governing structures. It is a mystery, a sacrament, the People of God.

Vatican II reminded us that the Holy Spirit is present in the whole Church, "in the faithful of every rank" (Constitution on the Church, n. 12).

By baptism and confirmation, all participate "in the saving mission of the Church itself" (n. 33).

There can be no inequality in the Church (n. 32). The laity, therefore, must be given "every opportunity" to "participate in the saving work of the Church" (n. 33).

In accordance with their competence and ability, the laity are not only permitted but sometimes even "obliged" to express opinions about matters that concern the good of the Church (n. 37).

The council proposed that such principles as these be implemented at every level: in parish and diocesan councils, in priests' senates, in synods, in associations of various kinds.

Such instruments of coresponsibility may not show the Church to be a democracy, but they clearly show it not to be a monarchy either.

Authoritarianism and Authority

(May 27, 1988)

I have a hunch that relatively few of my readers saw Eugene Kennedy's recent article in *America*, "The Problem with No Name" (April 23). The essay is too important to let pass.

The "problem" to which Kennedy refers is that of authority. More specifically it is the problem of discerning the difference between authoritarianism and genuine authority, and of making possible the transition from the one to the other. Most discussions of authority, he writes, are really condemnations or reassertions of authoritarianism.

What's the difference?

True authority is generative. It seeks to promote and nurture growth through guidance, encouragement, and support.

Unhealthy authority, or authoritarianism, is a phenomenon that uses techniques of shaming and debasement to gain its way. It is not interested in the growth of those under its supervision so much as in the control of their behavior.

The revolt against authoritarianism has made the recognition or recovery of genuine authority very difficult, Kennedy argues.

In psychology alone (Kennedy's own field of specialization), there are dozens of books and hundreds of articles and research projects on authoritarianism and its evils.

On the other hand, "there is hardly any interest, much less research or writing, about authority as a sound and indispensable element of human growth."

This is a very serious deficiency because "any institution, including the family and the church, charged with responsibility for fostering healthy development must be knowing about the nature of authentic authority."

The difficulty in identifying true authority is compounded, Kennedy continues, by the media's shorthand approach to the whole problem. Television and newspapers, focusing constantly on conflict, shape stories about the Catholic Church in the negative language of repression and rebellion.

"In fact," Kennedy insists, "very few Catholics want to rebel against church authority; hardly any want to overthrow the pope or, for that matter, be arbitrary in their judgments about curial decisions."

"Something psychologically far different is occurring," he notes, "and it is urgent for participants and observers to discern its proper nature."

Segments of the Catholic Church that seem to be in violent disagreement about authority are actually troubled by the same problem and are seeking, by different routes, some resolution of it.

Both liberals and traditionalists are searching for "a credible authority in which to invest their trust and to identify healthy leaders whom they can willingly follow."

The reason for the crisis of authority today is primarily cultural and historical, not theological or ideological.

The world has moved from a medieval, hierarchical model of reality, where everything is divinely organized from top to bottom, to a space-age world of collaboration and responsibility—of collegiality, if you will.

Authoritarianism is dying for many reasons, one of which is that authoritarians can no longer successfully control the flow of information in an age of communication. (That they still think they can is reflected in the preoccupation of some with the whole matter of "public" dissent.)

For example, because of space-age satellites, the nuclear accident at Chernobyl could not be hidden even by the ultraauthoritarian and ultrasecretive regime in Moscow.

"The church," Kennedy declares, "must come to terms with the same truth about its own inability to censor, disallow or render itself insensitive to the real meaning of human experience or the impact of new knowledge in realms as different as human sexuality, freedom of inquiry and the evolving understandings of theology."

But at the heart of the "problem" is the inability of authoritarian leaders to deal with the mystery that is at the heart of all true religion and all true human experience. They are simply ill at ease with that deeper, unquantifiable dimension of reality.

These leaders are comfortable only with "unambiguous concrete faith." And that is why they possess so little true spiritual authority, authority that "naturally attracts the attention of searching believers."

Nothing illustrates this problem better than the official Church's distinct awkwardness in its dealings with women.

"Religious life," Kennedy suggests, "is ending because it can no longer function as a male-dominated culture, not because human beings lack profound spiritual aspirations."

Just as the "male-bonded culture of clerical life is in ruins because it is a vestige of the great days of privilege, not because people lack interest in ministry."

"This turning away," Kennedy concludes, "represents a search for authority rather than a rejection of it."

"The more church leaders, still wearing its symbols in medieval court regalia, seek to reestablish authority as authoritarianism, the more surely they destroy their possibility of having any but remembered authority in the future."

And that's "the problem with no name."

Debate over Academic Freedom for Theologians, Institutions
(December 16, 1988)

We don't talk very much these days about infused knowledge, but the distinction between infused and acquired knowledge somehow always found a place in pre–Vatican II philosophy and theology courses.

Infused knowledge's decline in prominence parallels a similar decline in the fortunes of angels. Angels were the only creatures who were said to have infused knowledge, as a matter of necessity.

Since angels are pure spirits, they cannot attain knowledge as we do, by the use of concepts abstracted from the material world. Their knowledge is given to them directly by God. It is "infused."

The current debate over academic freedom for Catholic theologians and institutional autonomy for Catholic universities has unwittingly revived the notion of infused knowledge.

By implication at least, some of the critics of academic freedom and institutional autonomy are proposing that infused knowledge is not limited, after all, to the angels. Bishops also possess it.

Among the points being raised against academic freedom for Catholic theologians is that the bishops must make the "final" decision on what is true and what is false in theological "speculation."

Although theologians are encouraged to probe and to push back the frontiers of knowledge through painstaking scholarly efforts, they are also reminded that the "final" decision regarding the validity of those efforts rests solely with the hierarchy.

After there has been sufficient "dialogue, discussion and even disagreement," Pittsburgh's Bp. Donald Wuerl insisted in an address at the University of Massachusetts last summer, we "cross a line from discussion about various theological conclusions to the approbation and application of the conclusions."

"The work of theological development," he declared, "is to push our understanding of the faith to new and more profound limits. It is the task of the bishops to note when the limits have been crossed."

But such a claim raises an important question: How do the bishops know when "the limits have been crossed"?

Very few bishops are professionally trained and professionally active theologians. A mere handful of bishops earned a theological doctorate (or some comparable degree in Sacred Scripture) 20 or 30 years ago, but they have little or no record of teaching at advanced levels, of publishing scholarly articles and books, or of attaining leadership positions in professional societies.

When professionally active theologians and Scripture scholars seek after truth, they do so by examining the primary sources in the original languages, by studying all the relevant secondary literature, by engaging in careful textual exegesis, by sorting out the complexities and ambiguities of the historical record, by trying to fashion a sustained and compelling argument that will survive the critical scrutiny of a wider community of scholars, and then by defending that argument in a variety of scholarly settings.

If the bishops know when "the limits have been crossed," it must be because they already have the answers that the theologians have been searching for.

Since it is clear that the bishops have not attained the answers through their own scholarly efforts, they must have attained the answers through some other means. What is that means?

If there *is* another means, distinct from the rigorous methods of scholarship, why is it that the scholars themselves have never discovered it?

If it's possible to know that something is true or false without even cracking a book, so to speak, why isn't every member of the Church in on the secret, including especially doctoral students in theology?

Life would be much easier if we could come to an understanding of our faith without even working up an intellectual sweat, and we'd all have a lot more time for relaxation and prayer.

The only conclusion we can draw is that the bishops must have infused knowledge, while the theologians have to gain their knowledge the old-fashioned way. "They *earn* it!" as the late John Houseman used to say in the Smith Barney ad.

But why work when you don't have to? When a biblical scholar has a difficult problem with a particular text, why doesn't he just call up his local bishop and ask for the answer?

And why should Karl Rahner have struggled so long with the problem of the consciousness of Jesus? His bishop had the answer all the time.

Ditto for complicated questions in medical ethics and for all matters pertaining to human sexuality and reproduction.

Many years ago a committee submitted plans for a new seminary to the Vatican. Someone noticed there were no bathrooms. "*Suntne angeli?*" ("Are they angels?"), the Vatican asked.

Good question then—and now.

3

Catholics in Conflict

Introduction

Jesus commanded his disciples to love one another, as a sign of their fidelity to his message and mission: "This is how all will know you for my disciples; your love for one another" (John 13:34–35). Alas, in the history of the Church, ideal and reality have never completely overlapped. Even in those biblical communities that traced their origin to the author of the Fourth Gospel, the Gospel of love, there was sharp dissension and disunity.

So it was then; so it is now; so it has always been. Although the Catholic Church remains a community committed to reconciliation, healing, forgiveness, mutual understanding, justice, and all the other virtues, it is also a community of human beings prone to selfishness, greed, vindictiveness, insensitivity, and all the other vices.

The Catholic Church is at once a sacrament of unity and a community torn by internal conflict. That conflict has been described according to many different categories: left versus right, liberals versus conservatives, fundamentalists versus modernizers, traditionalists versus progressives, loyalists versus dissidents, orthodox versus heretics, and so on.

The columns in this chapter probe the problem of conflict within the postconciliar Catholic Church. They press beyond the media labels to uncover its underlying causes.

As I wrote in the column of July 1, 1988, "to admit that sharp differences of opinion can coexist in the Church is to admit the legitimacy of pluralism, which is to say that there is more than one orthodox way to understand and express our Catholic faith."

The Catholic Church is indeed a pluralistic Church. In such a Church, conflict is not simply inevitable, it is a sign of health.

Crisis Is Not as Simple as Catholic "Right" Thinks
(July 28, 1967)

Catholics should neither fear nor be disturbed unduly by criticism of the Church, particularly the criticism that has its source within the Christian community itself. Such criticism is a sign of life and health. People take the time and the trouble to criticize only what they regard seriously.

Most of these critics (and we can legitimately include the overwhelming majority of bishops at the Second Vatican Council) care deeply about the Church and are concerned only that she may conform more closely to the mandate she has received from Christ and that she may reflect more faithfully the reality of the Risen Lord, whose Body she is.

But wisdom and critical acumen are not the inherited birthright and private preserve of any single group inside the Church. Consequently frank and open dialogue between differing viewpoints is always essential. Such dialogue is possible when each of the participants fundamentally accepts the necessity of growth and development, of renewal and reform. They may differ only on methods and means, on pace and propriety.

However, the recent display of countercriticism from the right makes such dialogue awkward, if not impossible. The tone of complaint at the recent Wanderer Forum in Minnesota was both shrill and strident. The keynote address by an American official in the Roman Curia displayed a spirit of theological distortion and polemical exaggeration bordering on the hysterical.

To suggest, for example, that the proposal to change the law of clerical celibacy can only please the "Father of Lies" (presumably Satan) is patently absurd and inexcusably insulting to the Eastern Churches (not to mention the priests affiliated with or supporting the National Institute for Pastoral Renewal). That the statement was made by a member of the Oriental Congregation should be cause for deeper chagrin, if not pained amusement.

Occasionally members of the hierarchy react in a similarly extreme fashion, thereby compromising the potential effectiveness of legitimate conservative criticism. It is supremely provocative to suggest that "today the enemies . . . of the Catholic Church . . . are more likely to come from within," and that all such criticism springs from "intellectual pride."

When we begin questioning one another's motives rather than meeting fairly and fully one another's arguments, the dialogue has broken down.

In a recent article in the *Saturday Evening Post* (July 15) Frederick D. Wilhelmsen, professor of philosophy and politics at the University of Dallas, argues that "Catholicism is right, so why change it?" (See "Speaking out," pp. 10–12). Dr. Wilhelmsen constructs his case from a traditionalist posture, which is fair enough, but the result tends to discredit the intellectual seriousness and theological maturity of his position.

The heart of the article is that the papacy is the center of everything ("the very center of creation"). The pope alone has the keys of the Kingdom. Union with and submission to the pope is the sole guarantee of affiliation with the Kingdom; opposition to or independence from the pope leaves one in a spiritually precarious position indeed. For apart from Rome and the pope, there is nothing other than darkness.

Dr. Wilhelmsen is wrong when he argues that the pope alone has supreme authority in the Church. He seems unaware of the doctrine of collegiality, whereby the authority of the pope is theologically unintelligible apart from the college of bishops, of which he is the chief member. Wilhelmsen ignores the role of the charisms that have been conferred by the Holy Spirit upon the whole Church and not solely upon the ordained or consecrated minority. He offers no clue of familiarity with the biblical and theological meaning of the Kingdom of God of which, he insists, the pope holds the keys.

He resents all liturgical reform (Latin has been "sabotaged") and is especially touchy about laymen in the sanctuary ("Mickey Mouses"). Problems of academic freedom in Catholic colleges and universities are reduced to black-and-white proportions of orthodoxy versus heresy.

The elimination of clerical celibacy would mean the lowering of standards for the priesthood (again reflecting a peculiarly Western concept of the Church). And when he defends the position of an American cardinal on Vietnam, he is strangely silent about the corresponding position of Pope Paul VI, whose office he extols throughout the article.

Finally, Wilhelmsen reduces the whole critical spirit within the Church to a psychological problem: the critics are "educated prigs who have rejected their own lower-middle-class origin" (and they are anti-Italian besides!).

History and theology are against this spirit of postconciliar reaction. There is, indeed, a crisis of faith, as Dr. Wilhelmsen and others have insisted. But the crisis will be broader and deeper than they think. It may strike much closer to home than they now care to imagine.

Meanwhile the dialogue within the Church must proceed in an atmosphere that is at once intellectually responsible and theologically sound.

Threat of Catholic Fundamentalism

(July 26, 1985)

The U.S. Catholic bishops have been exceedingly energetic these past few years in the production of pastoral letters: on peace, on the economy, on women, on sexual ethics, and so forth.

One can hardly blame the bishops for not yet addressing every possible topic that someone somewhere might think important. But there has been one very obvious oversight: fundamentalism.

A prominent Catholic biblical scholar has observed that the number of Catholics who have been lost to the Church because of Hans Küng could hold a convention in a telephone booth, but the number lost because of fundamentalism is in the thousands.

Fundamentalism may be the most immediate threat to Catholic faith in the United States today.

Some of the television evangelists—all Protestant fundamentalists—boast that as much as 30 percent of their financial support comes from Catholic viewers.

In fact, when Jimmy Swaggart recently criticized certain points of Catholic doctrine, including the papacy, his fellow preachers urged him to back off for fear of alienating their Catholic supporters. He did not, by the way.

Thousands of Catholics belong to fundamentalist Bible-study groups and flock to preaching-and-prayer services in convention centers and outdoor stadiums all across the United States. And who can precisely calculate the number of ex-Catholics in the Jehovah's Witnesses, the Assembly of God, and various other Pentecostal churches?

These Catholics had found themselves defenseless against attractively simplistic interpretations of Sacred Scripture. The Catholic biblical renewal, launched by Pope Pius XII and given new impetus by the Second Vatican Council, has had no impact at all on such Catholics' catechetical formation (or, the truth must be told, upon the seminary education of some of their pastors).

Even today many, many Catholics remain completely unfamiliar with Pope Pius XII's encyclical *Divino Afflante Spiritu*, the Pontifical Biblical Commission's *Instruction on the Historical Truth of the Gospels* (1964), or the Second Vatican Council's Dogmatic Constitution on Divine Revelation (1965).

I had a letter recently from a reader of this column trying to prove that in order to be saved, all that we have to do is believe in the divinity of Christ. Her proof? The exchange between the so-called good thief and Jesus on Calvary. (And that is only one example in hundreds.)

With the biblical fundamentalist, however, it is almost always a mistake to be drawn into an argument over a particular text, because the effort to make the proper distinctions will be no match for the rifle-shot of certitude one receives in return.

A more practical tactic may be to distract the fundamentalist with a fundamentalist text of one's own. An example: "Not everyone who says to me, 'Lord, Lord,' shall enter the kingdom of heaven, but he who does the will of my Father who is in heaven" (Matthew 7:21). There are many others.

One can also remind the Catholic fundamentalist that his or her Protestant fundamentalist bedfellows are committed anti-Catholics.

One has only to ask them what they think of the papacy (not simply what they think of Pope John Paul II, whom many of them admire personally for his conservatism, but what they think of the very idea of the Petrine ministry).

Or what they think of Mary, the ordained priesthood, the Eucharist, the sacramental system in general, the intercession of saints, and especially the Church's authority to interpret Sacred Scripture.

The Catholic fundamentalist cannot have it both ways: bemoaning the erosion of traditional, orthodox Catholicism while throwing in his own spiritual lot with those who reject basic Catholic dogmas as unbiblical and therefore false.

Too many of us assume that because the biblical renewal has been with us now for 25 or 30 years, just about everyone in the Catholic Church has been exposed to it. This is not at all the case.

A pastoral letter on Catholic fundamentalism might help change the situation.

Split Among Catholics over Social Teaching
(March 14, 1986)

Recent surveys of U.S. Catholics have shown that Catholic laity are becoming more resistant to their bishops teaching initiatives in the social, economic, and political orders, as represented in the pastoral letters on nuclear war and the economy.

The survey results have been accompanied by warnings that the U.S. Catholic community may be facing a serious split between its increasingly conservative lay members and its more socially progressive clergy and religious.

But if that were to happen, it would not be the first time. In fact, it has always been the case that when pastoral leaders preach and teach Catholic social doctrine, they alienate many Catholics who have a vested interest in the social, economic, and political status quo.

One has only to look to the Philippines or to Latin America. When church officials were identified with the ruling classes, conservative laity were pleased. They enjoyed having "His Eminence" over to the house for dinner and showering him with "little gifts." The poor constituted a whimpering constituency at best.

But once the hierarchy, clergy, and religious began taking Catholic social doctrine seriously, everything changed. Suddenly the bishops, priests, and sisters were considered tools of the communists or were accused of mixing religion and politics.

American Catholics, too, were generally happy about Catholic social doctrine when they were nearer to the bottom of the economic ladder.

Defense of the right to unionize was a defense of *their* right to unionize.

Support for a just wage was support for thicker pay envelopes *for them*.

Arguments on behalf of distributive justice meant that *they* would get a larger slice of the economic pie.

But now many American Catholics have "made it." Many are not only well off. They are among the richest and most powerful people in the entire nation.

And many, many more are hoping and striving to "make it." Give them credit. They work hard for what they earn. And give them understanding. They resent others receiving for free what they have had to earn.

But understanding is one thing. Absolution is another.

No matter how it's sliced, selfishness is selfishness. And it is the antithesis of the gospel.

Jesus' message isn't an easy one to accept, especially if you've got something to protect. But it was never supposed to be easy.

Of course, the poor took to it. They had nothing to lose but their chains, as the saying goes.

But the real test of the poor person's acceptance of the gospel is what happens to him when he becomes a rich and powerful person.

And the real test of a poor immigrant community's acceptance of the gospel is what happens to it when it becomes a relatively prosperous and influential community.

It's no virtue to be generous with someone else's money or resources or talents.

Neither is it virtuous to be stingy with one's own money or resources or talents, particularly when there are others who cannot survive without our help.

And this doesn't apply only to individuals. It applies to nations as well.

Don't take my word for it. Pope John Paul II himself said so in his celebrated homily at Yankee Stadium in October 1979.

"For it is not right that the standard of living of the rich countries should seek to maintain itself by draining off a great part of the reserves of energy and raw materials that are meant to serve the whole of humanity. . . .

"We cannot stand idly by, enjoying our own riches and freedom, if, in any place, the Lazarus of the 20th century stands at our doors," he declared. "In the light of the parable of Christ, riches and freedom mean a special responsibility. Riches and freedom create a special obligation."

Socially, economically, and politically conservative Catholics take pride in their loyalty to the Church and in their fidelity to its teachings. They deplore even implied criticism of the Holy Father and applaud when a theologian like Father Hans Küng has his canonical mandate removed. They see nothing inconsistent, however, with their own criticism of bishops and their pick-and-choose approach to papal teachings.

When I last looked, the catechisms and textbooks from which these Catholics learned their religion still spoke of the bishops as shepherds and authentic teachers and consecrated men of God, with the sacramental grace of Holy Order, etc., etc., etc.

It didn't say anywhere that you could dismiss or ridicule them, at least not without having to go to confession afterward.

And nowhere did those books say that you had to accept the teachings of the pope, except when they have to do with social justice and human rights.

One doesn't demand conversion at this point. Just consistency.

Do Church Conflicts Have One Root?

(May 9, 1986)

Ask a well-informed Catholic to list a few issues that generate intramural conflict and the examples will flow:

1. How to deal with theological dissent, such as the Charles Curran case.

2. How to recognize and employ the gifts of women in the Church, especially the ordination debate.

3. How to exploit, to the fullest extent, the ministerial commitments of priests and sisters, for example, the questions of clerical celibacy and of religious vows.

4. How best to exercise pastoral leadership in the Church, for instance, the personal style of Pope John Paul II and the corporate style of the U.S. bishops.

5. How to translate moral principles into public policy, such as the debate surrounding the 1984 exchange between Archbp. John O'Connor and New York governor Mario Cuomo on abortion and the law.

   Each of these issues is important to the Church. The fact that they are also of abiding interest to the media doesn't make them any more or less important to the Church.

But the Church's agenda includes more than these issues, and more, therefore, than the media currently cares about.

For example:

1. How to improve the quality of preaching, without subordinating the liturgy of the Eucharist to the liturgy of the Word.

2. How to attract more and better candidates for the ordained priesthood, without lowering admissions standards.

3. How to deal justly and compassionately with retired and infirmed members of religious communities, without breaking the financial backs of their congregations or the dioceses in which they live.

4. How to improve the quality of religious education and catechesis, without sacrificing the needs of one constituency, such as adults, to another, such as children.

5. How to improve the quality of music in the liturgy, without violating the letter and spirit of the liturgical norms.

6. How to reach and serve the youth of our parishes, without reducing youth ministers to recreation directors.

7. How to provide a theologically and biblically rooted spirituality for adults and young people alike, for example, to teach them how to pray, without lapsing into psychologism, fundamentalism, or pietism.

8. How to identify and recruit better-qualified candidates for parish and diocesan councils and committees, without neglecting the needs and views of the vast majority of parish members.

9. How to develop better processes and structures of collaborative ministry, without blurring the lines of pastoral accountability.

10. How to provide just wages, salaries, and fringe benefits to church employees, without doing violence to other budgetary priorities.

11. How to connect the Eucharist and ordinary life, without robbing the Eucharist of its mystery or ordinary life of its rightful autonomy.

12. How to raise the consciousness of our parishioners regarding social justice, human rights, and peace, without seeming to reduce Christianity to a political program.

13. How to draw parishioners to a deeper union with Christ and a greater openness to the Holy Spirit, without seeming to reduce Christianity to an otherworldly religion devoid of interest in this one.

14. How to project a more compelling image of the Church as "a reality imbued with the hidden presence of God" (Pope Paul VI), without grasping for public relations gimmicks.

15. How to proclaim the good news to those outside the Church, without coming across like Protestant fundamentalists and conservative evangelicals.

16. How to be Catholic with a capital C, without sacrificing catholicity, that is, openness to all truth and to all people.

17. How to be catholic with a small c, without sacrificing Catholic identity.

18. How to raise money for the Church's missionary endeavors, without seeming to be concerned only with raising money.

19. How to face personal, social, national, and even global tragedies, without losing faith or hope.

20. How to express disagreements in the Church, without violating justice and charity.

If we could succeed at number 20, we'd have a big jump on numbers 1–19.

Letter Jesus Might Have Received from Critic
(June 12, 1987)

I receive a fair number of letters in response to my weekly column. Occasional articles in journals like *Notre Dame Magazine* (especially my recent piece that the editors, not I, entitled "The Hard-line Pontiff") also elicit some reaction. And so do occasional appearances on national television.

But in a class by themselves are letters I receive from people reacting to newspaper reports of a speech I've given somewhere or other.

On the basis of one or two sentences quoted out of context, these letter-writers draw all sorts of negative conclusions; for example, that I don't pray, that I don't believe in the Petrine ministry (they never use such precise terminology), or that I favor abortion.

I sometimes wonder what sort of letters Jesus might have received from the religious right of his day had a few of his talks been reported in the press.

Let's try the discourse on the hypocrisy of religious leaders in Matthew 23.

Headline: "Galilean Preacher Denounces Hierarchy, Calls Scribes and Pharisees 'Blind Guides' and 'Hypocrites.' "

Lead paragraphs: "Jesus of Nazareth, a well-known preacher from the Galilean town of Nazareth, carried his campaign against hypocrisy and legalism to the heart of the religious establishment today.

"Accusing the Pharisees and scribes of laying burdens on others that they would not carry themselves, he called them 'hypocrites,' 'blind guides,' 'fools,' 'whitewashed tombs,' 'serpents,' and a 'brood of vipers.' "

Irate letter to Jesus: "So, you're at it again! Don't you and all your dissenter friends ever get tired of banging the same old drum?

"Who set you up to judge God's law? Let me tell you: God won't take your arrogance lying down. You and your kind are going to have to face Him some day, and I'd hate to be in your sandals.

"How dare you accuse our beloved religious leaders of hypocrisy! God set them up as our authoritative teachers. They are the ones—the *only* ones—who can officially interpret God's word and God's law.

"It bothers you, doesn't it, that they get the first places in the synagogue and that they have the privilege of wearing special insignia of office?

"You'd love to be right up there with them, I'll bet. Well, it'll never happen. They've got your number now, Jesus. You couldn't be elected a money changer in the Temple after this latest tirade of yours.

"Don't you realize the scandal you are giving? If you had any self-respect, you'd quit teaching. Get out before they throw you out!

"Think of the little ones that you are leading astray. No wonder young people don't pay attention anymore to their elders. Even women are getting uppity these days. You've been giving some of them the idea they're equal to men. What nonsense!

"The trouble with you is that you don't pray. You'd better get down on your knees and ask God's forgiveness.

"It's pride that's doing you in. What makes you think you know more about God's law than the very men whom God Himself placed over us? It's their teaching, not yours, that we are bound to follow.

"Of course, you don't think the law applies to you. None of your kind does. I heard that you've broken the sabbath rules on more than one occasion. And you always have some damn-fool excuse about the sabbath being made for man rather than man for the sabbath. A cute turn of phrase, but it's still disobedience!

"I know that none of this is going to make the slightest bit of difference to you. You'll probably run off with one of those prostitutes you're always defending. Or perhaps one of your tax-collector buddies will give you a temporary hideout. You eat with tax collectors. You might as well live with them, too!

"You're something, all right! You claim to be a religious person, but then all you do is attack religion—our God-given religious laws, our God-ordained religious leaders, our God-sanctified religious traditions.

"Thank God for the Pharisees and scribes! Thank God for people who know what loyalty and obedience mean! Thank God for people who don't compromise their principles the first time they require sacrifice!

"I'll tell you one thing, Jesus. When the history of this time is written, all those God-fearing Pharisees and scribes you've so viciously attacked will be honored figures. You and your shabby crowd will be forgotten."

Meditation text: "They will put you out of the synagogues; indeed, the hour is coming when whoever kills you will think he is offering service to God. And they will do this because they have not known the Father, nor me" (John 16:2–3).

"Pick-and-Choose" Catholicism

(October 2, 1987)

As Pope John Paul II prepared for his second formal visit to the United States last month, there was much general discussion of a phenomenon known as "pick-and-choose" Catholicism, sometimes known as Catholicism à la carte.

Archbp. Jan P. Schotte, a high-ranking Vatican official, deplored "an increasing but gratuitous assumption that one can tailor one's church to one's own desires and turn it into a 'pick and choose' church where it is accepted that being a Catholic has little to do with adhering to all the church's teachings."

Public opinion surveys have consistently disclosed that U.S. Catholics have a highly favorable view of the current bishop of Rome, but by an even larger margin these Catholics also believe that they can disagree with the pope on certain issues of faith and morals and still be good Catholics.

The media—and perhaps Vatican officials like Archbishop Schotte— seemed generally to assume that such Catholics were all grouped somewhere on the left of the ecclesiastical spectrum.

The "pick-and-choose" Catholic, in other words, is one who disagrees with the pope on matters of sexual morality (contraception, divorce-and-remarriage, in vitro fertilization) or on matters of church discipline related to sex (ordination of women, clerical celibacy).

At a point further to the left is the Catholic who might also approve of homosexual behavior and of a woman's right to have an abortion.

True enough. Such Catholics do not accept every official church teaching and policy pertaining to matters of this sort. On the other hand, they continue to regard themselves as Catholics in good standing. In that sense they *are* picking and choosing.

But these liberal, or progressive, Catholics are not alone. Many conservative Catholics do the same thing.

They choose not to accept their Church's official teachings regarding social justice, human rights, and peace.

To be sure, they do not openly dissent from Pope John Paul II's encyclical on human work, *Laborem Exercens* (1981). They simply ignore it.

And when they recite their litany of papal teachings they support, the following papal pronouncements are always missing: Pope John XXIII's *Mater et Magistra* (1961) and *Pacem in Terris* (1963), and Pope Paul VI's *Populorum Progressio* (1967), *Octagesima Adveniens* (1971), and *Evangelii Nuntiandi* (1975).

Needless to say, Vatican II's Pastoral Constitution on the Church in the Modern World (*Gaudium et Spes,* 1965) and the Third International Synod's "Justice in the World" (*Justitia in Mundo,* 1971) are never mentioned.

The one exception to their rule of calculated silence is their response to the U.S. Catholic bishops' pastoral letters on peace (1983) and the economy (1986). Here these conservative Catholics are open, direct, and not a little sarcastic in their dissent.

They claim that they are not bound by the bishops' teachings because the matters under discussion are subject to prudential judgments and varied practical interpretations, as if matters of reproductive technology, for example, were not similarly complicated.

And they suggest, indeed they charge, that the bishops are not competent to speak on questions of peace and the economy, as if the bishops *were* competent to address matters of sexual morality.

But more to the point: these conservative Catholics are doing the very same thing that many liberal, or progressive, Catholics have been doing. They are picking and choosing.

They are deciding for themselves what is important in the body of official teachings and what is not, which official teachings they have to accept and which ones they don't have to accept, and whether the official teachers are even competent to pass moral judgment on the issues under discussion.

The pope and the U.S. bishops have never said that their teachings on sexual morality are more important than their teachings on social justice, human rights, and peace. Nor have the pope and the U.S. bishops ever said that the latter teachings are simply matters of personal opinion, to be taken or left according to the political whim of the individual Catholic.

On the contrary, the Second Vatican Council declared in its Pastoral Constitution on the Church in the Modern World:

> This split between the faith which many profess and their daily lives deserves to be counted among the more serious errors of our age. . . .

Therefore, let there be no false opposition between professional and social activities on the one part, and religious life on the other. The Christian who neglects his temporal duties neglects his duties toward his neighbor and even God, and jeopardizes his eternal salvation. (n. 43)

If anyone wishes to condemn pick-and-choose Catholicism, let him or her at least distribute the condemnation evenly across the entire spectrum of Catholics, conservative as well as liberal.

Kinship Among Religious Traditionalists

(January 22, 1988)

Early last month sharp divisions within the Church of England were dramatically and tragically exposed in the suicide of a conservative Anglican priest and Oxford don.

Twenty-four hours after his death, church officials reluctantly confirmed the rumors that the priest was the author of an anonymous attack on the archbishop of Canterbury, published a few days earlier as the preface to the new issue of a clerical directory.

The article's harsh tone had been denounced by the archbishop of York as "scurrilous, sour and vindictive."

But traditionalists in the Church of England hailed the priest as a martyr who killed himself in despair over the church's continued liberalization.

This unhappy story, minus the suicide, has been (and continues to be) played out not only in the Church of England but also just about everywhere else on the world's religious landscape.

Similar rifts, deep and acute, are to be found, for example, within the ranks of Southern Baptists, Lutherans, Jews, Muslims, and, of course, Catholics.

In every instance, traditionalists line up against moderates. They charge the moderates with corrupting the faith through compromise and accommodation. The moderates, in their turn, accuse the traditionalists of rigidity and unrealism. One wonders sometimes how traditionalists in one group regard their counterparts in another.

Does a strongly conservative Catholic, for example, feel any sort of intellectual and spiritual kinship with the Missouri Synod wing of American Lutheranism or with Hasidic Jews or with Southern Baptist fundamentalists, or with Shiite Muslims?

There is, after all, a common bond in the pursuit of a common cause.

Traditionalists of every religion are committed to purging their communities of the infection of heresy, modernity, accommodationism, compromise, call it what you will.

Their agenda is one of exclusion rather than of inclusion. Indeed, they seem to rejoice more over departures from the fold than they do over the entrance of new members. They're always trying to get their opponents to quit or else face expulsion.

Second, religious traditionalists prefer the method of censorship over dialogue. If individuals are teaching contrary to "the faith," get them fired, withdraw approval for their writings, deny them a public platform, make them nonpersons in the religious community, shun them.

Third, traditionalists think deductively rather than inductively. There are doctrines and there are rules. Don't ask how the doctrines got there or how the rules were formulated. Just obey them.

History, with its contingencies, doesn't count. Nonhistorical orthodoxy (to use a term coined by Michael Novak) is preferred to historical consciousness. Authoritative pronouncements, rather than historically grounded reasoning and arguments, provide the only sure access to truth.

Fourth, traditionalists seem to be particularly bothered by sex, whether it's Hasidic Jews burning bus-stop shelters in Israel because of advertisements featuring clothed but alluring females or Protestant fundamentalist preachers and Catholic prelates denouncing premarital sex, pornography, condoms, homosexual-rights bills, and abortion laws.

For some of them at least, it seems that sexual sins are the only sins that really count.

Thus, when the pope speaks about sex and marriage, loyal and faithful Catholics are supposed to listen and obey. But when the same pope speaks about economic justice and disarmament, Catholics can turn off the switch until the Holy Father returns to his spiritual senses.

Finally, traditionalists tend to lack a sense of humor, and especially the capacity for self-deprecating humor. They are too certain of their own righteousness and of the sinfulness of their adversaries. Indeed, they seem to believe that God has commissioned them personally to clean up the mess before the Final Judgment. Who has time for fun and laughter with a mandate like that?

Although traditionalists normally oppose ecumenical ventures, perhaps they're all part of an underground ecumenical movement, one with another.

In so many respects, they do think and act alike. In particular, they share a common aversion for dissidence and a common passion for a precisely regulated life.

But there may not be much of a future for their movement. If the common enemy were ever removed (namely, the moderates of every tradition), traditionalists would have no one else to fight except one another.

Protestant fundamentalists, for example, don't even regard Catholicism as a Bible-based Christian faith. And while some of them might admire the conservative posture of Pope John Paul II, as far as they're concerned he's still the beast of the Apocalypse.

But it's possible that such details of doctrine can be ironed out somehow. By accommodation and compromise perhaps?

Behind Liberal-Conservative Terminology

(July 1, 1988)

Some Catholics become very uncomfortable and even annoyed when terms like *liberal* and *conservative* or *left-wing* and *right-wing* are used to describe individuals and points of view within the Church.

They object for one (or both) of two reasons. Either they deny that differences of this sort exist in the Catholic Church or they resent the implication that one side (liberal) is good while the other side (conservative) is bad.

As you can deduce, those Catholics who object to the use of liberal-conservative/left-right terminology are almost always conservative themselves. Why is that the case?

Let's look first at the distinction between liberals and conservatives before trying to answer the question.

When in doubt, conservatives—whether in religion, in politics, in academic life, in business, even in sports—favor stability over change and order over freedom. Conservatives are people who literally want to "conserve" the good that we have achieved and now enjoy. They generally oppose change because they are happy with the way things are.

Given the same set of doubtful or ambiguous circumstances, liberals favor change over stability and freedom over order. Liberals are people who literally want to maximize our range of freedom over against the intrusions of institutions and figures of authority. Liberals generally favor change because they believe that things could be better than they are.

These tendencies—liberal and conservative—exist in every walk of life. Religion is no exception.

Liberals and conservatives, left-wingers and right-wingers, exist even in the Soviet Union, seemingly the most monolithic of societies and political regimes.

The *New York Times* carried a recent op-ed piece (May 21, 1988) by a sociologist who used to conduct polls for *Pravda, Izvestia,* and other Soviet newspapers. It was entitled "Why Soviet Conservatives Fight Reform."

What the author says about tensions within the Soviet Union are almost exactly parallel with tensions inside the United States, American corporations, and indeed the Catholic Church.

The author, Prof. Vladimir Shlapentokh, of Michigan State University, challenges the usual (superficial) view that tensions within the Soviet hierarchy today are reducible to personal rivalries among Politburo members and to the self-serving interests of other groups.

There is something more fundamental at issue. The conservatives who oppose Mr. Gorbachev's reforms, lumped under the terms *perestroika* (restructuring) and *glasnost* (openness), are acting as conservatives always act.

For these conservatives, the Soviet Union, despite its terrible flaws, has been able to achieve military parity with the West and to guarantee a standard of living that is much higher than those in most countries, because of its strong central authority, at both the political and economic levels.

In the conservatives' view, Gorbachev's new spirit of *glasnost* is undermining discipline. If people can now question and criticize those in economic authority, there will be a corresponding deterioration of economic performance. Workers will stop doing what their managers tell them to do.

And if the Communist party can be criticized and challenged, social order will break down.

For these conservatives, the Communist party has been the sole force of law and order in the Soviet system, coordinating at all levels the activities of various groups and organizations.

Finally, the conservatives maintain, by publicizing various social problems like drugs and prostitution, the advocates of reform have only acted to make these evils "normal" and have thereby encouraged young people to embrace them.

Sound familiar? Of course, it does!

There are Catholics who oppose the reforms and renewal inspired by the Second Vatican Council because, they maintain, these are leading to a general breakdown of discipline in the Church.

If Catholics are encouraged to think for themselves and even to raise questions about papal teaching, the moral order will inevitably fall apart.

And by encouraging open discussion of the faults and failings of the Church, the conservative argues, we are sending people, especially younger Catholics, a dangerous message that what can be openly discussed can also be openly practiced.

If the existence of liberal-conservative/left-right tendencies in all walks of life is self-evident, why, then, do some Catholics resist acknowledging their existence in the Church itself?

I offer a guess.

First, to admit that sharp differences of opinion can coexist in the Church is to admit the legitimacy of pluralism, which is to say that there is more than one orthodox way to understand and express our Catholic faith.

Second, the use of liberal-conservative/left-right language supplants the only real distinction such Catholics regard as legitimate; namely, the distinction between orthodoxy and heresy.

In other words, the only differences are between true Catholics and phony Catholics.

True Conservatives and Pseudoconservatives

(July 29, 1988)

The word *conservative* is a good word, both inside and outside the Church. Conservatives are people who want to hold fast to what is abidingly true and of enduring value in their respective traditions.

Within the Church, however, the conservative label is frequently misappropriated by people who are not conservative at all.

These pseudoconservatives talk and act like conservatives, but they differ from authentic conservatives in one crucially important respect: true conservatives know and understand the tradition they seek to preserve; pseudoconservatives are ignorant of the tradition they believe they honor.

The recent controversy over the excommunication of Archbp. Marcel Lefebvre (for ordaining four bishops without papal approval) is only the most recent case in point.

Although few of them will admit it openly, pseudoconservative Catholics feel a twinge of sympathy for Archbishop Lefebvre.

They share his disdain for many of the changes wrought by the Second Vatican Council, even if they would not go so far as he in defying the pope, especially this pope.

Pseudoconservative Catholics cannot understand why Pope John Paul II would excommunicate an archbishop with whom the pope obviously shares so much in common. Aren't both men deeply concerned about the moral, theological, devotional, and disciplinary trends that have been at work in Catholicism since the council?

Furthermore, if the pope felt that there was no alternative to Archbishop Lefebvre's excommunication, why did he not also excommunicate dissidents of the left: in particular, theologians who have been critical of one or another official teaching of the Church?

The pseudoconservatives' first complaint reveals their ignorance of canon law. They assume that the pope had a choice: to excommunicate or not to excommunicate Archbishop Lefebvre.

Pope John Paul II did not have such a choice. The excommunication is automatic in such cases.

Canon 1382 reads: "A bishop who consecrates someone a bishop and the person who receives such a consecration from a bishop without a pontifical mandate incur automatic (*latae sententiae*) excommunication reserved to the Apostolic See."

The pseudoconservatives' second complaint is the more interesting because it reveals a theological ignorance that is often masked as theological conservatism.

While he was at it, the pseudoconservatives ask, why didn't the pope also excommunicate theologians A, B, and C?

On what grounds? Heresy, they reply.

It's true that, according to canon law, heresy is one of the offenses subject to the penalty of excommunication (canon 1364, no. 1).

But what is heresy? Here is where the pseudoconservatives' theological ignorance glows in the dark.

For the pseudoconservative, heresy is dissent from any official teaching of the Church: infallible or noninfallible, definitive or nondefinitive, dogmatic or nondogmatic. (They conveniently forget their own dissent from official Catholic teachings on justice and peace.)

Theology, church history, and canon law are one on this point: Heresy is a technical term that applies only to the rejection of an infallibly defined dogma of the Church.

Since pseudoconservatives are more suspicious of theology than they are of canon law, let's take the definition of heresy that the code provides.

Canon 751 defines heresy as "the obstinate post-baptismal denial of some truth which must be believed with divine and catholic faith, or it is likewise an obstinate doubt concerning the same."

The term "divine and catholic faith" (*fide divina et catholica*) is also a technical term. It is one of the theological notes that anyone who studied theology before the council would be familiar with.

It refers to a doctrine taught with the highest authority; namely, an infallible teaching.

Not only must the alleged heretic *know* that he (or she) is rejecting an infallible teaching of the Church, but he (or she) must also be "obstinate" about it.

The implication here is that the denial or doubt must persist over time and even after a process of challenge or dialogue with church officials.

Not one theologian on the pseudoconservatives' "enemies list" has ever been accused of heresy, much less declared a heretic, by any church official or Vatican congregation—not Hans Küng, not Charles Curran, not Edward Schillebeeckx, not Leonardo Boff, not any of them.

Indeed, in spite of their respective difficulties with the Vatican, they all remain Catholic priests in good standing. That would be impossible if they were guilty of heresy.

On the other hand, Archbishop Lefebvre was excommunicated because he freely and deliberately ruptured the bond of unity with the Catholic Church. He committed the schismatic act of ordaining bishops without papal approval, indeed in open defiance of the pope.

Acknowledging Diverse Currents in the Church
(July 7, 1989)

Some Catholics react to the application of political categories to the Church the way most of us react to the scratching of fingernails on a blackboard.

They reject the very idea that the Catholic Church may be subject to the same social and systemic forces that generate conflict and diversity in comparable institutions.

For such Catholics, there is no left and right in the Church, only right and wrong. To their way of thinking, there aren't conservative Catholics and liberal Catholics; there are only good Catholics and "so-called" Catholics.

But now even Pope John Paul II has acknowledged the existence of diverse currents in the Church.

In a recent interview with an Italian journalist, the pope suggested that his many trips around the world have been providential in preventing a "confrontation" between liberal and conservative wings of the Church.

He claimed that by going directly to visit local churches, and by "avoiding being caught up in the confrontation between the 'right' and the 'left,' between 'conservatism' and 'progressivism,' " he was able to "introduce an element of balance in the implementation of conciliar reforms."

What is most significant about the pope's remarks, however, is not his recognition of the existence of right- and left-wing forces in the Church but the way in which he redefines the center.

The center of anything is relative to its extremities. The one who defines the extremes, therefore, also defines the center.

On the right the pope places schismatic Archbp. Marcel Lefebvre and those who are "afraid of 'change' as represented by the council."

On the left the pope places those who "already hoped for a 'Third Vatican Council' " or who are guilty of "reducing everything to the particular church."

Although the pope's reference to the left is much vaguer than his reference to the right (no names parallel to Lefebvre's are given by way of example), the pope's concept of the center isn't difficult to deduce.

If Archbishop Lefebvre and his sympathizers constitute the right-wing or conservative side of the Catholic Church, then it surely follows that the center belongs to Cardinal Ratzinger, movements like *Opus Dei* and Communion and Liberation, New York's Cardinal O'Connor and almost all of the U.S. archbishops appointed since 1980, the Fellowship of Catholic Scholars, *Crisis* and *Communio* magazines, critics of the U.S. Catholic bishops' pastoral letters on peace and the economy like Michael Novak and George Weigel, philosophers and theologians like Germain Grisez and William May, and on and on.

And if that is indeed the center, many of the Church's most active and influential Catholics must constitute the left—the opposite number presumably to Lefebvre-type resisters of Vatican II: Milwaukee's Archbishop Weakland and the working majority of the National Conference of Catholic Bishops, the Leadership Conference of Women Religious, the Catholic Theological Society of America, *America* and *Commonweal* magazines, drafters and supporters of the U.S. bishops' pastoral letters such as Cardinal Bernardin and Fr. J. Bryan Hehir, theologians like David Tracy and Richard McCormick, S.J., and on and on.

Are such individuals, groups, and journals really as extreme in their way as Archbishop Lefebvre is in his? Are they, in the end, comparable to one another?

I do not suggest that the pope had thought out the implications of his remarks to this extent. Clearly he hadn't. I suggest only that conclusions of this sort can be deduced from his interview.

And this is what troubles an increasing number of Catholics today. They note with dismay how the center has, in fact, been redefined.

The thousands, indeed millions, who have heretofore occupied the

Church's broad center ground have been displaced and, by implication at least, branded as extremists no less than Archbishop Lefebvre & Co. on the opposite side of the spectrum.

Although patently absurd and outrageously unfair, the tactic is the only way by which hard-line conservatives can redefine themselves as responsible centrists.

They recognize, after all, the validity of the old Scholastic axiom, *In medio stat virtus* ("Virtue stands in the middle"). Truth is to be found somewhere *between* the extremes, not *at* the extremes.

The redefinition of the center, however, is not only an injustice to the real center of the Church. It raises also a question of inclusiveness.

If Archbishop Lefebvre represents the right, Cardinal Ratzinger represents the center, and Archbishop Weakland is representative of the left, where does one place the Coalition of American Nuns or Catholics for a Free Choice or theologians like Daniel Maguire and Rosemary Ruether or activists like Fr. Daniel Berrigan or Catholic socialists like John Cort or the nameless thousands who scoff at any pronouncement from the magisterium or who defend the practice of celebrating the Eucharist without a priest-presider?

The redefiners evidently haven't thought of that.

Of Cafeteria Food and Oaths and the Force-feeding of Both
(August 18, 1989)

Cafeterias are places where you make your own individual food selections. From soup and salad to dessert you pick and choose whatever you want, pass by what doesn't please you, and, at line's end, pay the cashier for whatever happens to be on your tray.

Many Catholics are accused these days of practicing a kind of "cafeteria Catholicism." They are charged with picking and choosing among the Church's doctrines and disciplines, deciding entirely for themselves and in light of their own personal tastes what teachings they will accept and what rules they will observe.

Those Catholics who make this charge against their fellow Catholics are particularly bitter about the role of theologians in the emergence of cafeteria Catholicism. They are convinced that without the "bad example" of theologians, the "simple faithful" would never have taken up the cafeteria habit in the first place.

Their remedy is to force the theologians to take an oath to eat everything that's put on their plates.

Once the "simple faithful" see the theologians dutifully swallowing their last morsel of magisterial spinach, they will be properly motivated to clean their own plates.

But driving only the theologians out of the cafeteria, like money changers out of the temple, won't cure the problem.

The reason is that many of the same Catholics who raise the charge of cafeteria Catholicism are themselves secret cafeteria aficionados, so much so, in fact, that some of their critics wonder if they hate the sinner but love the sin.

Fr. Avery Dulles, S.J., reminds us in a short but important contribution to the January-February issue of *New Oxford Review* that dissent and even heresy are just as likely to come from the right as from the left.

"Historically," he writes, "rigorists and archaists have caused as much trouble for the Church as liberals and progressives.

"The Montanist and Novatian heresies, Jansenism, and the more recent disturbances connected with Fr. Leonard Feeney are cases in point.

"The Church today abounds in right-wing Catholics who dissent from the social teaching of popes and bishops or reject the liturgical reforms of Vatican II and Paul VI."

And that's just the point: Many Catholics who insist that theologians take an oath of absolute fidelity to Pope Paul VI's birth-control encyclical, *Humanae Vitae,* for example, can give you all kinds of reasons why they themselves are not similarly bound by Paul VI's encyclical on social justice, *Populorum Progressio,* issued only one year earlier.

But consistency has never been their strong suit. And one can understand why it is not. Just consider for a moment what the new oath would commit us all to, if taken at face value. The text released this spring by the Vatican allows for no exceptions. Doctrines at three levels are covered: teachings solemnly defined, teachings "definitively" proposed, and teachings of the ordinary magisterium that are neither solemnly defined nor definitively proposed—in other words, everything else.

Take just a few of the examples given by my colleague Father James Burtchaell, C.S.C., in a devastatingly whimsical piece on the oath in the April 7 issue of the *National Catholic Reporter.*

The Council of Trent taught that sacramental confession is by divine law necessary to salvation. Outside the confessional, no salvation? Really? Even for non-Catholics?

The Council of Nicaea established once and for all that bishops must be elected by all the bishops of a province, with final confirmation by the metropolitan, and that no bishop can be transferred to another diocese. Shall theologians swear to that, too?

The same council also held that clerics who receive interest on their funds should be deposed ("a sobering thought," Father Burtchaell notes, "for all who hold savings or interest-bearing checking accounts").

The Second Council of Nicaea decreed "definitively" that no one can be made a bishop without knowing the Psalter by heart and without having read the entire Bible, "thoroughly, not cursorily."

And what of the teaching of the Holy Office (and of popes Alexander III, Innocent III, Leo X, Paul III, and the Third Lateran Council) that slavery is "not at all contrary to the natural and divine law"?

Boniface VIII taught that no one can be saved except in obedient subjection to the Roman pontiff, while Leo XIII declared that free thought and speech and publication must not be allowed by civil governments. Do we swear to these, too?

Before badgering theologians into taking an oath of fidelity to everything the magisterium has ever taught, our oath advocates ought to go up into the Church's attic and have a closer look around.

If they come back downstairs and tell us that some things (like Father Burtchaell's examples) we can forget about, ask them on what basis they distinguish between teachings of the magisterium we have to accept and teachings we don't have to accept.

And when they finish explaining, hand them back their cafeteria trays.

Drawing the Line on What to Believe

(March 30, 1990)

Four weeks ago I did a column on the Universal Catechism in which I recommended that the project be abandoned.

One of my colleagues at Notre Dame—someone outside the theology department—expressed a friendly concern about the essay.

He neither challenged my characterization of the document nor questioned the validity of the criticisms leveled by the theologians, biblical scholars, and religious educators I had cited.

He wondered, however, if such criticisms were directed only at this particular document or if they were indicative of a more sweeping opposition to all such initiatives—indeed, to the very idea of drawing any lines whatever between valid and invalid expressions of Catholic faith.

He observed that theologians no longer seem to acknowledge that there are lines that a Catholic cannot cross and still be Catholic. It's as if one can believe whatever one wishes to believe.

He asked how a Catholic—any Catholic, not just the so-called traditionalist type—is to know what is essential to Catholic faith and what is not.

We recite the Creed every Sunday at Mass, I replied. The core of Catholic faith is contained right there.

But I could see that he was not satisfied. I thanked him for his gentle prodding and promised I'd do a column on the subject. This is it.

For the record, there *are* lines beyond which a Catholic cannot step and still be Catholic.

Catholics cross the line if they deny the reality of a loving and providential God. One cannot be a Catholic atheist.

Catholics cross the line if they deny the triune nature of God. It is of the essence of Catholic faith that God created us (Father), redeemed us (Son), and sanctifies us (Holy Spirit). One cannot be a Catholic unitarian.

Catholics cross the line if they deny the divinity of Jesus Christ and the saving effect of his death, resurrection, and ascension. One cannot be a Catholic Liberal (in the 19th-century meaning of the word).

Catholics cross the line if they deny the necessity of the sacraments or the Real Presence of Christ in the Eucharist. One cannot be a Catholic antisacramentalist.

Catholics cross the line if they deny the resurrection of the body and eternal life. One cannot be a Catholic Sadducee.

But not everything essential is in the Nicene Creed, even if the core is there.

Catholics also cross the line if they deny the reality of grace, reducing everything to the purely natural. One cannot be a Catholic materialist.

Catholics cross the line if they deny the necessity of faith for salvation, arguing instead that everything has to be rooted in human reason. One cannot be a Catholic rationalist.

On the other hand, Catholics cross the line if they deny the use of reason in studying the mysteries of Christianity, arguing instead that everything must be taken simply "on faith." One cannot be a Catholic fideist.

Catholics cross the line if they deny the essential goodness of the created order, arguing instead that there are two coequal creative forces in conflict in the world, Good and Evil. One cannot be a Catholic Manichaean.

Catholics cross the line if they deny the necessity of grace for salvation, arguing instead that human effort and strength of will are sufficient. One cannot be a Catholic Pelagian.

On the other hand, Catholics cross the line if they deny the necessity of human freedom for salvation, arguing instead that God has already determined our fate for us, independently of our own responsible thoughts and actions. One cannot be a Catholic predestinationist or determinist.

Finally, Catholics cross the line if they deny that we are all our brother's and our sister's keeper, that we are bound in charity and justice to share what we have with those in greater need and to forgive even our enemies. One cannot be, in the end, an un-Christian Catholic.

Ironically, in collapsing the distinction between what is essential and what is debatable in Catholic faith, it is the drafters of the Universal Catechism, not modern theologians, who have erased those lines.

"Heresy" Alive and Kicking on the Right
(June 8, 1990)

Heresy is a technical theological term. It refers to the rejection of a solemnly defined teaching of the Church, known as a dogma.

But there are Catholics who mistakenly believe that a rejection, or criticism, of any official teaching is heresy.

In their view, heresy is an everyday occurrence, like the common cold, and only liberal or progressive Catholics seem to catch it. But is that really the case?

The following items, culled from Catholic newspapers and from my own mail, suggest that "heresy" is alive and kicking on the right as well as the left.

1. A Florida priest's column in the nationally distributed *Our Sunday Visitor* (March 4) offers comfort to an Indiana resident who complained that the cross atop the local church steeple had been replaced by a rooster, a symbol, he (or she) was told, of the resurrection.

"The Resurrection," the columnist replied, "is not at all necessary for our redemption and is, if the phrase is not too flippant, icing on the cake." (The phrase is not just flippant, Father. By your theological standards, it's "heretical.")

"The great central act of human history is the redemption of the human race, accomplished by our Lord and Savior, Jesus Christ, through his passion and death. Jesus was not born to be resurrected. He was born to die on the Cross in order that we might have eternal life."

One wonders what the columnist makes of First Corinthians 15:17. Or of the Easter Vigil, for that matter.

2. Another christological gem, this time in a letter from Connecticut in response to a recent column on Satan and Mary: "Facing Jesus is still tough, but we can get our breath. Jesus is still a little remote; after all, his Father owned the store. But Mary is one of us, and yet somehow in their family, too."

Jesus, our Mediator? True God and true man? Like us in all things except sin?

3. But just how effective has Christ's redemptive work been on our behalf? Take note of this dire warning in a letter from Maine, which chastised me for spreading "the ultimate in heresy: universal salvation."

Indeed, the writer was "scandalized" to read in my column that the human race may be an essentially saved community from which only a relative few may be lost.

"Christ clearly taught that few will be saved,' because few would find the narrow gate of salvation, and that many will be lost through the wide path.

"Through Christ's sacrifice on the cross [no resurrection here either!] there is universal redemption," my correspondent conceded. But—"Salvation must be earned." The "heresy" of Pelagianism?

Jesus, I was told, "did more preaching to warn against hell than anything else. The fear of hell is a hallmark of his message."

That puts love of neighbor pretty much in its place, I guess. In any case, if most of us are going to hell, it was only fair of Jesus to give us some advance warning. Good news, indeed.

4. Speaking of love of neighbor, try this one. It's an excerpt from a published interview with a well-known and very successful Catholic businessman,

who has ridiculed (there is no other word for it) the bishops for their supposedly naive 1986 pastoral letter on the U.S. economy and the social teachings of the Church.

"You can't get rid of the poor. I mean, no matter what you do for them, some people are either ill, or unmotivated, or mentally screwed up, and you're never going to eliminate poverty.

"I have three or four homes," he continued. "I don't feel at all guilty about this. I was brought up in a huge household with 68 servants and a yacht and 28 crew members and a place in Scotland with 80 or 100 people. I was brought up that way.

"Questions like . . . Why do you have a place in Florida? Give it to the poor. Baloney.

"Why do [the bishops] think that other people should be saints and work their _____ off morning, noon and night to give away everything they don't need? Now, you suggest this to St. Augustine or St. Francis. *They'd* do that. But how many saints are there?" (*New York Daily News,* September 24, 1989).

Don't look this way, please. There's no one over here but a few of us hard-working camels trying to pass through the eye of a needle.

5. Most right-wing "heresies" probably have to do with the structure and government of the Church. Such "heretics" commonly assume that Jesus left the Church a precisely detailed organizational chart, in the shape of a pyramid.

And so another letter-writer from Connecticut complains: "I feel it is unfortunate that some do not realize, or ever accept the fact, that the Catholic Church is an absolute monarchy."

"Orders, Rev. McBrien, come from the top down," he admonished me. "The truly humble accept that fact."

Yes, sir. Excuse us for thinking, sir. Any further instructions, *sir?* (Click of the heels, with stiff salute.)

4

Ordained Ministry

Introduction

Ministry is, literally, a service. Since the whole Church is a servant Church, the whole Church is also a ministerial Church. In principle, every member of the Church is called to ministry.

For certain specially designated ministries, however, the Church has the right and the duty to determine who should exercise them and who should not. Among the Church's many designated ministries are those few that require ordination: episcopacy (the ministry of the bishop), presbyterate (the ministry of the priest), and diaconate (the ministry of the deacon).

The Second Vatican Council has had an impact on all three ordained ministries. Bishops are now seen as members of a college of bishops, responsible to one another and not only to the pope. Priests are now described as collaborators of bishops and as servants of their people. And, in response to the crisis brought about by a precipitous decline in vocations to the priesthood, the permanent diaconate has been restored—with mixed results, it must be said.

The columns in this chapter address some of the practical problems that have arisen since the council: the large number of resignations from the priesthood, the decrease in vocations to the priesthood, the declining morale of priests who stay, the challenge of closer collaboration between priests and laity, the restoration of the permanent diaconate and the tensions it has created in parishes and dioceses, especially among women, and the changes in the way bishops are selected.

As I pointed out at the end of the column of August 11, 1989, "Only when the broad center of the Church is willing to discuss realistic solutions openly will the situation begin to change. In the meantime, we should cherish, encourage, and support those thousands of good priests we already have."

Is Attitude Changing Toward Priests Who Leave?
(January 25, 1974)

The Vatican will have to make up its mind. For the last few years its attitude toward priests who resign from the ordained ministry has been ambivalent at best.

On the one hand, the Roman Curia has processed many requests for "laicization" with both courtesy and dispatch. For a time few people had any legitimate complaints about the handling of such cases.

On the other hand, Pope Paul VI himself has made some very severe remarks about these same priests, referring to them in a now infamous Holy Thursday homily as "Judases" and thorns in his own crown of suffering. And, in the meantime, the Vatican flip-flopped in its policies and began making it very difficult indeed for priests who wished to resign.

And now we have a curious, unsigned article in *L'Osservatore Romano* urging priests to remain at their posts, even if they aren't truly measuring up to traditional standards. More significantly, the article adopts a relatively benign and sympathetic attitude toward those priests who do in fact leave.

"Every person is a mystery, every life is a unique destiny," the official Vatican daily conceded. Priests who resign deserve understanding, not condemnation. Their decisions are usually painful, the interior process "grueling and anguished."

The quickest way for a parent to destroy the psychological equilibrium of a child is to punish then reward the child for one and the same act of behavior. That is also a classic technique in brainwashing.

Which is it now to be: the act of a "morally mediocre" Judas (to quote Pope Paul VI's 1971 homily) or the act of a unique individual struggling to determine the best course toward our common goal, the Kingdom of God?

But even if the *Osservatore Romano* piece reflects a new official sentiment (some have ascribed the article to the pope himself!), it does not go far enough.

Compassion and understanding are always appropriate virtues for Christians, particularly in their relations with one another. But in this instance the application of such virtues deals only with the symptoms of the problem, not the root causes.

The fundamental issue is not the treatment of priests who wish to leave (usually to marry), but the viability and even the moral justification of present canonical restrictions on the exercise of the ordained ministry.

How is it possible that in this day and age the Roman Catholic Church continues to exclude married people and women (married or not) from its most important positions of pastoral leadership, namely, the priesthood and the episcopacy?

There is certainly no basis for such exclusionist policies in doctrine or theology. I am not suggesting, of course, that there never was, or never could be again, some peculiar historical or cultural basis for celibacy as an ad hoc condition of ordination, but the burden of proof always rests upon those who seek to impose the restriction or, in the present instance, on those who wish to maintain it.

I should argue that they have not established a case, and certainly not a case strong enough to justify the suppression of what the Second Vatican Council called a "universal and inviolable" right (Pastoral Constitution on the Church in the Modern World, n. 26).

Nor is there any foundation for the present discrimination against women. Apart from the appallingly naive view that women can't be ordained because Christ, the High Priest, was a male, the usual argument against such ordinations is one that should be called "the argument from inertia": we've never done it before; therefore, we can't do it now.

I should suggest that the situation in the Catholic Church, at least with respect to this issue of priestly ordination, took a definite downward turn at the end of 1971, after the adjournment of the Third International Synod of Bishops in Rome.

Many Catholics invested their profoundest hopes in the deliberations of that synod. All the world knew that the question of the priesthood was uppermost on the synodal agenda; some thought, too optimistically, that the bishops would vote to make celibacy optional and to open ordination to women.

The synod did neither. On the contrary, it adopted a position perceptibly to the right of Vatican II and sharply to the right of contemporary theological and biblical scholarship. I think that many gave up hope at that point. Certainly the attrition process has not ebbed since then.

Until something more substantial is done in the way of institutional reform, we Catholics are going to be continually embarrassed by those seemingly repetitious journalistic pieces on the romantic adventures or misadventures of our clergy: the "Father Bills" of the *New York Times Sunday Magazine* or the "third way" priests of *Newsweek*.

In the meantime, the quality of replacement personnel will remain on its depressingly sloping course.

On the Selection of Bishops

(February 7, 1975)

Archbp. Jean Jadot, apostolic delegate to the United States, is so much of an improvement over his two immediate predecessors that some of us may be tempted to immunize him against all criticism lest he abandon his encouragingly open manner and progressive outlook.

But criticism, when courteous and fair, is itself a sign of respect. Indeed, there is nothing more contemptuous than a silence born of indifference and disdain.

In a year-end interview for the *Washington Post,* Archbishop Jadot pointed to a new trend in the appointment of bishops: younger men more oriented toward change, with wide and strong pastoral experience.

He noted that in March 1972 the Vatican directed its papal representatives to consult much more broadly than before. Many people—priests, religious, and laity alike—are now asked for their views on the needs of the diocese and on the kind of person they would like to have as their bishop.

The consultations, he added, are "always on a one-to-one basis."

It is this latter circumstance that, for all practical purposes, invalidates the process as a genuinely consultative one.

What one usually accumulates in such personal conversations is raw and unrefined opinion. In the absence of public argument, our hidden theological and pastoral presuppositions rarely, if ever, emerge.

There is an ancient canonical principle that "he who governs all should be elected by all." And there is an ancient and long-standing practice to back it up: the popular election of bishops by clergy and laity (see John E. Lynch, "Co-Responsibility in the First Five Centuries: Presbyteral Colleges and the Election of Bishops," in *Who Decides for the Church?*, J. A. Coriden, ed., Canon Law Society of America, 1971).

If the Catholic Church is to adhere once again to both the principle and the practice, it is essential that the process be public and broadly participatory, that is, it should include all the major elements within a given local community, selected by the diocesan pastoral council from its own members: diocesan priests, religious men and women, laywomen and laymen. (Of course, this presupposes that there is a functioning pastoral council in the diocese—still a rarity today.)

The committee for the selection of bishops should have a limited term of office, although for the sake of continuity the terms of the individual members ought not to terminate all at the same time.

It is also essential that this selection committee be fully informed of the needs of the diocese and have access to every kind of information it may require to make responsible judgments about the various candidates.

It is equally imperative that the committee consult as widely as possible and encourage public discussion.

Earlier recommendations for reform in this area are inadequate because they leave unchallenged the power of outside bishops, papal delegates, and the pope himself in the final selection process.

A bishop should be the choice of the community he is to serve. An agreed-upon nominee who meets opposition from external sources should not thereby be rejected, except after public discussion involving the full disclosure of reasons for such opposition.

In the end, the pope accepts rather than approves the decision of the local church.

Objections to the widening of the episcopal selection process are based on two assumptions, one theological and one practical: (1) that the pope alone has the right to appoint bishops, because he is the Church's absolute monarch, and bishops are only his delegates and vicars; and (2) that no electoral system, apart from the present method, could work.

I have considered both of these objections at some length in my book *The Remaking of the Church: An Agenda for Reform* (Harper & Row, 1973).

First, the belief that the Church is, by the will of Christ, an absolute monarchy is without biblical, doctrinal, or theological foundation. Indeed, the teaching of Vatican II on the collegiality of the Church is irreconcilable with the notion of absolute monarchy.

Second, there were, in fact, other selection systems in the earliest days of the Church. The present system, which allows no effective voice for the clergy and people of a community, is the one without adequate historical foundation.

It was not until the sixth century that the election of bishops by clergy and laity began to decline, and it was not until the Council of Trent, in the 16th century, that the papal prerogative in the selection process was finally systematized.

We are still a very long way indeed from the practice of the first five centuries of the Church, and equally distant from the ecclesiological principle of coresponsibility upon which this practice was based.

"Consulting" more and more people on a "one-to-one basis" brings us no closer to either the principle or the practice.

Parish Councils: Nuisance or "The Answer"?

(June 6, 1975)

There are two extreme views of parish councils. The first is that they are an incredible nuisance; the second is that they are "the answer" to the parochial crisis.

The first attitude is, of course, contradicted by the teaching of Vatican II and contemporary Catholic theology. Councils have been encouraged as one way in which to implement the principle of coresponsibility.

The mission of the Church, in other words, has not been given to the pope or to the bishops or to the clergy alone. It belongs, by reason of our common baptism, to every member of Christ's Body.

A parish council provides a vehicle by which each member of a local Christian community can exercise that baptismal responsibility in a representative fashion.

Those who continue to understand the Church as a monarchy will not, and cannot, accept parish councils as an important, or indeed legitimate, part of the Church's pastoral life.

Councils, in their minds, can only interfere with the unilateral decision-making power of the pastor, or, at the diocesan level, the monarchical authority of the bishop. In that sense, councils are indeed a nuisance.

The second attitude—that councils are the solution to all our pastoral problems—is contradicted by our experience. Even where councils have flourished, Christian perfection has remained elusive.

The parish council movement is not a panacea for all the Church's ills. Councils aren't bringing lapsed Catholics back into the Church. They aren't heightening the social consciousness of the rank-and-file membership. They aren't a semimiraculous device for achieving ecclesiastical detente between young and old, rich and poor, hierarchy and laity, and so forth.

Parish councils, on the other hand, are at least one significant and useful way in which to bring to practical expression the principle that the Church consists of all the baptized, and that all members participate directly in its saving mission (Dogmatic Constitution on the Church, n. 33).

A parish without a council is a parish without a broadly representative outlet for this universal missionary obligation. No matter how open-minded and benign the pastor of such a parish might be, his ministry will be one exercised upon, rather than in collaboration with, his fellow Catholics.

It is clear to those who have conducted nationwide surveys of the parish council movement that parish councils are always, and only, as good as the pastor of the parish.

Even in a diocese where you have vigorously progressive leadership at the top, a parish council will founder if the individual pastor is not really committed to it.

It is the pastor, after all, who in almost every case appoints the steering committee, which in turn draws up the blueprints and supervises the election. It is the pastor who in many cases appoints additional members "to balance it off a little."

Because of this problem and some others, many of the first-wave members of parish councils have long since departed from the conciliar ranks. According to recent studies, the second-wave membership is often less qualified (there are, of course, exceptions) and is more likely to include the "old institutional stand-bys."

A parallel can be drawn here with the experience of many priests' senates around the country. The enthusiasm of priest senators in the early post–Vatican II years waned as soon as it became apparent to many of them that their senates were not being taken very seriously.

Although there are impressive exceptions here and there, diocesan priests' senates are no longer dominated, as many once were, by the most gifted leadership-types in the local clergy.

If we are to preserve and strengthen the parish council movement and the important theological principle it embodies, then what we need today is some solidly scientific research. We need reliable answers (not hunches and gut feelings) to such questions as these:

What is a parish really like? Who comes, and why? Who stays away, and why? What are the alternatives to the "traditional" parish?

What are the stated goals of individual parish councils? How do these compare with the insights of Vatican II and contemporary Catholic theology on the question of the Church's mission?

What is the precise relationship between the stated goals and the actual performance of such councils? To the extent that there is a gap between rhetoric and reality, what factors explain the gap?

The parish council movement is only one part of the total renewal and reform of the Catholic Church in our time. Parish councils can and will thrive, as Vatican II intended that they should, only to the extent that other institutional and structural reforms occur.

Restoring Permanent Diaconate

(November 25, 1983)

The restoration of the permanent diaconate was one of the least momentous changes encouraged by the Second Vatican Council. Why was it done and what have been the results?

It was done because certain ministerial activities associated with the office of deacon were "in many areas [being] fulfilled only with difficulty according to the prevailing discipline of the Latin Church" (Dogmatic Constitution on the Church, n. 29). And the results have been mixed.

It would seem that the diaconate first came into being, in the earliest days of the Church, in response to a specific pastoral need.

The 12 apostles and some other Hebrew disciples of Jesus had been criticized by the Hellenists (Greek-speaking converts) because the Hellenists' widows "were neglected in the daily distribution" of food and other material necessities (Acts of the Apostles 6:1).

The apostles summoned the body of disciples and shared their dilemma with them. "It is not right that we should give up preaching the word of God to serve tables. Therefore, brethren, pick out from among you seven men of good repute, full of the Spirit and of wisdom, whom we may appoint to this duty. But we will devote ourselves to prayer and to the ministry of the word" (Acts 6:2–4).

And so it was done. The seven men were brought before the apostles, who prayed and laid their hands upon them. "And the word of God increased; and the number of disciples multiplied greatly in Jerusalem" (Acts 6:7).

This account is extremely important. It reminds us that the diaconate was established to meet a pastoral need, not for the spiritual enrichment of the potential deacon nor as a reward for service to the Church.

Deacons exist to relieve pastoral leaders of those ministerial burdens that, although important in themselves, make it difficult for the pastoral leader to do what is even more important.

The implication is clear for today's pastoral situation: If in a particular diocese or parish there already are ministers, ordained or not, who are taking care of these other pastoral burdens, there is no need for deacons in those places.

The Second Vatican Council listed some of the pastoral duties that the restoration of the permanent diaconate was designed to fill: the solemn administration of baptism, the distribution of Holy Communion, the blessing of marriages, bringing Viaticum to the sick, reading Sacred Scripture at the liturgy, instructing and exhorting the faithful, presiding at prayer services, administering sacramentals, and officiating at funeral and burial services.

In North America such duties as these, when not fulfilled by bishops and priests, are fulfilled by lay persons and nonordained members of religious communities. Thus, there are ample numbers of lay lectors, ministers of the Eucharist, religious educators, and so forth.

Where a diocese or a parish already has qualified lay or religious ministers taking care of these pastoral duties, in association with the bishop or pastor, there is no need at all for a deacon. Indeed, the introduction of a deacon where he is not needed can be intrusive, disruptive, and demoralizing to the ministers who are already on the pastoral scene.

The restoration of the permanent diaconate, therefore, makes sense in countries where no tradition of lay ministry has as yet been developed, unlike the United States and Canada, or in North American dioceses and parishes that have inadequate ministerial personnel.

History confirms this principle. The diaconate began declining in importance as early as the latter part of the third century, when the Church's membership moved outside the cities and into smaller towns and villages.

The deacon, who was originally an assistant to the bishop, either moved up with the bishop in the now larger diocesan structure or stayed behind in a local community as assistant to the presbyter (pastor).

In both instances the importance of the diaconate was lessened. The deacon's administrative responsibilities were gradually taken over by the presbyters, and deacons in parishes lost prestige.

Again, the point is clear. Where deacons are needed, their ministry is received with gratitude. Where deacons are not needed, their ministry declines in importance. And always the criterion is pastoral need, not the personal consideration of the deacon.

What about the "mixed" results of the restoration of the permanent diaconate in North America? There are too many deacons who are not needed. There are too many men who become deacons out of strong personal motivation rather than in response to demonstrated pastoral needs. And there are too many of those types of deacons who have become more clericalized than the very priests with whom they serve.

It is one of the great unpublicized complaints of today's Church that we are getting deacons we don't need, and deacons whose clericalism (and antifeminism) is more than mature, effective lay and religious ministers can reasonably bear.

Permanent Diaconate Revisited, Part I

(April 6, 1984)

If fools rush in where angels fear to tread, what do you call fools who rush back in a second time after barely escaping with their skin?

I return this week to the subject of the permanent diaconate. My last venture into this dangerous terrain evoked more than the usual amount of reader response.

I and my papers heard from deacons who firmly but politely disagreed, from deacons and deacons' wives who said that I had touched an exposed nerve, from laypersons who verified the experience implied in the questions my column raised, from priests who pronounced an "Amen," and from other priests, especially directors of diaconate programs, who thundered, Anathema sit!

I have no intention this week of retracting anything in that earlier essay. I attacked no one in that column. My purpose then, as now, was to advance the suggestion that the permanent diaconate program, whatever its strengths and weaknesses, needs to be reviewed.

It is the same point made in the February 25 issue of *America* magazine by one of Milwaukee's auxiliary bishops, Richard J. Sklba, a biblical scholar in his own right and president of the Catholic Biblical Association. I refer to his credentials not to load the dice but simply to call attention to the special competence he brings to the subject.

Although his encounters with permanent deacons have been "generally quite positive," it is the "emerging role of our baptized and confirmed laity" that prompts him (and others) to call for "a refocusing of the ministry presently assigned to the permanent deacon."

After all, you don't have to be an ordained deacon to bring Communion to the sick or to become involved in preparation for baptism or marriage.

Lay ministers become confused when they see the permanent deacon placed in the role of a mini-priest, that is, where his ministry is confined to the liturgy.

As Bishop Sklba notes, the permanent deacon evokes a negative reaction in these circumstances "since it is precisely in liturgical areas that he is least skilled and trained.

"It is my fond hope," he continues, "that the reappraisal [of the permanent diaconate program] will result in a return to the manner in which deacons functioned in the early church, particularly in Rome.

"They coordinated and supervised works of charity; as such the community could not imagine celebrating the Eucharist without the visible presence of the deacon."

When the deacon assisted at the baptism of candidates, they were not just any candidates for Christian initiation. Rather it was the baptism of those who had been involved in the social ministry.

When the deacon proclaimed the gospel, it was to motivate the rest of the community to continue their service to the needy.

In other words, the original ministry of the deacon was "an extension of Christ's care for the sick and hungry of his day. Such a focus would clearly separate the deacon from other ordained ministers of the church."

The diaconate, therefore, is not a rung on the canonical or liturgical ladder.

Deacons are ordained to provide an essential service to the Church. But if that service is already being provided by others, then the Church has to ask itself some questions.

Do these ministries require ordination to the diaconate? If not, there would be no reason to ordain a deacon to do them.

If these ministries do require ordination, why not ordain those laity who are already engaged in them?

Insofar as those who have been ordained to the permanent diaconate were already involved in the Church's ministry to the needy, the sick, and the oppressed, their ordination is pastorally intelligible.

Where candidates for the permanent diaconate have never shown any interest, much less involvement, in various diaconal ministries, the appropriateness of their ordination and of programs that sponsor them are at the very least subject to review.

Permanent Diaconate Revisited, Part II

(April 13, 1984)

When the Second Vatican Council mandated the restoration of the permanent diaconate, it assumed that most of the new deacons would be ordained in and for the Third World, where there were few priests.

Progressive bishops were prepared to see many parishes throughout the world presided over by these married pastoral leaders. This would have been consistent with the council's general desire to broaden the ministerial base of the entire Church.

Those conservative bishops from Europe and North America who opposed the restoration of the permanent diaconate never expected it to take hold in their own countries. Their opposition reflected instead a fear that the very existence of a married diaconate might undercut the obligatory celibacy of priests.

Events since the council have shown both sides to have been wrong. By and large, married deacons have not assumed positions of pastoral leadership in areas without priests (more than two thirds, in fact, have been ordained for the United States), and the married diaconate has had very little, if any, impact on the celibate status of priests.

But with the passage of time and a careful review of the permanent diaconate program, the situation could change. The instincts of both camps might yet prove to have been closer to the mark than now appears.

There is evidence, for example, that the shapers of the permanent diaconate program in the United States are concerned about the excessively liturgical cast the program may have taken in some instances, giving rise to the phenomenon of the permanent deacon as "mini-priest."

In its origins the diaconate was primarily a ministry of social service. Deacon means, literally, "servant." All of the deacon's activities, including involvement in the liturgy, were connected with his social ministry.

What the Church must look for, therefore, are candidates with strong track records in the social apostolate. Failing that experience, candidates should at least demonstrate some potential for social ministry and some capacity for leadership in its exercise.

If such candidates can be identified and formed in sufficiently large numbers, they would constitute a new reservoir of talent for broader pastoral leadership in the Church.

Which leads to a further point. Some of the highly qualified men who have been ordained to the permanent diaconate since Vatican II probably shouldn't have been ordained as deacons.

Is it a contradiction to speak of them at the same time as "highly qualified" and yet not suited to the permanent diaconate? Not if one takes into account the hidden role that obligatory celibacy plays in this whole matter.

Is it not the case that some of the men ordained as deacons are really better suited to the priesthood and that the only reason they become deacons rather than priests is their marital status?

If celibacy were not a requirement for priesthood in the Latin rite today, how many men now considering the permanent diaconate would redirect their thinking toward the priesthood? And how many present deacons would apply for a change in ministerial status?

Priesthood and diaconate are both important ministries, but they are also different ministries. The latter is far more specialized than the former and has a more restricted latitude of pastoral leadership.

The Church should be able once again to choose people for each of these ministries on the basis of their suitability for the ministry, rather than the presence of the charism of celibacy.

If permanent deacons themselves and those who lead their programs recognized the pertinence of the celibacy law to the present discussion, the review that is called for might be even more constructive because more forthright.

If so, the review would lead in directions that the original opponents of the permanent diaconate feared from the outset.

Veils and Collars Only Tip of Iceberg
(April 8, 1988)

The bishop of an Eastern diocese (one not directly reached by this column) recently sent all of his priests a copy of an article on clerical dress, written some time ago by a Jesuit who says he's been wearing the Roman collar for 50 years.

You don't have to have very much perspicacity to figure out that the article favored the collar's retention. Otherwise, why would the bishop have circulated it?

Arguments over relatively trivial matters like sisters' veils and clerical collars can be fun and exciting for some people (a dwindling minority, one would hope), but such arguments are usually engaged at the tip of a theological iceberg.

There is a deeper issue below the surface, both in the article and in the bishop's decision to reproduce it.

That deeper issue is the nature and purpose of the ordained priesthood and, more fundamentally still, the nature and purpose of ministry as such.

The article's author reported that he had asked the readers of his newsletter a simple, "unweighted" question: Do you want priests to wear Roman collars?

He received 202 responses: 192 in favor of the collar, 5 against, and 5 don't cares.

I'm not interested here in the final tally. The survey was clearly unscientific, and its author never claimed it to be otherwise.

What catches the attention are some of the reasons given in support of the collar. They reveal far more than the writers realized or intended.

"When priests dress like laypeople, they act like laypeople."

How do laypeople "act"? Is one supposed to infer that laypeople are usually poor, or at least inferior, models of Christian behavior?

Do we have here a throwback to the discredited pre–Vatican II notion that laypersons are somehow second-class Christians, that the only *real* Christians are priests, nuns, monks, and other celibates, marriage being a concession to weakness of the flesh?

"Keep the collar. It's about the only Catholic symbol we have left."

That's even more disconcerting. What about the Eucharist, which Vatican II called the summit and the source of the whole of the Church's life? The baptismal font? The cross? The papacy?

More revealing still is this third response: "Priests, like doctors, are our reassurances. Both are emergency people. Both should wear identifying insignia."

Bad theology? Right, but bad medicine, too. It's a totally outdated and uninformed idea that we should go to the doctor only when we can't stand the pain any longer or can't stop the bleeding. Preventive medicine isn't a liberal plot.

Where do we get this notion that priests are primarily for emergencies? Is presiding and preaching at the Eucharist an emergency situation (I suppose it is if you're not prepared).

Is working with parish ministers and parish organizations on a day-to-day and week-to-week basis to carry out the mission of the Church an emergency matter?

That's a peculiar concept of ministry itself. But, then, many Catholics still don't look upon the priesthood as a ministry first and foremost.

They still see it as a state in life invested with extraordinary supernatural and spiritual powers. Because the priest possesses these powers through ordination, he deserves special respect and privileges.

In return, however, he must not—not ever—"act like laypeople"!

Occasionally the argument from emergency gets blended with the argument from convenience: "I went to confession to a strange priest on a plane during a storm and was glad he could be identified."

Perhaps the most ambiguous reply came from a reader whom the Jesuit author describes, significantly, as "a fair young maiden."

"Priests look so handsome and distinguished in the Roman collar," she wrote.

Then again, how about this one: "Invariably, I smile when I see a Roman collar."

Our Jesuit friend, not content to let his readers carry the whole burden of the case on behalf of the Roman collar, contributed his own rationale to the mix. It isn't of a much higher order than those of his respondents.

He argues that "since we priests are fed, clothed, sheltered, bedded, health-cared for and put on wheels by the people of God, it behooves us to attend to their marked preference in the matter of our attire.

"Bluntly, if the laity who support us want this outward sign from us, then, by George, we ought to comply."

Sounds more like the job description of a mistress than of a minister.

And that's the point, by George!

Priest Profile Responsible, Real

(July 15, 1988)

Every so often a book or an article appears that has "special" written all over it. You think it should be required reading for this or that group of people.

The June 13 issue of the *New Yorker* contains such a piece. It's entitled "Parish Priest," by Paul Wilkes.

The article is a profile of a priest in the archdiocese of Boston, Fr. Joseph Greer, pastor of St. Patrick's in suburban Natick.

It is one of the most realistic and responsible pieces ever done on the priesthood. Every candidate for ordination should be encouraged to read it and then to discuss it fully and frankly in some supervised setting.

Father Greer is 56 years old (about the median age of U.S. priests today) and was ordained just a few years before the Second Vatican Council.

St. Patrick's, like its pastor, is also fairly typical of a large number of American parishes that have fallen on hard times. Once considered a pastoral plum of the first order, the parish "plant" is now simply too big to manage on an acutely shrunken financial base.

In addition to the church itself, there is a 16-acre cemetery, a huge elementary school building and adjoining hall, an 18-bedroom convent, and a 27-room rectory.

Today the school is closed, and the old parish clubhouse in back of the church has been remodeled into a residence for the homeless. The number of resident priests is vastly reduced, and the nuns are gone.

When Father Greer arrived in 1984 he found the church badly in need of repair, outside and inside, upstairs and downstairs.

The spiritual state of affairs didn't seem much better. Sunday Mass was a lifeless ritual. People hurried out through the vestibule, heads down, even before the Mass had ended.

How Father Greer undertook the process of renewal is vividly described in the article. The more striking story, however, is his own, as a middle-aged priest, prepared for duty in a pre–Vatican II Church but expected to serve just as effectively in a vastly changed postconciliar Church.

The description of his seminary training and the clerical culture that it fostered is unfailingly accurate. (I know. I attended the same seminary at about the same time.) It explains a lot about the gap between pastoral challenge and pastoral performance that many laity find in some of their priests.

One Boston priest, quoted in the article, put it bluntly: "For eight years, they dressed you like a girl and treated you like a child. And then they expected you to be a man."

There is something of the "a-day-in-the-life-of" genre about this profile, and to that extent it would make particularly instructive reading for all those Catholics and non-Catholics alike who have ever been known to ask, "Just what *do* priests do all day anyway?"

But there is much more than that in this piece. Somehow Paul Wilkes has also been able to penetrate through to the personal and priestly core of his remarkable subject.

Father Greer comes across as a profoundly committed Christian, a dedicated priest, and a no-nonsense yet sensitive and compassionate human being, tempered by his own weaknesses, physical and spiritual alike.

"Sometimes this is a Church that expects too much of her people," Father Greer told his interviewer. "I never thought I'd live to see the day I'd say that, because at one time it was so easy to judge: I was right, and everyone who disagreed with me was wrong."

During the turbulent 1960s and 1970s, however, he found that he was "just as weak as the weakest of them."

"Now I'm not so quick to judge," he admitted. "I don't want to be judged that harshly myself."

"Maybe I'm a little late," he continued. "I'm rounding third and heading for home—but I hope I'm learning that the true sign of the Church is forgiveness, not making the wounds deeper."

He spoke, by way of example, of those who have resigned from the priesthood but whose petition for laicization was denied. They remain outcasts in their own Church.

He spoke, too, of the victims of broken marriages who are supposed to live as monks and nuns the rest of their lives. And he spoke of a Boston priest dying of AIDS, banished from sight.

"God is kinder to man than man is to himself," he suggested.

"I learned, from my own mistakes, that people don't really *want* to sin," he concluded. "And through it all—this is strange to say—I knew that I was born to be a priest. And that I would die one."

The good news is that there are thousands of Joe Greers still active in the priesthood throughout North America. The bad news is that there aren't enough like him coming along to take his place.

Prayer and fasting alone won't change that situation. Only change itself will, change that many continue to resist.

Reflecting on the Low Morale of Priests
(February 10, 1989)

"Reflections on the Morale of Priests" is one of the most important documents ever released by the U.S. Catholic bishops. Unfortunately it will never achieve the public recognition of their earlier, and justly celebrated, pastoral letters on peace and the economy.

Prepared by a subcommittee of the bishops' Committee on Priestly Life and Ministry, the report concludes that "there exists today a serious and substantial morale problem among priests in general."

This finding should concern every committed member of the Catholic Church, because, as the report correctly points out, "when the morale of priests is high, the mission and ministry of the church becomes a positive experience for all within the Christian community.

"When the morale of priests is low," on the other hand, "the quality of ecclesial life diminishes and almost every area of church life suffers, from evangelization to vocations, from liturgical celebrations to service with and to the people of God."

According to the report, priests are simply exhausted. But theirs is more than a merely physical exhaustion.

Many priests feel caught between two forces: their own sound pastoral instincts, often honed over 20 to 40 years of priestly ministry, and the directives and policy statements they regularly receive from on high.

"Some priests feel that at times they are passing on to parishioners, who clearly disagree, pastoral decisions which they sense their bishops do not fully endorse and which they themselves personally question. 'Caught in the middle' is an apt description."

The bishops' report puts its finger directly on the problem: "Many [particularly in the 45 to 60 age group] feel they have worked hard and long to implement, or at least adjust to, the practical consequences of Vatican II. They sense that much of that effort is now being blunted or even betrayed and they elect to drop out quietly."

The bishops are reluctant to identify the blunters and the betrayers of the conciliar mandate, so I will.

The priests, especially in this 45-to-60 generation, are demoralized by the Church's current papal/curial administration. They see it as driven by a rigid, ideologically conservative agenda that brooks no disagreement of any kind.

They are particularly discouraged by the recent pattern of episcopal appointments in which ideologically "safe" men are selected over priests who, because of truly enviable pastoral records, enjoy the confidence and respect of their brother priests, religious, and lay ministers.

Let me express the frustration of this middle generation of priests (and others) in unambiguous terms.

If, for example, the priests and lay ministers of the diocese of Brooklyn were allowed to elect the successor to their much-beloved Bp. Francis J. Mugavero, Aux. Bp. Joseph M. Sullivan would probably win in a landslide.

But anyone who knows the score will tell you that a Joe Sullivan doesn't have a chance in this regime. "He's too good," everyone says, sadly.

What kind of Church are we running here when bishops and priests as outstanding as Joe Sullivan are blocked while other bishops and priests, safely "orthodox" in theology and securely "loyal" to the Holy See, are promoted, frequently to gasps of disbelief from fellow priests, from lay ministers, and even from fellow bishops?

The episcopal-appointments phenomenon is not unrelated to another aspect of the priestly morale problem: ecclesiological conflict.

According to the bishops' report, priests (and parish staffs) are frustrated and demoralized when they have to live and work side by side with fellow priests with whom they differ strongly about the very nature and mission of the Church.

The problem is magnified when they find themselves in ecclesiological conflict with their bishop. Given the recent pattern of episcopal appointments, this problem is going to get worse, not better.

Now Is the Time to Act on the Problem of Priestly Morale

(February 17, 1989)

"Reflections on the Morale of Priests," a report issued last year by a subcommittee of the U.S. Catholic Bishops' Committee on Priestly Life and Ministry and recently published in *Origins* (January 12, 1989), ranks as one of the most important documents ever to come out of the national episcopal conference.

It should be read not only by every priest but by every person who cares about the future of the Catholic Church.

"When the morale of priests is low," the report observes, "the quality of ecclesial life diminishes and almost every area of church life suffers, from evangelization to vocations, from liturgical celebrations to service with and to the people of God."

Priests are demoralized today because they feel themselves "caught in the middle": pulled in one direction by their own pastoral experience and the needs of their people, and pulled at the same time in another direction by official policies and directives from on high.

The problem is exacerbated by the tone and style of the Church's current papal/curial administration and especially by the pattern of recent episcopal appointments, which leads many priests to conclude that the future will even be worse than the present.

But there are other sources of discouragement and demoralization as well.

According to the report, good priests are demoralized by the constant carping attacks from the right—from "unreasoning and often well-organized opposition of the self-styled orthodox and of those who simply do not believe in the decisions and directions of Vatican II."

This creates a "debilitating wear" on priests, whose calling is to exercise a ministry of healing and reconciliation. Instead, they often find themselves engaged in battle with determined and mean-spirited people.

But there is even more to the morale problem. Our priests are also discouraged by the durability of the problem priest, that is, the type who didn't work very hard in the pre–Vatican II Church and who still isn't working very hard in the post–Vatican II Church. These are men of "limited energy and regular absenteeism," to use the report's own words.

In the past, with so many other priests on the job, the deficiencies of the problem priest could be "easily disguised or replaced." Not so today.

Unfortunately these problem priests take up much of the valuable time and energy of diocesan personnel boards and bishops as they seek to find assignments for them where they will do the least amount of harm to the Church.

What really discourages many hard-working priests is the knowledge that some possible avenues of relief are not even allowed to be discussed, much less implemented.

These avenues include the ordination of married men, effective use of laicized priests, the ordination of women, and the elimination of obligatory celibacy.

Indeed, the bishops' report acknowledges that virtually "every study or commentary done on the priesthood and shortage of vocations mentions sexuality (and specifically mandatory celibacy) as a major reason a) for leaving the priesthood, b) for shortage of vocations, and c) for loneliness and personal unhappiness of those who stay."

But most church officials seem to act as if these studies didn't even exist. And that in itself is cause for further demoralization.

The report offers a number of recommendations, only a couple of which are given here by way of example.

"A major factor in low morale," the report concludes, "is the perception by priests that they have no control, that they are impotent before major events and directions of their lives and of their church."

Therefore, priests must have a meaningful voice in the formulation of diocesan policies regarding such important matters as sacramental practices and parish structures.

Bishops, furthermore, must be "frank and honest" with priests about their own frustrations and questions. Priests must be able to feel that a bishop "really understands" because he himself is "in the same boat."

Indeed, bishops must also be honest and frank with one another, not only about personal pressures and frustrations but also about "the hard issues that confront the living church" regionally, nationally, and internationally.

Not surprisingly, the report falters when it tries to fashion recommendations regarding the abiding and utterly crucial problem of obligatory celibacy.

The report admits that the traditional rationale for obligatory celibacy is inadequate. But the bishops lamely recommend that "new language be found."

Such language doesn't exist, and priests and laity alike know it. The challenge is not finding new words but facing reality.

By and large, however, Bishop John McRaith and his subcommittee have done a good job of addressing the problem of priestly morale, and they should be commended for their report.

It's time now to do something about it.

Early Church Had Great Variety

(March 10, 1989)

Fr. Frederick Cwiekowski's *The Beginnings of the Church* (Paulist Press, 1988) is an important and valuable survey of current biblical scholarship as it affects our understanding of the origins and early history of the Church.

His fellow Sulpician, Fr. Raymond Brown, one of this country's foremost New Testament scholars, describes the book as "intelligent," "respectful," and "centrist."

He assures us in his foreword that he knows of no other popular work that covers the biblical background for Christology and ecclesiology as well and in so short a compass as Cwiekowski's. Neither do I.

Father Cwiekowski, a professor at St. Mary's Seminary and University in Baltimore and a priest of the archdiocese of Hartford, surely did not intend his work as a debunking enterprise. He carefully nuances whatever conclusions he draws from the findings of contemporary Catholic and Protestant biblical scholars.

Nonetheless, the scholarship that Father Cwiekowski surveys so well in this book thoroughly undermines what he calls "the pre-critical approach" to understanding the beginnings of the Church.

Still assumed by many Catholics (including some in the hierarchy) to be the only orthodox view, the pre-critical approach is based on biblically and historically untenable assumptions.

It incorrectly assumes, for example, that Jesus clearly and deliberately intended to "found" the Church as we have it today; that he "ordained" 12 apostles as priests and then as bishops; that he explicitly instructed the apostles to ordain successors and to exclude women from ordination; that Peter was the founder and first bishop of the Church in Rome and was recognized from the beginning as the Church's first pope; that the threefold ministry of bishop, priest, and deacon was directly established by Christ and then set in place right from the start everywhere in the early Christian world; that Jesus explicitly instituted the seven sacraments, even giving precise directions on how they were to be administered and by whom.

Did Jesus envision a Church that would last for (already) 20 centuries? Father Cwiekowski's survey discloses that "we have no evidence to support the view that Jesus envisioned a lengthy period with a span of centuries before the fulfillment of God's plan" (p. 44).

But didn't Jesus know everything about everything? After all, wasn't he divine? "Today biblical scholarship and sound contemporary Christology hold that Jesus' human knowledge was truly human and hence limited. Recognition of this limitation does not imply that Jesus was not divine; limitations in his human knowledge were fully a part of his being human" (p. 63).

Was the Last Supper the first ordination ceremony? "A careful reading of the texts does not indicate that at the Last Supper Jesus saw himself 'ordaining' the apostles or that he regarded them as 'priests' who were to preside at a sacrifice" (p. 58).

Did Jesus leave a precise blueprint by which the Church would organize and structure itself, sacramentally, hierarchically, and pastorally? "Biblical evidence does not support the idea that Jesus in his ministry set up a new community with its own internal structures and its own identity distinct from other Jews" (p. 59).

Did Peter found the Church in Rome and become its first bishop? "The strong case for Christianity's arrival [in Rome] in the early 40s (while Peter was still in Jerusalem) discredits the idea that Peter was the original missionary to Rome and the founder of the Roman Church. Our best evidence, Paul's letter to the Romans, suggests that Peter did not have any significant association with the Roman church before A.D. 58" (p. 99).

Indeed, there is "no evidence that any one individual in the mid-80s actually functioned in this Petrine role for the universal church either at Antioch or anywhere else. (Available evidence suggests that Rome at this time did not have any one such leading figure.)" (p. 156).

Given Jesus' supposed insistence on the exclusion of women from offices of pastoral leadership, many have assumed that women were silent and submissive in the early Church. "But clearly Paul takes for granted that women pray and prophesy (1 Cor 11:5, 13) in the liturgical assembly and he finds no objection to this" (p. 125). There is even some evidence that women functioned as deacons in the early Church, such as Romans 16:1.

Did women, then, also function as priests in these early years? "Christians of the 50s lacked church buildings or temples, cult statues or traditional sacrifices. They had no cultic leaders who were called 'priests' " (p. 126). Women or men!

The point is that there was far more variety, diversity, complexity, and development in the early Church than the authors of our 1940s and 1950s theology manuals and catechisms realized. Father Cwiekowski's *The Beginnings of the Church* is an important and useful corrective.

If you read no other book on theology this year, read this one.

Reactions to the Downturn in Vocations to the Priesthood
(August 11, 1989)

All the surveys, including a front-page story in the July 7 Sunday edition of the *New York Times,* continue to report a steady downturn in the number of vocations to the ordained priesthood. Although the U.S. Catholic population grew by 15 percent over the last 20 years, the number of seminarians in graduate-level studies declined by more than half.

What these surveys cannot statistically capture is something that is usually acknowledged only in private; namely, the concomitant change in the quality of the candidates. A disconcerting number have been found to be passive, dependent, rigid, and authoritarian. And more and more candidates are gay and/or sexually immature.

There are at least two unhelpful reactions to this negative trend.

The first comes from those on the Church's left who jubilantly predict the impending demise of the priesthood altogether. At long last, they declare, Catholicism is about to be liberated from its clerical chains.

The second reaction comes from those on the Church's right who see the decline of vocations as the inevitable outcome of moral laxity and doctrinal compromise. Only through an uncompromising return to traditional piety and orthodoxy, they insist, can the Church once again attract the numbers it requires for the priesthood.

Both reactions are unhelpful because neither has anything realistic to offer by way of a solution.

There are times, of course, when one is tempted to believe that those on the left may be correct.

Many of the Church's most effective priests are getting older, and they're not being replaced, man-for-man, because the factors that once stimulated and shaped their own vocations are no longer at work.

The priesthood hasn't been attracting the best and the brightest of Catholic high school graduates in recent years. According to a recent study by Sr. Katarina Schuth, of the Weston School of Theology in Cambridge, at least "the top tenth" intellectually has been lost (*Reason for the Hope,* Glazier, 1989).

Well-educated and increasingly affluent Catholic families no longer view the priesthood as the status symbol it once was perceived to be. Their sons have more choices before them now, beyond joining the police force, the fire department, the FBI, or entering a seminary.

And because of a serious morale problem within the ranks of the priesthood, confirmed by a recent subcommittee report from the National Conference of Catholic Bishops, priests themselves no longer encourage young men to follow in their footsteps.

But a priestless Church is no "solution" to a major pastoral problem.

The Church needs qualified and gifted people to preside at the Eucharist and to coordinate the multiple activities of a parish community. The ordained priesthood is utterly crucial to the life and mission of the Church.

But need they be celibate males? That's a question that some Catholics refuse even to discuss.

The Church's ultraconservative wing doesn't want the priesthood to disappear, only certain kinds of priests. To produce the "right" kind, the recipe is simple: Get back to basics. Open wide the seminary doors to prayerful, devout, and obedient young men. And purge the faculties of dissenters.

The "basics" they have in mind is an advanced version of the Baltimore Catechism, untouched by Vatican II and the last 25 years of theological and catechetical thought.

But that is a prescription for going backward, for repudiating the Second Vatican Council or at least for pretending it never happened.

Opening wide the seminary doors means, as anyone with any experience in seminary work knows, admitting intellectually inadequate and psychologically unstable people. They may satisfy a hunger for numbers in the short run, but they create havoc for the Church in the long run.

Many bishops and pastors have discovered this too late, much to their sorrow and regret. More pragmatic than ideological, they're not likely to make the same mistake over and over again.

Purges, finally, are more scandalous than the alleged evils they are designed to eliminate. People today, especially an increasingly well-educated Catholic public, are appalled by efforts to muzzle and censure those who dare to think or express views at variance with an official line.

They believe in the biblical Gamaliel principle: if it's not of God, the dissident view will fall of its own weight, but if it is of God, we would be found "opposing God" (Acts 5:38–39).

Accordingly, an increase of passive-dependent and rigid-authoritarian clerical types via lower seminary admission standards is no solution either. Such individuals prove ineffective in parish ministry because, among other things, their theology and personalities render them incapable of exercising ministry in a truly collaborative way, especially with women.

Only when the broad center of the Church is willing to discuss realistic solutions openly will the situation begin to change. In the meantime, we should cherish, encourage, and support those thousands of good priests we already have.

5

Laypersons in the Church

Introduction

Before the Second Vatican Council the so-called lay apostolate was understood in terms of Catholic Action, that is, the participation of the laity in the work of the hierarchy. Whatever laypersons did in the Church was always by way of assisting the hierarchy with *their* ministry. The hierarchy, in turn, determined when and under what circumstances the laity would be called upon to cooperate in that ministry.

With the Second Vatican Council, however, the lay apostolate was reconceived as a direct sharing in the mission of the Church itself. The laity participate in that mission not because of some act of delegation by the hierarchy but by reason of their baptism and confirmation.

The story of postconciliar Catholicism, therefore, has been the story of increasing involvement by the laity in the life and work of the Church. Laity now serve on parish councils, on diocesan pastoral councils, as directors of religious education, as youth ministers, as directors of liturgy, even as chancery officials.

And laity, conservatives and progressives alike, are also more vocal about the internal affairs of the Church. Laypersons have more than ideas about the Church; they have specific plans for its reorganization, as were offered at the Call to Action Conference in Detroit in 1976 (see the columns of June 17 and June 24, 1977).

And laity no longer derive their spirituality from that of priests, monks, and nuns. Since Vatican II they have been engaged in a sustained search for a more personal relationship with God (see the columns of July 13 and 27, 1973, on the charismatic renewal).

Whatever the post–Vatican II laity are, they are definitely not "the simple faithful" (see the column of October 17, 1980). The laity have come of age, because the Church, which they are, has come of age.

Diocesan Pastoral Councils Essential

(May 1, 1970)

Within the last several weeks there have been two major conferences on the problem of coresponsibility in the Church. The first, sponsored by the

National Council of Catholic Men, met in Dayton, Ohio, in mid-March. It centered its attention on diocesan pastoral councils. The second, sponsored by the Canon Law Society of America, convened in New York City during Easter week. This latter symposium addressed itself to the larger problem of core-sponsibility as such. Papers were given by Hans Küng, Andrew Greeley, Charles Curran, John Meyendorff, Thomas O'Dea, and others.

These and other similar meetings indicate that the Catholic Church in the United States intends to implement the theological perspective and pastoral implications of the Second Vatican Council. These two levels, the theological and the pastoral, converge in the conciliar teaching on the People of God.

Chapter II of the Dogmatic Constitution on the Church reminds us that Christ instituted the new covenant "by calling together a people made up of Jew and Gentile, making them one, not according to the flesh but in the Spirit. This was to be the new People of God . . . a chosen race, a royal priesthood, a holy nation, a purchased people" (n. 9).

Its heritage is the "dignity and freedom of the sons of God"; its law is "the new commandment to love as Christ loved us"; and its goal is "the kingdom of God." The new People of God exists as "a lasting and sure seed of unity, hope, and salvation for the whole human race."

Christ established this community as "a fellowship of life, charity, and truth" and as "an instrument for the redemption of all." The Church is sent forth into the world as light and salt for the whole of mankind. Furthermore, this community, as the new People of God, continues the priestly, prophetic, and kingly ministry of the Lord.

Chapter IV of the same document draws out some of the pastoral impli-cations. "Everything which has been said so far concerning the People of God applies equally to the laity, religious, and clergy" (n. 30). That is to say, every Christian is called to participate in the life and work of the whole Church. The laity, religious, and so-called lower clergy do not simply assist the hierarchy in its responsibilities, as if the mission of the Church belonged to the hierarchy in the first instance and to the rest of the Church only by favor of the hierarchy.

On the contrary, "the laity, by their very vocation, seek the kingdom of God" (n. 31), and that, after all, is the point of the Church's life and mission. The lay apostolate is not to be regarded, therefore, as given to the hierarchy (which is the way in which the lay apostolate was described in "Catholic ac-tion" days), but rather it is "a participation in the saving mission of the Church itself" (n. 33).

The theological basis for this follows immediately in the constitution: "Through their baptism and confirmation, all are commissioned to that apos-tolate by the Lord himself. Moreover, through the sacraments, especially the Holy Eucharist, there is communicated and nourished that charity toward God and man which is the soul of the entire apostolate. . . . Thus every layman, by virtue of the very gifts bestowed upon him, is at the same time a witness and a living instrument of the mission of the Church herself, 'according to the measure of Christ's bestowal' (Eph. 4:7)."

That is why the Second Vatican Council urged the establishment of a pastoral council in each diocese (see the Decree on the Bishop's Pastoral Office in the Church, n. 27), and why the Dogmatic Constitution on the Church urges pastors to "recognize and promote the dignity as well as the responsibility of the layman" and to "willingly make use of his prudent advice" (n. 37).

Diocesan and parish councils are not "frosting on the cake." They must exist because the mission of the Church is the responsibility of each member, ordained or not. All baptized Christians, as the new People of God, are called to proclaim, embody, and realize the Kingdom of God among men.

The Church is a single community with a single mission. Its life and work must reflect this. If all are responsible for the mission, even though in different ways and to different degrees, then all must have some proportionate share in those decisions whereby the Church commits itself to the work of Christ. And the Church itself must be so structured that it is manifestly one community in Christ.

These recent conferences on coresponsibility in the Church are not only signs of hope but also reminders that the work is only beginning.

The Catholic Charismatic Renewal, Part I

(July 13, 1973)

One is readily impressed by the extraordinary outpouring of delegates to the 1973 International Conference on the Charismatic Renewal in the Catholic Church at Notre Dame University—23,000 participants nearly filled the southern half of the school's massive stadium.

But newspaper photos of men and women—a generous sampling of priests and sisters included—with eyes closed and arms outstretched can also have a disconcerting effect: mildly disconcerting when the total delegation is only 90 (as it was at the first conference in 1967), but acutely disconcerting when the delegation has been multiplied more than 25 times.

Undoubtedly there may be some among us who have been hoping all along that by ignoring the movement we might somehow induce it to go away quietly.

There may be others who will persist in ignoring the numerical facts, but they are destined to wallow in disappointment for some time to come. The movement is not about to fall apart, at least not so long as this transitional period in Catholic history perdures.

A once-vibrant Catholic prayer life (novenas, rosary, stations of the cross, forty hours, benediction, and assorted private devotions) has fallen under the shadow of a question mark. Little has come along to fill the spiritual void.

The reformed eucharistic liturgy remains central in Catholic worship, as it should be, but it was never intended to stand alone. It is shorn now of its ancillary satellite system of paraliturgical devotions.

The charismatic movement is supplying for that deficiency. And it is doing so with remarkable success.

As I have argued in previous columns, the charismatic movement is strong because it is based on several durable theological principles: the Church is first and foremost a community and it should be experienced as such; the age of the Holy Spirit is not over, his gifts are available to all; the Word of God as it has been proclaimed in the Bible is the Church's abiding source of nourishment alongside the Eucharist itself; the mission of the Church essentially includes the fostering and celebration of fellowship (*koinonia*), which is the distinctive gift of God's Spirit.

But nothing, including the Church at large, is exempt from criticism. The charismatic movement is no exception to the rule. For if the Body of Christ is not identifiable with the Kingdom of God, neither is any movement within that Body.

The charismatic movement is no longer purely charismatic. It is already on the way to becoming institutionalized, and thoroughly so. Conferences of this size do not simply happen. National publications are hardly ad hoc, spontaneous ventures. Leadership is assumed; power is acquired and exercised.

This was to be expected. We have learned enough from the sociologist Max Weber to know that all charisms are eventually institutionalized—or they die. The question, therefore, is not whether the charismatic movement should be institutionalized, but rather what kind of institutional form will, and should, it take.

Even Protestantism, after all, has never made a serious attempt to create a church order that reflected the Pauline doctrine of charisma, but has left this task instead to the sects. Why? Because, as the distinguished Protestant New Testament scholar Ernst Käsemann has argued, "such an attempt would inevitably open the doors wide to fanaticism."

"For it can scarcely be denied," Käsemann continues, "that the Pauline communities . . . were, within one generation, swallowed up by Enthusiasm" (*Essays on New Testament Themes,* p. 93).

If Catholic charismatics were to ingest the illusion that they are part of a movement solely and completely prompted by the free, unpredictable activity of God's Spirit, then that movement will develop, in due course, the same kind of triumphalistic imagery that enjoyed rather wide currency within the Catholic Church before Vatican II.

They shall also prove themselves incapable of dealing with the inevitable structural and institutional problems that will beset the movement as surely as such problems have beset every other movement of its kind in human history.

The Catholic Charismatic Renewal, Part II
(July 27, 1973)

It has been repeated so often that it may already have become something of a platitude: True renewal of the Church requires not only structural reform but spiritual rebirth. The converse is also true.

To be sure, the repetition of such principles does not necessarily trivialize them or negate their validity. Indeed, its vigorous reaffirmation may have been the most important thing said at the recent Notre Dame conference on the Catholic charismatic renewal, judging by news reports and the testimony of several participants. It was Cardinal Suenens of Belgium who insisted that the postconciliar Catholic Church needs a spiritual renewal as well as coresponsibility.

"I see a profound complementarity between the achievement of true coresponsibility and the development of an authentic charismatic renewal among the whole People of God," he said. "We need this renewal for coresponsibility to become a reality."

Cardinal Suenens's judgment on this point is theologically and pastorally unassailable.

An improvement in the process by which we select our bishops will have little effect on the life of the Christian community if it is not accompanied by a renewed sense of commitment on the part of all ecclesiastical leaders to the abiding mission of the Church.

What is the point if laity are more directly involved in the decision-making process of a diocese or a parish if, when all is said and done, neither laity nor clergy are sufficiently motivated to give of themselves generously for the coming of God's Kingdom?

What is the point of involving more laity more directly in the weekly eucharistic liturgy if such participation contributes not a bit to the deepening of the community's awareness of God's presence in their midst and of their common responsibility to render apt worship?

What is the point of tampering with the pope's term of office or accelerating the practice of government-by-synod if, in the final accounting, the pope's primary ministry—that of strengthening the faith of the brethren (Luke 22:32)—is set aside as relatively unimportant?

Indeed, what would be the point of fostering intercommunion among separated Christian churches if their coming together contributed in no way to the unity of the whole Church, thereby enhancing her corporate witness to the reconciling power of God's Holy Spirit?

But, of course, it works the other way, too. Spiritual renewal that leaves ecclesiastical structures completely intact cannot really take root in the life of the Christian community.

The charismatic renewal, to be specific, has given Catholics a much greater sense of participation in the Body of Christ, not as second-class Christians but as full partners with God in the proclamation, signification, and facilitating of the Kingdom.

Structures that inhibit the exercise of this responsibility eventually generate oppressive conflicts in the souls of the "spiritually renewed." This is no idle supposition. It has already happened, again and again.

If the thunderous applause and standing ovation accorded the remarks of Fr. Harold Cohen, S.J., were indicative of the sentiment of most of the 23,000 participants at Notre Dame—and there is no reason at all to suppose otherwise—then one can surely conclude that the institutional implications of the charismatic renewal are clearly on the minds of the charismatics themselves.

What is troubling, however, is the way in which this concern is expressed. There is no call for greater freedom in liturgical expression nor for fuller participation in the decision-making process or in the leadership-selection process. Rather, they appeal for more explicit episcopal approval. Is it that they want their bishops to reassure them that what they're doing is really all right?

What kind of "guidance" does the charismatic movement need from the bishops that is not already available to its members? What kind of "discipline" does the charismatic movement require from the bishops that is not already imposed by the Word of God and baptism?

Indeed, the official statements of the American hierarchy on the subject of charismatic renewal have been models of restraint, patience, and measured sympathy. One might suggest—I hope not unfairly—that a previous generation of bishops might have come down harder, demanded rigid scrutiny of the movement's activities, and even actively discouraged its continuance, if not nationally, at least in several of their own dioceses.

But this did not happen, and it is to the credit of the bishops' good judgment that it did not happen. To expect more from the bishops, however, may be a sign of ecclesiastical naïveté. To want more—even to demand more—may reveal something about the underlying ecclesiology of many in the charismatic movement.

"Call to Action" Response, Part I
(June 17, 1977)

I attended last October's "Call to Action" conference in Detroit as an observer and immediately thereafter did a series of interpretative pieces for this column and a longer single article for the *National Catholic Reporter*.

Now that the American bishops have had their meeting in Chicago and have offered their first official response to "Call to Action," I find no reason to change the judgments or the predictions I made last fall. The bishops have accepted (in spirit, if not in letter) almost all of the conference's recommendations in the broad fields of social justice and ecclesiastical responsibility: racial and ethnic discrimination, due process, financial accountability, concern for the elderly, pastoral care for the divorced, and so forth.

But on no issue where Detroit was asking the bishops to oppose present Vatican policy or discipline did they affirmatively respond.

They rejected the recommendations regarding the abolition of priestly celibacy and the ordination of married persons.

They stood firmly on the side of the recent Declaration on the Question of the Admission of Women to the Ministerial Priesthood.

They expressed anew their fidelity to the papal teaching on birth control.

They made no concessions regarding the readmission of divorced-and-remarried Catholics to sacramental fellowship.

And they sidestepped the distinction between deliberative (policy-making) and consultative (advisory only) power for diocesan and parish councils.

But the seventh and final draft of their collective response to Detroit is an essentially positive document, much better by far than the initial draft prepared in March by a United States Catholic Conference staff journalist.

Had that first draft prevailed, the bishops would have strongly reaffirmed their own authority within the Church, downplayed the ecclesial image "People of God" in favor of a more "ontologically hierarchical" emphasis, and generally kept the Detroit conference at more than an arm's length from episcopal favor.

Instead the bishops, by an overwhelmingly positive vote, have now issued a statement in which they recall that they themselves had invited the process of "structured public discussion."

They insist that they were, in fact, moved by the voices of those hundreds who came before them "to describe how their lives are troubled by social injustice" and to express their hope that the Church can be more effectively "a sign and source of social justice and peace in the world today."

The bishops admit that the two-year process of consultation was not without imperfections and that some of the conclusions were either problematical or untenable, according to their own perception of theology and Church discipline.

But the consultation process, they observe, was marked by "trust and respect." It gave many people "a good opportunity to speak directly to church leaders." It identified issues and proposed several constructive suggestions for action.

"We reaffirm our commitment to the principle of shared responsibility in the contemporary church," the bishops declare, "and we assert our intention to improve consultation with our people in the future."

The bishops draw upon the Second Vatican Council's ecclesiology in formulating their response to "Call to Action." Basic to the council's theological vision is its description of the Church as People of God.

All of us—clergy, religious, and laity alike—derive our dignity from the same source: the free love of God manifested in the risen Christ. "At this most fundamental level of the life of the church," they write, "there are no distinctions among us."

The hierarchical ministry, therefore, is ordained entirely to the service of the whole People of God, making it possible for the Church to respond faithfully to its call to holiness.

"As pastors who are teachers," the bishops continue, "we are called both to listen and learn from our people." And when they presume to speak, it is to be done "sensitively, intelligently, and compassionately."

"Call to Action" Response, Part II
(June 24, 1977)

For a while it looked as if the American Catholic bishops were going to pronounce a plague upon the Detroit "Call to Action" conference of last October.

Rumors of severe intramural debate recently spread across the ecclesiastical grapevine and then into the press.

At issue was the statement being drafted for the May meeting of the bishops in Chicago. The document would provide their first official reaction to the bicentennial program's climactic event.

Had the first draft prevailed, those less enthusiastic about the Detroit proceedings would have been vindicated. The statement, it is said, was strong on episcopal authority and weak on shared responsibility.

The bishops would have been disowning their own handiwork, for the "Call to Action" conference was an official, USCC-NCCB operation from its inception.

To reject Detroit with some measure of theological vehemence would have required a similar, though more subtle, rejection of Vatican II itself. And that is precisely what some critics of the first draft perceived.

The statement the bishops finally approved with near unanimity not only endorses the basic concept of "Call to Action" but links it explicitly with Vatican II's ecclesiological self-understanding; namely, that the whole Church— laity, religious, and clergy alike—is the People of God.

"As members, they share a common dignity from their rebirth in Christ. They have the same filial grace and the same vocation to perfection. They possess in common one salvation, one hope, and one undivided charity. . . .

"And if by the will of Christ some are made teachers, dispensers of mysteries, and shepherds on behalf of others, yet all share a true equality with regard to the dignity and to the activity common to all the faithful for the building up of the Body of Christ" (Dogmatic Constitution on the Church, n. 32).

It would have been one matter to have criticized or even rejected particular resolutions passed by the Detroit conference (and the bishops did do that, in the end), but it would have been another matter entirely to have criticized the collegial process itself.

And it would have been another matter still to have fragmented (and therefore weakened) that process by parceling out the "Call to Action" resolutions to standing committees of bishops.

Instead the bishops established a special committee whose charge will be "to develop the five-year Plan of Action in consultation with our NCCB and USCC committees."

This committee will have "responsibility for oversight of [the Plan of Action's] implementation" and will "submit a written public report on the implementation process at each of our general meetings in November for the next five years."

"Call to Action" clearly has not been swept under the rug. The process is ongoing, and its guidance and supervision will be at once public and regular.

This is not to suggest, however, that most of the delegates to Detroit or that many other active Catholics throughout the United States are going to be completely satisfied.

The bishops—even the so-called progressives and moderates—are seriously mistaken if they believe that the particular resolutions they rejected outright will eventually recede from Catholic consciousness and no longer be a source of discussion and controversy.

Optional celibacy for priests, the ordination of women, policy-making authority for diocesan and parish councils, readmission of many divorced-and-remarried Catholics to sacramental fellowship, and a critical reinterpretation of *Humanae Vitae*—all of these are issues that, until resolved, will continue to impede the Church's progress toward effective reform and renewal.

The Laity Question Again

(April 28, 1978)

Several months ago a group of Catholics in Chicago issued a statement of concern regarding the decline of lay participation in the mission of the Church.

The document looks back nostalgically to the days when the U.S. Catholic Church had such lay organizations as the Association of Catholic Trade Unionists, Young Christian Students, Young Christian Workers, and the Catholic Council on Working Life.

The underlying argument of the piece is that the Catholic Church is under the spell of a new clericalism, this time of the left.

Priests have taken over the direction of various social action movements and no longer encourage laypersons to assume positions of leadership in the struggle for justice, freedom, and peace.

To the extent that laypersons are drawn into the active life of the Church, their energies and abilities are channeled into work traditionally assigned to priests or sisters, such as religious education, pastoral care for the sick and elderly, and lectors at Mass.

The newly restored permanent diaconate, in fact, tends to reinforce a common notion that one must be ordained to do the really significant work of the Church.

But "in the last analysis," the document argues, "the Church speaks to and acts upon the world through her laity. . . . No amount of social action by priests and religious can ever be an adequate substitute for enhancing lay responsibility."

Not even the recent "Call to Action" conference in Detroit elicits full approval. The signers of the Chicago statement suggest that "Call to Action" devoted too much of its attention to the internal affairs of the Church, for instance, parish and diocesan councils, ordination of women, a married clergy, and the election of bishops.

The signers are "deeply concerned" that the Church's energies are now being diverted from the challenge of lay responsibility to an "almost obsessive preoccupation with the Church's structures and processes."

"Reform for what purpose?" the Chicago statement asks. "It would be one of the great ironies of history if the era of Vatican II which opened the windows of the Church to the world were to close with a Church turned in upon herself."

I have devoted most of the space for this week's column to summarizing the "Chicago Declaration of Christian Concern" so that the critical remarks that follow will have some point of reference. It's been almost five months since the Chicago statement first appeared, and many may not have read it then or since.

The principal problem with the document is that it is ecclesiologically unbalanced.

It assumes that questions of structure and process are not only entirely secondary to questions of mission but that they are entirely separate as well.

The mission of the Church includes, to be sure, the pursuit of justice and the transformation of the world, as the Third International Synod declared in its "Justice in the World."

But the Church is also called to proclaim in word and sacrament its faith in the Lordship of Jesus Christ and all that this implies, and it is called furthermore to offer itself as a sign or sacrament of what it preaches and celebrates.

To be indifferent to the quality of ordained ministry is to be indifferent to the quality of preaching and worship.

To be indifferent to the conditions under which a Catholic is eligible for ordination is to be indifferent to the composition and indeed the size of the priestly community that serves the Church.

To be indifferent to questions like due process is to be indifferent to the manner in which the Church as institution treats its own members, and ultimately to be indifferent to the impression the Church makes upon the rest of the world as an authentic or inauthentic community.

To be concerned about justice outside the Church and not about justice inside the Church suggests a strangely selective understanding of the virtue of justice.

It also ignores a principle forcefully declared by the Third International Synod: The Church cannot effectively work for justice in the world if she is not herself just in the eyes of the same world.

This is not the time to pit Church reform against the social apostolate. Both have to do with the mission of the Church.

Role of Laity in the Church, Part II
(May 5, 1978)

The "Chicago Declaration of Christian Concern," issued as a joint statement at the end of last year and freshly circulated among key members of the U.S.

Catholic Church, urges a restoration of lay initiative in the mission of the Church.

The document worries about a resurgence of clericalism and about a growing notion that laypersons can effectively apply the gospel to the social order only when they move outside their present occupational roles.

What the signers of the "Chicago Declaration of Christian Concern" want is a return to the idea that Christian values are embodied and communicated mainly by laypersons and at the point where they work as lawyers, businessmen, factory laborers, teachers, and the like.

In last week's column I raised a question about the document's ecclesiological balance, without prejudice to the validity of many of its critical insights.

The declaration seems to suggest a dichotomy between concern for social justice, freedom, and peace outside the Church and the quest for these same goals inside the Church.

However, the Church exists not only as an agent of social justice and freedom but also as a model of both. The Church is called not only to be a servant community but to be a sacrament of Christ as well.

The Church—and in whatever mixture of lay and clerical leadership—may work unstintingly for a change in a city's housing code or for a reform of the local banking establishment's policies on mortgages, but if her own personnel policies elicit (as they occasionally do) public charges of unfairness and anti-unionism, the effect of the Church's social involvements is considerably weakened.

And how do we get the Church to change the way she reaches decisions regarding personnel policies, for example, without attending to the nature and operation of her internal structures?

The same kind of question can be put to some of the Latin American liberationists. How can you insist, on the one hand, that the Church ought to be a more effective institutional force for social justice, and, on the other hand, disregard the manner in which pastoral leadership is conferred in the Church or the process by which key decisions are made regarding the allocation of resources?

And just as the social actionist should not pit church reform against social reform, so he or she should not pit ordained leadership against lay leadership, even by implication.

But the declaration tends in this direction, too. "In the last analysis," it concludes, "the Church speaks to and acts upon the world through her laity."

Substitute the words "United States" for "Church" in that sentence and see how it reads.

Granted, the ideals, goals, values, and hopes of the people of the United States are addressed to and affect the rest of the world through nonofficial channels: literature, art, television, films, business operations, even tourism. But the United States is not limited to these channels of impact, nor are these channels self-sufficient.

Tourism presupposes treaties and other international arrangements regulating travel, diplomatic immunity, enforcement of laws, protection of rights, standards of health, and the like.

The export of films and other business commodities is governed by international economic factors: rise and decline in currencies, interest rates, tariffs, taxes, loans, mortgages, bonds, and the like.

And however well known and widely appreciated Barbra Streisand or Woody Allen might be, neither makes so much difference to international relations as President Carter, Secretary of State Vance, U.N. Ambassador Young, Sen. Russell Long, or a number of other officials.

Who gets elected or appointed, and how, to such positions as these is a matter of great importance to the nation. Similarly, who gets ordained, and by what process, is a matter of great importance to the Church.

"In the last analysis," I should suggest, the Church speaks to and acts upon the world through her total membership, but especially through persons of high visibility and influence, whether lay, religious, or ordained.

In the words of Vatican II, it is the "noble duty" of the ordained leader "so to shepherd the faithful and recognize their services and charismatic gifts that all according to their proper roles may cooperate in this common undertaking with one heart" (Dogmatic Constitution on the Church, n. 30).

Where Did You Get on the Train?

(June 22, 1979)

As time passes, it becomes clear that there is more diversity within the ranks of Catholic renewalists and reformers than first appears.

Other Catholics, who are less happy with the changes in the post–Vatican II Church, are sure there is a monolithic bloc they have to contend with, but that is not the case.

Those who are actively involved in various contemporary movements, such as social ministry, ordination of women, ecumenism, charismatic renewal, and marriage encounter, know that there are sometimes sharp differences of view among those who attend the same conferences, workshops, and programs.

And yet from the outside, that is, from the vantage point of the Catholic who resists further "tampering" with the Church, they all look about the same.

If there are differences, what is their basis?

I should suggest here at least one reason for diversity and even conflict within the reformist segment of the Catholic Church, and it is closely related to age.

Although all renewalists are riding the same train, not all boarded at the same station or even on the same day. The route has been long and winding, crossing national and even continental borders. The passenger list reads like a United Nations quorum.

Catholics over 50 or 55 got ecclesiastically involved at a time when the key issues were liturgy and social action. They are people for whom papal documents, for example, were friendly sources, not embarrassments to be ignored or challenged.

This older group was inspired by the great social encyclicals of popes Leo XIII, Pius XI, and various statements of the U.S. Catholic bishops on race relations and labor unions.

They also drew a full measure of direction and support from the two encyclicals of Pope Pius XII: *Mystici Corporis* (1943), on the Church as the Mystical Body of Christ, and *Mediator Dei* (1947), on the liturgical life of the Church.

These Group I Catholics have a highly refined sense of the Church as a community in which the unification of the apostolate is a major value. It is not a matter of clergy working against the laity, or vice versa, but of all working and worshiping together, head and members, as one body.

Catholics between the ages of 35 and 50 (and these are rough estimates, admitting of numerous exceptions) entered their ecclesiastical prime during the Second Vatican Council. All had just become adults or were still in their early thirties when the council adjourned in 1965.

These Catholics boarded the renewal-and-reform express when liturgy and social action were no longer the focal concerns, although they were still very important.

By 1960 or so, adjustments had to be made in the baggage car. The liturgy-and-social-action parcels had to be moved nearer to the rear and against the wall to accommodate some new pieces of luggage: ecumenism and the biblical, theological, and canonical renewals in particular.

And Group II Catholics had their tickets punched by a new and truly extraordinary conductor, Pope John XXIII, who perhaps did more to shape their attitude to the nature and mission of the Church than any other single human force.

This is a group, then, for whom the Church is wider than the Catholic Church and for whom various doctrinal assumptions, theological positions, and disciplinary arrangements were eminently revisable.

It was the group, indeed, that questioned *Humanae Vitae,* which called for greater participation of laity and the so-called lower clergy in the decision-making processes of the Church, optional celibacy for priests, election of bishops, and so forth.

The third, and youngest group (under 35), came to adulthood after the Fathers of Vatican II had left St. Peter's Basilica for the last time in December 1965. For some in Group III, the council is a dim memory, like John F. Kennedy's assassination. And Pope John XXIII is just a textbook hero.

These Catholics haven't experienced a Church where the pope and the hierarchy were often out front of the laity and clergy on issues that really count: liturgy and social action (in the case of Group I) and collegiality, ecumenism, and the servanthood of the Church (in the case of the council's impact on Group II).

Many in Group III were only 10 or 12 when Pope Paul VI was elected in 1963. He was "the pope" for the next fifteen formative years of their Catholic lives.

They lived through the controversies over birth control, changing canonical practices regarding marriage and divorce, the rise of the women's liberation movement, the disillusionment with the institutional path to renewal and reform.

And so Group III often "doesn't see why" this or that can't simply be done. "It makes sense. The only ones stopping us are the conservative people who are in power. If they won't approve, we'll do it anyway."

Or they set themselves apart entirely from structural concerns, focusing instead on the movement of the Spirit and the call to personal holiness.

There is a sense of freedom here that may be at once consistent with the gospel and somewhat oblivious to the process by which the gospel has been "handed on" (which is the meaning of "tradition").

The life of the Church is undoubtedly enriched by this diversity, but the reform and renewal movements themselves might be better served if the passengers on the train realized that not everyone of them got on at the same station.

Two Worlds: Sacred and Temporal

(June 6, 1980)

The controversy surrounding the enforced withdrawal of Fr. Robert Drinan from the U.S. House of Representatives is many-sided.

The case touches the theology of the ordained priesthood, the concept of collegiality, the issue of church and state, and, indirectly at least, the question of government funding of abortions for the poor.

I do not intend to continue raking over the ground on this recent Vatican directive. But there is one additional topic that transcends the Drinan matter and that also merits some specific attention; namely, the relationship of the lay apostolate and the temporal order.

This, of course, is a fairly traditional theme in Catholic social teaching. The Second Vatican Council's Dogmatic Constitution on the Church declared that "the laity, by their very vocation, seek the Kingdom of God by engaging in temporal affairs and by ordering them according to the plan of God" (n. 31).

But the theological sword is double-edged. If we insist too strongly on the point that the laity, by reason of their place "in the world," are called to work for the Kingdom of God in the temporal sphere, we may also be led to the conclusion that laity have no place at all in the sacred order. This view cannot be supported by an appeal to the Second Vatican Council.

Whatever one's opinion of the Drinan case, one should not assume that there is something unequivocally clear about this sacred-temporal dichotomy; namely, that there is a sacred order administered entirely by priests (sacraments, ecclesiastical governance, etc.) and a temporal order populated only by laypeople, but always under the guidance and direction of the clergy.

First, the council does not teach that the temporal order is for laity alone. "Secular duties and activities belong properly *although not exclusively* to laymen," the Dogmatic Constitution on the Church declares (n. 43, emphasis mine).

Second, "As sharers in the role of Christ the Priest, the Prophet and the King, the laity have an active part to play in the life and activity of the Church" (Decree on the Apostolate of the Laity, n. 10).

Third, the Church's pastors must recognize the laity's rightful place within the Church as well as in the temporal order: "Pastors also know that they themselves were not meant by Christ to shoulder alone the entire saving mission of the Church toward the world. On the contrary, they understand that it is their noble duty so to shepherd the faithful and recognize their ministries and charismatic gifts that all according to their proper roles may cooperate in this common undertaking with one heart" (Dogmatic Constitution on the Church, n. 30).

Fourth, there are laypersons who, "by reason of [their] knowledge, competence, or outstanding ability," are permitted "and sometimes even obliged" to express their opinion on matters that affect the good of the Church itself (n. 37).

Fifth, such involvement on the part of the laity in the life of the Church cannot be confined to the parish or even the diocese, but must extend to the "interparochial, interdiocesan, national, and international fields" (Decree on the Apostolate of the Laity, n. 10).

Sixth, the council mentions specific areas and/or activities within the Church where lay involvement is both welcome and expected: parish, diocesan, national, and international councils (Decree on the Apostolate of the Laity, n. 26; Decree on the Bishop's Pastoral Office in the Church, n. 27); the management of ecclesiastical resources (Decree on the Ministry and Life of Priests, n. 17); evangelization (Decree on the Apostolate of the Laity, n. 31); the administration of various ecclesiastical organizations and agencies (n. 20); foreign missionary work (Decree on the Church's Missionary Activity, n. 41); liturgical planning (Constitution on the Sacred Liturgy, n. 44); and so forth.

Finally, although the involvement of the laity in the life of the Church is often under the direct supervision of the hierarchy, the Church's pastors are also urged by the council to encourage the laity so that they "may undertake tasks on [their] own initiative" (Dogmatic Constitution on the Church, n. 37).

The laity may have a proper role in the temporal order, but that role does not prejudice their right and responsibility to participate fully in the life of the Church itself. Any theological assumption to the contrary would only add to the unfortunate implications of the whole Drinan matter.

Treating Laity as "Simple Faithful"

(October 17, 1980)

Some 15 years after Vatican Council II one of its fundamental teachings remains inoperative for many Catholics; namely, that the whole People of God is the Church, laity as well as clergy and religious.

The People of God shares directly in the total mission given the Church by Christ: preaching, teaching, sanctifying, worshiping, and so forth.

Laity, women and men alike, participate in the saving mission of the Church itself, not by an act of pastoral largesse on the part of the hierarchy but through their own baptism and confirmation.

Indeed, "all are commissioned by the Lord Himself" (Dogmatic Constitution on the Church, n. 33).

Why is it, then, that in so many places laywomen and laymen are still not full partners in the task of shaping the life and mission of parishes and dioceses?

Laity are in no realistic sense partners where there are no parish councils or diocesan pastoral councils or where these agencies are little more than hand-picked, rubber-stamping groups.

Why is it that in so many places laypersons still have no significant role in the weekly celebration of the Eucharist?

Laity exercise no meaningful liturgical ministry where they cannot serve as acolytes, lectors, music ministers, liturgical planners, or ministers of the Eucharist.

And why is it that in so many places laity are still regarded as if they were too unsophisticated to be given more than the simplest, even childish, explanations of Christian faith, whether in the weekly homilies, sermonettes in the parish bulletin, or in material provided in the book and pamphlet racks?

Why is it that those who regard themselves as the intellectual and pastoral elite of the Church so often assume that they, and they alone, are in the only position to judge what the laity can safely be exposed to and what they must be protected against?

Whoever coined the term "the simple faithful" to describe and characterize about 95 percent of the Catholic community was working from a very clericalist and patronizing concept of the Church.

This is not to deny the existence of those laypersons who are not prudent, whose ears are itching for unsound doctrine (as the New Testament would put it), and whose idea of participation in the life of a parish is to make life as miserable as possible for the pastor and others with busy jobs to perform.

But these are the exceptions, and it is exceedingly unfair to generalize on the basis of these exceptions.

The laity in North America today are not immature. Many are highly educated, and most of those who have not had the advantages of formal study at college or university levels are nonetheless people of common sense, with an enormous body of information at their disposal, drawn from television, radio, the press, and their own richly diverse fund of experience.

To speak as if one can keep something unpleasant or controversial from their attention is to pretend that we are still living in a premodern age when people were born, lived, and died within an acutely confined geographical setting, with little or no substantial contact with the world beyond, through travel, telephone, or print and electronic media.

The "simple faithful" who live in such a modern world are far more scandalized these days, not by the diversity of opinion within the Church, but by the clumsy attempts of officials and their agents to suppress the free flow of information throughout the Church.

Weekend after weekend this mentality is displayed in too many pulpits all across North America. Sermons whose intellectual level would be offensive to a bright junior high school student are delivered as a matter of routine.

Occasionally a preacher will use the pulpit to vent his own frustrations (not those of the "simple faithful") about changes in the Church, and especially changes in the theology he once so grudgingly studied in seminary, some 20 or 30 or 40 years ago.

Sensible people know that it's more "Father's problem" than it is theirs or the Church's. They know, too, that there is more to most issues than what the "party line" may say about them.

They're not looking, on the other hand, for silly, arbitrary, or pastorally irresponsible solutions. That is not what attracts them to the kind of theology that some regard as too rich and dangerous a diet for them.

People who take their faith seriously are searchers, learners, inquirers. To tell them they haven't the capacity to search is to insult their human dignity. To tell them they haven't the right to search is to insult their status as full members of the People of God.

On Christian Initiation of Adults

(April 20, 1984)

The restoration of the adult catechumenate was potentially one of the most significant decisions taken by the Second Vatican Council. One must continue to say "potentially," however, because the high promise of the council has not yet been fulfilled.

In the minds of many, if not most, Catholics baptism is still seen as something "done" to infants, by an individual priest, for the sake of personal liberation from Original Sin.

There is, for all practical purposes, no connection between baptism and conversion, baptism and community, or baptism and mission. The restored Rite of Christian Initiation of Adults unequivocally makes all three links.

Although the Constitution on the Sacred Liturgy mandated the restoration of the catechumenate for adults (n. 64) and called for the revision of the rite of baptism for adults and infants alike (n. 66), it was the Decree on the Church's Missionary Activity that provided the underlying theological and pastoral rationale.

Entrance into the Church presupposes conversion to Christ and the gospel. Conversion itself is a process. It is a beginning, not an end.

A person turns away from sin and toward Christ. That may occur in a single dramatic moment, but without some follow-through and support it will not last. People who have begun diets or tried to quit smoking can testify to this fundamental principle.

The council, therefore, described the period *before* baptism as transitional, bringing with it "a progressive change of outlook and morals." This change is "gradually developed during the time of the catechumenate" (n. 13).

The catechumenate is not "a mere expounding of doctrines and precepts, but a training period for the whole Christian life" (n. 14).

When the candidate for admission into the Church is judged ready for the rite of initiation, the council recommended that the candidate be initiated during the Easter Vigil when the Church celebrates the passage of its Lord from death to new life.

Since the candidate is being initiated into a community of faith and not simply freed from the "stain of Original Sin," the whole community must be involved in the process of preparation, the rite of initiation, and even the follow-up period of continuing formation.

It is not just the priest who inducts the candidate, "but the entire community of the faithful, especially the sponsors. Thus, right from the outset the catechumens will feel that they belong to the People of God."

But even that is not enough. Baptism is linked not only with conversion and community but also with mission. "Since the life of the Church is an apostolic one, the catechumens should also learn to cooperate actively, by the witness of their lives and by the profession of their faith, in the spread of the Gospel and in the upbuilding of the Church" (n. 14).

But how has the restored catechumenate for adults actually worked out since it was officially promulgated in 1972 and in the 10 years since an English version of the Rite of Christian Initiation has been available for use?

The record is spotty at best. For many parishes and dioceses the effort required exceeds resources and will.

In some other cases, it must be said, there has been resistance to a process that substantially modifies the traditional role of the priest as sole preparer, baptizer, and subsequent Father-Confessor of the "convert."

One still finds in a Catholic newspaper the week after Easter photos of bishops or priests baptizing infants at the Vigil service. However, the point of the restoration was not only to situate baptism within the Easter celebration but to underscore baptism's essential links with conversion, community, and mission.

Indeed, the National Catechetical Directory, issued by the National Conference of Catholic Bishops, identifies adult initiation as the norm rather than the exception.

Where the RCIA has been implemented with reasonable success, entire parishes have begun to experience a new self-awareness as a community of disciples in mission to the world.

And that is precisely why the restored catechumenate for adults is at once so important and so threatening.

It is of crucial importance because it calls each community of faith to become more fully what it is by divine grace and election.

But it is also threatening because the pastoral stakes are so high. To fail at the restored catechumenate for adults is to fail at bringing one's community to maturity of faith and action.

Laity Are Integral Part of Church
(March 3, 1989)

In the days before Vatican II, the lay apostolate (sometimes known as Catholic Action) was defined as the participation of the laity in the work of the hierarchy. Laypersons served the Church and its mission as helpers and deputies of the bishops.

Although it was surely better for the laity to have been involved in the mission of the Church as helpers and deputies of the hierarchy than not to have been involved at all, the definition (and the theological mentality behind it) happily did not survive the council.

According to Vatican II, the laity are as much a part of the Church as are the hierarchy: "Everything which has been said so far concerning the People of God applies equally to the laity, religious, and clergy" (Dogmatic Constitution on the Church, n. 30).

"The lay apostolate," therefore, "is a participation in the saving mission of the Church itself. Through their baptism and confirmation, all are commissioned to that apostolate by the Lord Himself" (n. 33).

For the council, laypersons are not simply helpers of the hierarchy, nor is their engagement in the mission of the Church made possible only by episcopal deputation. The laity's call to mission and ministry is sacramentally rooted: in baptism and confirmation.

Some laypersons, however, have expressed concern about certain postconciliar developments in the Church because of their apparent effect on the lay apostolate.

Catholics associated with the National Center for the Laity in Chicago, for example, have consistently warned against a clericalization of lay ministry within the Church and a clericalization of social ministry outside the Church.

Such Catholics complain that when the laity are invited to ministry, too often it is only for the sake of keeping the Church's internal machinery going.

Laypersons, they say, are not being encouraged to transform political, social, and economic institutions beyond the Church, nor to assume positions of intellectual leadership in science, literature, and the fine arts.

What is worse, the clergy, and especially bishops, have taken over the laity's proper role in the temporal order.

Thus, while many U.S. Catholics have applauded the bishops for their leadership on issues of peace and economic justice, Catholics associated with the National Center for the Laity seem to view these episcopal initiatives as an invasion of the laity's rightful apostolic territory.

If one presses such complaints too far, however, we could find ourselves once again trapped in the false clergy-laity, Church-world, sacred-temporal dichotomies of the past.

All of us, clergy and laity alike, are coequal partners in the life and mission of the Church. It's not the clergy's job to mind the Church store, while the laity mind the world store.

The clergy (including the bishops) have an important role to play in the so-called temporal order. They have "the right to pass moral judgment, even on matters touching the political order, whenever basic personal rights or the salvation of souls make such judgments necessary" (Pastoral Constitution on the Church in the Modern World, n. 76).

Conversely, the laity have an important role to play in the internal life of the Church: in its worship, in its religious education, in its ministry to the needy, and, yes, even in matters of governance (Dogmatic Constitution on the Church, nn. 34–37). Indeed, in earlier centuries the laity had a decisive role in the selection of bishops.

If we draw the line too sharply between the Church and the world, we run the risk of excluding laypersons (and especially women, who constitute the great bulk of the Church's ministerial force) from any meaningful involvement in the internal life and work of the Church.

Moreover, by rejecting any significant temporal leadership role for clergy (and for bishops in particular), we run the risk of individualizing the social apostolate.

It would no longer be a matter of the Church speaking and acting officially (and therefore with some political clout) but more often of individual members of the Church striving to Christianize a particular plot of temporal ground on which they happen to stand.

The internal life of the Church is every Catholic's business. And so, too, is the Church's external mission to the world at large.

The two are not mutually opposed. On the contrary, the transformation of the world is essentially linked with the transformation of the Church.

Because of its sacramental nature, the Church must practice internally what it preaches externally. The one is ineffective apart from the other.

Explaining Recent Challenges by Laity

(March 17, 1989)

There have been several highly publicized instances recently where laity have challenged bishops over the appointment or transfer of their parish priests.

Significantly, a few of these challenges have even been mounted within so-called national parishes, which some people have mistakenly regarded as the most subservient to the hierarchy's will.

Many observers aren't sure what to make of the phenomenon. Some have speculated that it reflects a struggle for power in the post–Vatican II Church: an increasingly democratic-minded laity against a traditionally authoritarian hierarchy.

While a desire for power may be at issue in one or two exceptional cases, the entire phenomenon cannot be explained on that basis alone. There is something much more profound at work in these recent developments.

Vatican II does have a lot to do with it, of course. It was the council that described the Church as the People of God, every member of which shares in Jesus' threefold mission as prophet, priest, and king.

Laypersons are not mere instruments of the hierarchy; their Christian responsibilities are rooted in their baptism and confirmation (Dogmatic Constitution on the Church, n. 33).

But the council asserted something more than that: "The laity have the right, as do all Christians, to receive in abundance from their sacred pastors the spiritual goods of the Church, especially the assistance of the Word of God and the sacraments" (n. 37).

The council encouraged laypersons to "openly reveal their needs and their desires to [their pastors] with that freedom and confidence which befits a son [or daughter] of God and a brother [or sister] in Christ."

Pastors, in their turn, were urged to "recognize and promote the dignity as well as the responsibility of the lay person in the Church." They are to "make use of [the laity's] prudent advice," and also to encourage them to "undertake tasks on [their] own initiative."

In light of such conciliar teachings, let me offer a tentative explanation of these recent little explosions at the parish level.

What is happening cannot be reduced to a power struggle between a restive laity and a possessive clergy. Very few laypersons are naive enough to believe that they have either the time or the skills to assume pastoral control of a parish.

Sensible, healthy laypersons are content to leave that task to their priests, religious, and lay ministers.

What these laypersons do want, however, is caring and competent pastoral service. They want—and have grown to expect—good liturgy, good preaching, good religious education for their children, good pastoral care for their sick and aged, organized service to the needy and handicapped, and a sincere concern for their own spiritual welfare.

We are often sourly reminded by Catholics who have never been happy about the council that a smaller percentage of Catholics goes to church now than was the case before 1962.

That may be true, but those Catholics who do "go to church" go because they want to go, not because they are afraid of committing a mortal sin and risking their immortal souls.

Catholics who once attended Mass primarily out of a sense of obligation weren't noticeably concerned about the quality of Eucharistic celebration or preaching, for example. As far as the Mass was concerned, the faster, the better. And if the priest decided to cancel the sermon, all the better still.

Those who come to church today come because they want to come. If they didn't want to come, they wouldn't. And many don't.

Those who do come are attracted by the presence of God that they find in the liturgy, in the community itself, and in the ministers who serve them.

Indeed, effective pastoral service, especially (but not exclusively) from their priests, usually defines the difference between a good parish and a not-so-good or bad parish.

When parishioners become accustomed to effective pastoral service, they notice the change at once if suddenly deprived of it.

In the past they might have simply accepted the change as the will of God. Today they don't. They want and expect quality pastoral service, and when they don't receive it, they want to know why.

The Second Vatican Council said they have a right to such service, and a right as well to express their needs and desires for it.

Unfortunately, bishops and diocesan personnel boards aren't always in a position to accommodate the laity's legitimate needs and desires. The sad truth of the matter is that there just aren't enough good priests to go around, and the situation is getting worse.

These latest rumblings over clergy appointments and replacements are only the first stages of a more violent storm to come.

Sensible people don't prepare for storms by filling their picnic baskets. They take the weather reports seriously and act accordingly.

What We Think of Our Saints and Ourselves as Humans

(October 6, 1989)

Two of the most basic sets of questions in theology have to do with sanctity and sinfulness.

What is holiness? Who is a saint?

What is sin? Who is a sinner?

In attempting answers to such questions, we reveal what we really think of ourselves as human beings and of the life of grace bestowed on us through Jesus Christ.

Take the matter of human sexuality as a case in point. Is sexual intimacy as expressed in marriage an integral, God-given dimension of human existence? Or is it simply a necessary evil for the sake of human reproduction?

Even great figures from the Church's past like Gregory of Nyssa and Augustine regarded the sexual impulse as a cause for shame, and moral theology textbooks, still in use as recently as a couple of decades ago, continued to refer to the genital organs as indecent and dishonorable (*partes inhonestae,* in the Latin).

For Augustine, they were the bodily instruments for the transmission of Original Sin. Indeed, Augustine's ideal society was one devoid of sexual passion, where male and female would join for reproduction not through the "eager desire of lust, but the normal exercise of the will" (*City of God,* 14:26). The highest ideal for him and for other Fathers of the Church was consecrated virginity.

This kind of thinking is generally rejected today, but its spirit lingers on in many of the churches.

There are Christians, Catholics and Protestants alike, whose list of serious sins is still dominated by moral transgressions related to human sexuality and human reproduction: homosexuality, premarital sex, birth control, abortion, masturbation, pornography, sterilization, in vitro fertilization, surrogate motherhood.

They regard the Church's and the Bible's teaching on these issues to be clear, absolute, and nonnegotiable, that is, not subject to any exception or compromise.

Theologians and other church leaders who step "out of line" on any one or more of these topics deserve whatever punishment they receive, even banishment for life from the practice of their academic or pastoral vocation within the Church.

What doesn't usually show up on such lists of sins—at least not in great quantity—are those moral transgressions having to do with injustice, violence, greed, self-righteousness, bigotry, vindictiveness, and the like.

For such Christians, the Church's and the Bible's strictures on matters sexual are unmistakably clear and binding, admitting no variation in degree (*parvitas materiae,* the old Latin textbooks called it), while the Church's and the Bible's teachings about these other moral issues are subject to all sorts of qualifications and exceptions.

A theologian (or any Catholic, for that matter) who raises a difficulty about some aspect of papal teaching on birth control, for example, is to be told that he or she is simply in error and that the criticism must be withdrawn, or else.

But a theologian (or any other Catholic) who raises a difficulty about some aspect of papal teaching on the obligation of governments to the unemployed would be left in peace. These are, after all, debatable matters about which Catholics can in good conscience disagree.

This difference in understanding the nature of sanctity and sinfulness is "cashed out" in the canonization process.

(The word *canon* means "list." To canonize someone is to add him or her to the official list of saints.)

No matter what else we say as a Church, if the vast majority of people we canonize as saints are priests, nuns, single laypersons, or widows who later founded their own religious order, we're telling our fellow Catholics and the rest of the world that the surest way to sanctity is through sexual abstinence.

In other words, the sexual expression of love, even within the sacrament of marriage, is a less "holy" form of Christian life than is virginity.

The Church also says something important to the world when it *fails* to canonize other types of Catholics: married men and women who didn't happen to enter a convent or seminary upon the death of their spouse but whose whole life was one of heroic sacrifice for their families, friends, associates, and the wider human community.

The readers of this column could supply hundreds of candidates for sainthood on this criterion alone: mothers and fathers, grandparents, siblings, relatives, friends, acquaintances.

Their nominees might never have founded a religious order or lived a life of sexual abstinence. On the contrary, their lives may have been fired with a sexual passion that was inspired and sustained by their profound love for another human being.

If we insist nonetheless on canonizing mostly priests and nuns, then why not someone whose sanctity is rooted in a courageous commitment to justice rather than in the mere avoidance of intimate human contact.

Why not someone like Archbp. Oscar Arnulfo Romero of El Salvador?

6

Women in the Church

Introduction

Before Vatican II, women were seen in the Church but generally not heard. Nuns were hidden behind veils and convent walls, and laywomen never entered the sanctuary except to be confirmed and married or to fix the flowers and replace the altar linens.

Today women serve as ministers of the Eucharist, lectors, servers, pastoral associates, directors of religious education, chancery and tribunal officials, and the like. And many are ready to be ordained.

No event has dramatized this change more memorably than Sr. Theresa Kane's chiding remarks about church attitudes and policies regarding women, given in the presence of Pope John Paul II at the Shrine of the Immaculate Conception in Washington, D.C.

As I pointed out in my column of November 2, 1979, "Anyone who thinks Sister Kane is just one nun in a thousand (or even ten thousand) doesn't know the religious landscape of the Catholic Church in the United States and Canada. The 'good sisters,' as they have condescendingly been called, are no longer a monolithic breed."

And neither are Catholic women in general. Pope John XXIII anticipated the change in his remarkable encyclical letter of 1963, *Pacem in Terris* (Peace on Earth): "Since women are becoming ever more conscious of their human dignity, they will not tolerate being treated as mere material instruments, but demand rights befitting a human person both in domestic life and in public life."

The 1971 World Synod of Bishops' document *Iustitia in Mundo* ("Justice in the World") broadened Pope John's XXIII assertion to include the Church as well: "We also urge that women should have their own share of responsibility and participation in the community life of society and likewise of the Church."

"Feminism takes a particular form in the Catholic Church," I wrote in my column of August 16, 1985. "It rejects the use of sexually exclusive language in the liturgy and in ecclesiastical documents. It insists on respect for the experience, competence, and judgment of women in ministerial positions of every kind. And, of course, it argues for equal access to all ministries, including those one enters through ordination."

Postconciliar Catholicism looks very different indeed. It has a feminine as well as a masculine face.

Women's Role in Life of the Church
(November 10, 1972)

Controversy about the place of women in the Church has been simmering anew ever since the release of a papal decree early in September.

The impression was clearly given over national network news and in the press that the pope had finally voted no on the question of women's rights, in much the same way, it was made to appear, as he had voted no in July of 1968 on the question of liberalizing the Church's traditional opposition to birth control by artificial means.

Consequently the debate has been clouded from the outset. Reporters misinterpreted the meaning of the papal decree on the reform of the Church's minor orders. In this regard, the Vatican press office ought to assume some responsibility for the confusion.

Contrary to the widespread impression, the pope did not definitively rule on the issue of women's rights. In keeping with the liturgical directives of the Second Vatican Council, the pope has been systematically revising various forms of Catholic worship, including ordination rites.

This latest decree was relatively progressive in character. The pope decided to abolish certain obsolete ceremonies and offices, such as the rite of tonsure, the minor orders of porter and exorcist, and the major order of subdiaconate. The remaining minor orders, now called ministries, are now also open to laity and are no longer reserved exclusively to candidates for the priesthood.

The pope chose not to change at this time the traditional practice of the Catholic Church regarding the exclusion of women from these ministries, except under extraordinary circumstances. There was no intent, however, to remove women from those ministries they were already exercising, such as the distribution of Holy Communion and the reading of Sacred Scripture at Mass. Authorization for such practices can still be granted.

The debate was further clouded by the decision of the Administrative Board of the National Conference of Catholic Bishops not to publish the theological study on the priesthood that the bishops had commissioned at least two years earlier.

Among the unofficial reasons given for the vote was the majority's unwillingness to be identified in an official or even quasi-official way with certain conclusions reached by the theologians. One of those conclusions concerned the possibility of accepting women for ordination to the priesthood. For some observers, that decision served to strengthen the mistaken impression of a renewed antifeminist bias on the part of the pope and the bishops.

When, about a month later, the Vatican finally responded to the criticisms of the original decree, it emphasized the point with which I began this column: The papal action "did not intend to make innovations." It was not making a final, irrevocable stand on the possibility of the ordination of women and other related problems. It was simply maintaining the present practice until such time as additional studies might make a change possible or necessary.

The Vatican spokesman said that the pope did not want to "anticipate or prejudice what might subsequently be established at the end of the study on women's participation in the Church's community life."

According to the Catholic news services, this was the first public indication that the Vatican had indeed accepted the request of several participants in last year's International Synod of Bishops for a serious theological study of this question, but it was still unclear whether or not the study has already begun.

Another Vatican source, however, disclosed that a commission has indeed been formed and the study is under way. Although this second source would not reveal the composition of the commission, he predicted that the study group will not recommend any change in the present practice.

Thus, we have a third unfortunate aspect to this new debate about women in the church: the imposition of secrecy on the very process of study and discussion.

If such a commission has in fact been established, by what criteria were its members selected? Are there any women on the commission, as the 1971 International Synod of Bishops recommended? Will the commission's findings be submitted only to the pope? Or will they be made public and thereby become a matter of open debate?

The issues related to the place of women in the Church are highly controversial. Many Catholics have strong feelings about them. Unfortunately, the recent distortions surrounding the papal decree and the apparent imposition of secrecy on the formal study of the matter will not make it any easier for the Church at large to accept whatever decision is finally reached.

Pastoral Side of the Women's Rights Debate
(November 17, 1972)

The contemporary debate about the place of women in the Church is of recent origin.

It was the cause of some surprise when, in 1963, Pope John XXIII referred to the growing concern for women's rights as one of the three distinctive characteristics of the present age.

"Since women are becoming ever more conscious of their human dignity," the pope wrote in his last encyclical, *Pacem in Terris,* "they will not tolerate being treated as mere material instruments, but demand rights befitting a human person both in domestic and in public life" (n. 41).

There was some minimal but pointed reference to the same development in the documents of Vatican II: "Since in our time women have an ever more active share in the whole life of society," the council declared, "it is very important that they participate more widely also in the various fields of the

Church's apostolate" (Decree on the Apostolate of the Laity, n. 9; see also the Pastoral Constitution on the Church in the Modern World, nn. 9, 20, and 60).

But it seems to have taken the pressure of a wider public debate beyond the borders of the Church to bring theologians and pastoral leaders more fully into the discussion. Because the rhetoric and style of some women's liberation representatives tend to provoke a strongly negative reaction among women as well as men, it is difficult for such people to admit that this movement, emotionally charged style notwithstanding, has forced us all to confront the issue openly and directly.

Accordingly, the theological and official literature on the subject is sparse in comparison with, let us say, the discussion on the causality of the sacraments or the doctrine of Original Sin.

Of all the bilateral ecumenical conversations that have been in progress in the United States since 1965, only one, the Reformed Presbyterian–Roman Catholic Consultation, has addressed itself to the problem of the ordination of women.

The consultation takes note of a growing consensus among theologians of both Roman Catholic and Reformed traditions that there is "no insurmountable Biblical or dogmatic obstacle to the ordination of women" and asserts that "ordination of women must come to be part of the church's life." Furthermore, it calls for the establishment of an ecumenical commission composed of women and men to study the role of women in religion and society.

In its evaluation of the Reformed Presbyterian–Roman Catholic Consultation, a special committee of the Catholic Theological Society of America agreed, in July of this year, that "there are no clear obstacles to [ordination of women] in revelation or Christian dogma."

The CTSA committee noted how closely the recommendations of the consultation paralleled a proposal of the 1971 International Synod of Bishops that "women should have their own share of responsibility and participation in the community life of society and likewise of the Church."

The principal word of caution offered by the CTSA evaluating committee is that women, once admitted into the Church's ministerial life, ought not to be forced "abruptly into patterns of ministry that have been developed with a view to an exclusively male clergy."

Similar conclusions were reached in the unpublished theological study of the priesthood commissioned by the American Catholic bishops. That study finds that the scriptural, historical, and theological evidence concerning the exclusion of women from Holy Orders is "inconclusive."

"The question," the theologians suggest, "is basically a pastoral one. The Church is free to ordain women if it so decides, and that decision rests upon a determination of what form of ministry is most conducive to the mission of the Church in our times. It should be noted, however, that if women are admitted to the ordained ministry, they cannot be expected to follow a masculine model of ministry, but will have to develop their own style and spirit of ministerial service."

In my judgment, the strongest argument against the ordination of women, at least at this particular time in the Church's history, is the pastoral one; namely, that this change would have such a disruptive effect, ecumenically and within the Catholic community itself, that the negative results would tend to outweigh the positive. I do not subscribe to that argument, but one must recognize that a case can be constructed from that pastoral starting point.

Opponents of the proposal would be well advised not to employ the usual simplistic argument that women can never be ordained because Christ did not ordain women. (I leave aside the coarsely unchristian argument that women are, by the will of God, inferior to men and therefore cannot appropriately exercise any significant authority in the Church.)

Such arguments fail to take into account the necessary historical, cultural, and social limitations imposed upon the Lord by the incarnational principle. They also tend to forget that many elements in the life of the Church today cannot be traced directly back to Christ, such as the division of the Church into dioceses and the convening of ecumenical councils.

"The Philadelphia Eleven"

(August 9, 1974)

On Monday, July 29, four bishops of the Episcopal Church defied their church's law and ordained 11 women to the priesthood in Philadelphia.

Under present Episcopal Church practice, women may seek ordination to the diaconate alone. Last year's General Convention defeated efforts to open the priesthood and the episcopacy to women.

It should be pointed out, however, that those efforts were defeated not by a majority vote but by a constitutional technicality (somewhat, but not exactly, akin to the electoral college system employed in presidential elections in the United States).

The majority of bishops voted in favor of such ordinations, and the majority of lower clergy and laity, in their turn, also supported this reform. But because of a special unit-rule system in the House of Deputies, the verdict of the latter two groups was recorded as negative even though a numerical majority of both clergy and laity agreed with the majority of bishops.

Three of the ordaining bishops and the 11 women rejected pleas to desist on the part of the presiding bishop of the Episcopal Church, the bishop-presidents of the church's eight U.S. provinces, and the president of the Episcopal House of Deputies.

What is, or can, be said of this unusual occurrence?

Even though I have consistently supported the ordination of women, this particular ordination troubles me on three counts.

First, this must be regarded, according to every reasonable pastoral standard, as an act that is potentially, if not actually, disruptive of church unity. That does not mean that such an act could never be justified under any set of circumstances. But it does mean that such an act requires more than ordinary justification.

It is a fact, and not mere conjecture, that a majority of bishops, clergy, and laity—at least those who represent the Episcopal Church in General Convention—support the ordination of women. There is reason to believe that this reform will be approved at the next General Convention in Minneapolis two years hence.

Unlike the situation in the Roman Catholic Church, it is clear that the Episcopal Church is relatively close to a positive decision on this controversial matter. This change is likely to occur in the very near future. No appeals to "the long run" are necessary.

Given these circumstances, it is difficult, if not impossible, to justify an act of such pastoral desperation.

Second, I am disturbed that the ordaining American bishops were, in each case, without present pastoral responsibility. Each is a retired and/or former bishop.

None of the three bishops is in a position to accept any of these women for service in a diocese. What these bishops supplied, when all is said and done, is simply "validity."

The ecclesiological mentality reflected therein is truly abominable: If only we find a "validly consecrated" bishop to ordain us, then of course our "priesthood" will be "valid."

Where is the call of the community? Indeed, where is the need of the community expressed? What diocesan pastoral councils were consulted? What process preceded the decision to ordain the "Philadelphia eleven"?

This ordination would have been far more credible if the ordaining bishops were active bishops who, after consulting their own people, were prepared to accept one or several of these women for ministerial service in their own particular dioceses. But this was not the case at all.

Third, I am dismayed to see that one of the women is already 79 years old. This makes something of a mockery of the ordained ministry. The priesthood is not a reward for a lifetime of faithful Christian practice. It is not a spiritual value to be appropriated by an individual to meet one's individual needs.

The priesthood is for service, a service that involves presiding over the liturgy, celebrating the sacraments, preaching the gospel, and generally exercising pastoral leadership within a given Christian community.

By all accounts, the priestly ministry requires not only spiritual and theological resources but physical vigor as well. Indeed, the latter consideration has prompted the Catholic Church in recent years to suggest, and even enforce, retirement of its older clergy, certainly those over 70 or 75 years of age.

Even if every other standard were being met, the ordination of a woman (or man) of that age is pastorally indefensible.

Indeed, the pastoral ineptness of this whole affair may very well have delayed rather than hastened the change that most Episcopalians (and many Roman Catholics) apparently support.

"Washington Four" Ordination

(October 3, 1975)

For the second time in just over a year, a group of Episcopalian women have defied their church's law and have accepted ordination to the priesthood. The ceremony took place early last month in Washington, D.C.

This year four were ordained; last summer in Philadelphia there were 11. This year there was only one ordaining bishop; last summer there were four.

This year the women had some form of prior approval from diocesan standing committees; last year none of the women had approval of any kind.

On the other hand, both ordinations were unauthorized and therefore "irregular," according to Episcopalian standards.

Both ordinations were performed by retired bishops.

And both groups of ordinands turned deaf ears to the pleas of their ecclesiastical sympathizers to delay so drastic a pastoral move at least until after the next General Convention of the Episcopal Church in 1976.

I opposed the Philadelphia ordinations last summer, and I oppose this latest Washington ordination.

First, both acts are, by any reasonable measurement, pastorally provocative and divisive at best and schismatic at worst.

I should not want to argue that individuals or groups within the Church can never pursue a course that may endanger the unity of the Church.

But if such a course of action is initiated and if indeed the risk of serious disruption is clearly present, then the burden of prior justification clearly lies upon the shoulders of the initiators.

At the very least they have to consider these questions: Is there an issue of justice at stake? Is this the only course available to rectify an unjust situation? Is there a reasonable hope that other, less drastic, solutions can be developed? Are the demands of justice denied if one waits for a less disruptive solution? How long can one reasonably wait?

It appears that the Washington four failed this first test.

There is a majority view within the Episcopalian community to allow ordination of women. There is good reason to predict that the next convention will vote in favor of such ordinations.

I should suggest that a delay of one more year is not an unreasonable alternative to what is, by most accounts, a pastorally extreme solution.

Second, even if one were to grant that circumstances required a pastorally extreme solution, the women are open to criticism for having accepted ordination at the hands of a retired, rather than an active, bishop.

It would appear that these women, intellectually qualified in so many other respects, have succumbed to the theologically deplorable assumption that "validity" is all that really counts in the end.

Thus, an emotionally distressed priest could "consecrate" all the bread in a bakery just by storming in and saying the "right words."

Or, indeed, a group of Christians can become priests simply by having "validly" consecrated hands imposed upon them.

If pastorally extreme solutions are required now and again, so be it. But it is disastrous in some circumstances to imitate—and therefore implicitly accept—the worst values of the so-called oppressing side. A pacifist obviously damages his cause if he pulls a gun on a would-be robber.

The Washington four may be well read in feminist literature, but they may also have some homework to do in sacramental theology and ecclesiology.

The Washington ceremony has hurt, not helped, the work of those in the various churches—men and women alike—who have been working hard these past several years on behalf of the ordination of women.

There is nothing either admirable or courageous about what happened in Washington last month. To suggest otherwise is simply to compound an act of serious pastoral irresponsibility and bad theological judgment.

NCCB Statement on Ordaining Women

(November 14, 1975)

Several weeks ago Archbp. Joseph L. Bernardin, president of the National Conference of Catholic Bishops, issued a statement concerning the ordination of women. He did so on behalf of the NCCB Administrative Committee.

The argument (or perhaps better, the counterargument) of the Bernardin statement is twofold: (1) There is indeed a "serious theological obstacle" to the ordination of women; namely, that "women have not been ordained up to now"; and (2) the disqualification of women from ordination is not an injustice since "no one, male or female, can claim a 'right' to ordination."

It seems now that the argument from historical practice is the only theological argument left on the anti-ordination side. The Bernardin statement itself admits, in agreement with the 1972 report of the NCCB Committee on Pastoral Research and Practices, that "many of the arguments presented in times gone by on this subject may not be defensible today."

I should suggest that none of the arguments presented "in times gone by" is defensible today. (See, for example, Fr. Haye van der Meer's *Women Priests in the Catholic Church?* Philadelphia: Temple Univ. Press, 1973.)

Indeed, not a single argument from "times gone by" is brought forth in the Bernardin statement, other than the problematical view of some earlier theologians and canonists that the prohibition is of divine law, and not of ecclesiastical law alone.

Accordingly, the only theological obstacle is the one created by the practice of the Catholic Church itself from its beginnings. Not an inconsiderable obstacle, to be sure. But not an insurmountable one either.

It is exceedingly curious that those of us who think in terms of eternity (*sub specie aeternitatis*) on so many other theological and pastoral questions are apparently less inclined to do so on this issue.

How much time, after all, is 2,000 years in the history of the Church, not to say in the history of humankind or the world? By what process of reasoning, theological or otherwise, do we assume that 2,000 years represents the bulk of the Church's total historical existence, so that the practice of these years must serve as an absolute norm for all subsequent ecclesiastical practice?

Let us suppose, for example, that we shall not collectively pollute ourselves to death until the year 20,000 (an optimistic estimate, perhaps).

How, then, would some historian of the year 19,975 characterize the first 2,000 years of the Church's history? Would he or she not be justified in referring to this period as one of the Church's infancy or very early childhood?

We readily accept innovations that were made in the "early Church" ("early" from our present perspective) because we regard that period to be one of formation and tentative consolidation.

But could not someone looking at the Church of 1975 from the vantage point of 19,975 come to the same conclusion about us?

The argument from historical practice is not a groundless argument. I do not want to suggest that. The constant practice of the Catholic Church casts at least a short shadow of doubt over the arguments advanced by the advocates of ordination.

But when seen in the perspective sketched above, the argument from history is relativized considerably.

Regarding the second counterargument: because no one has a "right" to ordination, the Church does women no injustice in preventing them from being ordained.

I do not think we ought to press that kind of argument too far. By the very same reasoning, the Catholic Church could exclude black males from ordination or Indians or Chinese or—given an extraordinary inversion of circumstances some day—even white males.

If no one could possibly have a "right" to ordination, then no one can unjustly be excluded from ordination.

I do not want to trivialize the argument advanced in the NCCB statement. Of course, the bishops' primary concern is with the will of God. But the content of God's will on this matter is precisely what is at issue.

There is a debate about this issue today because there are theologians, canonists, and women themselves who do in fact challenge the assertion that for all practical purposes the will of God is both clearly and finally negative.

Do we know for certain that God is not calling any women to ordination in the Catholic Church? If God were in fact calling some women to ordination and if, at the same time, the Church were preventing them from heeding God's calls, then would there not be a question of justice involved?

One can only applaud Archbishop Bernardin's exhortation that the various parties to this controversy should not engage in recriminations and that we should approach one another with charity and mutual respect.

Using the Gift of Leadership

(December 26, 1975)

Those who issued pessimistic predictions about the recent Ordination Conference in Southfield, Michigan, were proved wrong.

The conference was not taken over by "castrating witches," as one observer thought might happen.

There were no unordained "concelebrants" at the conference's closing liturgy.

There was no public call for irregular ordinations by retired Catholic bishops according to the Episcopalian mode.

This was all the more remarkable in light of the exceedingly high enrollment (well over 1,200, with a few assorted gate-crashers).

The conference was a well-organized and carefully structured event.

Why was it so responsible? How was such a controversial topic handled so constructively before so large—and potentially so unwieldy—a crowd?

My own view, as one of its minor participants, is that the conference was blessed with exceptionally good leadership. Each of the women in charge of major segments of the conference's overall design was, without exception, a person of theological and pastoral maturity.

The good impression that Sr. Nadine Foley, O.P., coordinator of the Conference Task Force, made on the national television news was grounded firmly in fact.

The other members of the executive committee were similarly effective in their respective areas: Sr. Joan Campbell, S.L., director of communications, and Patricia Hughes, chairperson of the publicity committee.

The same kind of smooth professionalism permeated the rest of the conference network: liturgical planning, registration, finances, housing, hospitality, and all else that goes into the making of a successful convention.

The short-term success of this Ordination Conference was thereby insured. (The only measure of its longer-term effectiveness will be known later on by the quality of the discussion the conference generates within the Roman Catholic Church and, longer term still, by the ordination of qualified women to the Catholic priesthood.)

A traditional axiom has been reinforced, it seems to me, for the benefit of the entire Church in North America and for the Church universal as well: With good leadership even complicated organizational efforts can be effective; without good leadership such efforts are doomed almost from the start.

Year's end always prompts us to look back and take the measure of our achievements and failures. At the threshold of a new year we grope for second chances and fresh opportunities.

It would be grossly simplistic to identify any one or two factors as explaining the crises and setbacks experienced by the Catholic Church over the past 10 years.

That a failure of leadership played a major part, I should nonetheless strongly insist.

It was the Church's leadership that, in the first place, refused to encourage (not to say "allow") the Church's scholars and educators to discuss controversial topics freely and openly before the Second Vatican Council.

And it was the Church's leadership again that proved inept at the task of preparing the Church's rank-and-file membership (not to mention her clergy) for the changes Vatican II was in the process of initiating.

Indeed, such failures were operative even during the council itself. The pope, for example, forbade the bishops from debating the issue of birth control, a matter that would erupt in all its fury in the summer of 1968 and significantly change the face and character of 20th-century Catholicism for God knows how long.

And there were bishops who returned from the council with vague and confused ideas not only of what they had voted on but, what is more important, of the implications of their votes.

Thus, we entered the immediate postconciliar period with the ironic spectacle of bishops arguing with theologians insisting that they (the bishops) had really not intended to do any more than change some vocabulary and adjust a few ecclesiastical fixtures.

The problem was multiplied at the lower pastoral levels, where priests unsympathetic with the conciliar changes did not even have the basic advantage of attendance at the council meetings, as the bishops had.

If some of the American bishops at Vatican II had names like Nadine Foley, Monica Brown, Joan Campbell, Anne Mary Dooley, Patricia Hughes, Mary B. Lynch, Mary Schaefer, et al., I suggest that the last 10 years might have been less disruptive and unproductive than that decade was.

The Ordination of Women Movement

(December 8, 1978)

The Second Conference on the Ordination of Women in Baltimore followed by three years its forerunner in Southfield, Michigan. Having attended portions of both and having had an opportunity to speak at both, I am drawn to make a few comparisons.

First, the organizers of this conference seemed younger and the level of lay participation seemed higher.

The principal coordinator, Dolly Pomerleau, herself a layperson, publicly took note of the fact that about 30 percent of the delegates this time were laywomen (60 percent were religious women).

Another speaker, Dr. Elisabeth Fiorenza of the University of Notre Dame, italicized the point in her own address, leaving one with the impression (and I call it only an "impression") that some of the laywomen were at least mildly resentful of the dominance of nuns at the Michigan conference and in the early stages of the ordination movement generally.

The youthfulness of some of the principal organizers and the broader representation of laywomen in the leadership group had some disadvantages as well. The more experienced sisters who convened the first conference in 1975 were thoroughly versed in the ways of community organization and ecclesiastical "diplomacy." Lines of authority and responsibility were more clearly drawn, and a very complex process was executed with remarkable smoothness and success.

A second, and much more important, difference was evident in the nature of the major papers. Alongside the Southfield presentations, the Baltimore talks were less substantive, theologically and historically.

Generalizations about capitalism and even ministry itself were not balanced with critical reaction and analysis. There was a consistent reluctance on the part of the speakers to disagree with anything that had been said by anyone else.

The youthfulness and lay status of many of the delegates (again, a good sign and a positive trend in itself) may also account, however, for the wooliness of ecclesiology underlying some of the talks, some of the resolutions, some of the group discussions, and the liturgies.

A "free church" ecclesiology was the only discernible focus for a solid minority of the delegates. Ministry for them is something communicated directly by Jesus Christ and the Holy Spirit, and if it is "mediated" at all, it is mediated by the affirmation of a small group of like-minded Christian friends and associates.

The notion that ordination relates one sacramentally to a larger Church, that the interests and supervisory authority of the larger diocesan and universal churches also have to be taken into account, that the Church has to issue a "call" to ordination, and that the mere desire to be a priest is not enough—such points as these were viewed as marginal at best, irrelevant at worst, by some at the conference.

Few proposals were received with less favor by this segment than one that insisted on criteria and standards for the selection, formation, ordination, and performance evaluation of the Church's priests.

It was suggested, in fact, that such a consideration is something only a man would press, and that for a woman to do so would serve only to undermine the unity of the women's movement.

What some women apparently do not realize is that the application of standards is just as threatening to unqualified or weak male candidates for the priesthood.

The Church is not well served by any incompetent or psychically unhealthy ministers, be they female or male.

Resistance to such standards weakens the credibility of those who press for ordination of women on the grounds that it will not only meet the requirements of justice but enrich the life and mission of the Church as well.

If there is to be a change in the present discipline regarding the exclusion of women from ordination (or in the present discipline regarding celibacy), it will come as a direct result of the efforts of those—women and men alike—who strive to reform structures from within the Catholic theological tradition.

Just because the Catholic Church remains officially opposed at this time cannot justify abandoning the Catholic tradition itself.

Perhaps the most hopeful element at this Second Conference on the Ordination of Women was the noticeably positive response this very argument received from an apparent majority of the delegates.

It's unfortunate that there weren't some representatives present from the National Conference of Catholic Bishops to sense that spirit and to enter into open and constructive dialogue with those women of faith who embody it.

In the meantime, the issue is not going to "go away," nor are those women. This conference, and others like it, serve to keep the question alive. That may be their principal purpose and primary justification.

Sr. Theresa Kane and the Pope

(November 2, 1979)

Sr. Mary Theresa Kane is the president of the Leadership Conference of Women Religious. She is better known these days as the sister who publicly urged the pope in the National Shrine of the Immaculate Conception to reconsider his stand on women's ordination.

Only those who have no extensive contact with the religious women of North America could have been taken completely by surprise.

Sister Kane's was a courageous gesture, according to some observers. But there are hundreds of other sisters just like her—and many who are heads of congregations and coordinators of provinces—who would have done exactly the same thing given the same opportunity.

Anyone who thinks Sister Kane is just one nun in a thousand (or even ten thousand) doesn't know the religious landscape of the Catholic Church in the United States and Canada. The "good sisters," as they have condescendingly been called, are no longer a monolithic breed.

Many thousands of American sisters are highly educated, culturally sophisticated, and uncomfortably dedicated to the poor and the oppressed—"uncomfortably" so from the perspective of those of us whose commitments are more calculated and restrained.

But neither Sister Kane nor the many thousands like her need this column's praise. "Carrying coals to Newcastle," and all that.

What prompts these reflections this week is the undercurrent of discussion not about what she said but about the propriety of what she did.

Was it appropriate for her to use the occasion and the platform as she did, with the pope sitting there as a captive audience?

The answer, it seems to me, is "It all depends." It depends on the larger context of the whole papal visit.

Did the pope himself raise controversial issues, like women's ordination? If he had not, then surely it would have been out of place for Sister Kane or for anyone else to introduce a polemical spirit in an entirely nonpartisan, goodwill visit.

But the pope did insert controversy into his public statements in Philadelphia and again in Chicago. He himself raised the question of women's ordination, as well as birth control, clerical celibacy, and divorce.

But even if the pope did first raise the issues, would that necessarily have justified Sister Kane's gesture?

The answer is no if the papal visit had already provided the pope with opportunities to meet with women seeking wider responsibilities in the life and mission of the Church, with married couples whose experience conflicts with the official teaching on birth control, with divorced people, and with married priests.

The pope is a man whose whole theological and philosophical vision, so magnificently expounded at the United Nations, centers on the infinite value and worth of each individual person.

No one is to be regarded as a mere cog in the wheel or a number in a system. No one is to be written off as a "typical" this or a "typical" that. Each man and woman has a concrete individuality that must be respected and accounted for in every public policy decision.

The planners of this U.S. trip, therefore, might usefully have recognized the pope's need to implement his excellent principles and to learn about the Catholic Church in the United States not only through contact with mammoth crowds or with bishops and other ecclesiastical officials, but also through more intimate personal contact with those whose views would not have been reflected by his various hosts.

In short, if the pope had already had an opportunity to hear directly from the Sister Kanes of the U.S. Catholic Church, then Sister Kane's remarks at the National Shrine should have been more perfunctory and diplomatically antiseptic than they were.

But in spite of the fact that the pope gave almost 70 speeches and sermons, never once—except at the Shrine in Washington, D.C.—was there even the slightest opportunity for him to receive feedback or to enter into dialogue with those whose convictions and experience led them to a view different from his own.

Accordingly, the question is not whether Sr. Mary Theresa Kane was justified in what she did and said. The question really is whether or not she could conscientiously have remained silent.

If she was courageous, she was courageous in doing her duty. Given her convictions and the structural deficiencies of the trip itself, she had no other choice.

The Role of Women in the Church, Part I

(February 8, 1980)

One of the most significant recent statements on the place of women in the Church appears in the October 1979 issue of the *Catholic Biblical Quarterly.*

The general readership of the Catholic press is not likely to see this task force report of the Catholic Biblical Association, but it deserves wider circulation and attention.

"The Christian priesthood as we know it began to be established no earlier than the end of the first or beginning of the second century," the report declares (contrary to a popular notion that the Last Supper was in effect an ordination ceremony). "In the primitive Church before this, ministries were complex and in flux, and the different services later incorporated into the priestly ministry were performed by various members of the community."

Lest some readers wonder, the biblical scholars are not saying that priesthood has no basis or place in the Catholic Church. They are saying only what is recognized generally today by theologians and biblical scholars alike: that the priesthood and the episcopate did not have the same exact form in the earliest years of the Church's history as they have now.

Bishops and popes did not always exercise the kind of authority they have today. The New Testament evidence "does not indicate that one group controlled or exercised all ministries in the earliest Church. Rather the responsibility for ministry, or service, was shared by various groups within the community."

What was unequivocally central to the early Church's faith and vision was its conviction that the Kingdom of God had broken into history and that the old social order was transformed. By virtue of baptism into Christ, "there is neither Jew nor Greek, there is neither slave nor free, there is no 'male and female' " (Galatians 3:28, with reference to Genesis 1:27).

"That this conviction was implemented with respect to women both in Jesus' ministry and in the early Church, to the extent allowed by cultural possibilities, can scarcely be doubted," the task force notes.

Thus women were among the disciples of Jesus from the beginning and were faithful to the end (Mark 15:40–41, 47; 16:1; Luke 8:1–3). Women were the first to discover the empty tomb on Easter morning (Mark 16:2–8; Luke 24:1–11) and, according to some Gospel traditions, the first to see the Risen Lord (Matthew 28:1–10; John 20:11–18).

Women were among those first designated by the Lord to be his witnesses (Luke 24:48). Given the accepted criteria for apostleship, namely, seeing the Risen Lord, receiving a commission to proclaim the gospel, and having accompanied Jesus during his ministry, women could have been apostles if the Church wished them to be. Indeed, Junia may have been one (Romans 16:7).

(Again, some readers may wonder how a Catholic could even consider such a possibility. But the apostleship was larger than the circle of the

Twelve. All of the Twelve were apostles, but not all apostles were among the Twelve).

There is evidence, according to the scholars, that many of the functions later associated with the priestly ministry were in fact exercised by women, and no evidence that women were excluded from any of them.

There were women who were instrumental in the founding of churches (Acts 18:2, 18–19, with First Corinthians 16:19 and Romans 16:3–5); women in leadership roles (Romans 16:1–2, 6, 12; Philippians 4:2–3); women with liturgical responsibilities (First Corinthians 11:5); women engaged in teaching converts (Acts 18:26); and women prophets (First Corinthians 11:5; Acts 21:9).

"The limitations presently placed on women's role in the Church and on the arguments advanced in support of those restrictions must be evaluated in light of the evidence for ministerial coresponsibility and for the presence of women in ministries in the Church of the NT [sic] period."

The apostles, for example, were not the only ones who presided at the Eucharist in the early Church (although we have no explicit evidence that they did so at all). The New Testament reports that prophets and teachers also presided (Acts 13:1–2; also the Didache 10:7).

Prophecy was a charism second only to the apostleship (First Corinthians 12:28), and it is certain that prophecy was given to women (First Corinthians 11:5; Acts 21:9).

> Other ministries, apparently more significant in the earliest period, such as missionary preaching, teaching of new converts, administration and service of local churches, were exercised by persons who were not members of the Twelve and in many cases not appointed by the Twelve, and who evidently were not exclusively male.
>
> Thus the claim that the intention and example of Jesus and the example of the apostles provide a norm excluding women from priestly ministry cannot be sustained on either logical or historical grounds.

"The conclusion we draw," the report declares, "is that the NT evidence, while not decisive by itself, points toward the admission of women to priestly ministry."

The Role of Women in the Church, Part II

(February 15, 1980)

"What do you people want anyway?" That's the sort of question many a spokesperson for minority causes has often encountered.

The "you people" shows that the group has been stereotyped in the questioner's mind, and the "What do you . . . want anyway?" reveals the questioner's sense of confusion and frustration.

Blacks in particular have suffered the "you people" routine in the past. Women are being subjected to it today.

Most of the time the question never gets answered. The one to whom it is directed usually counters with one of his or her own: "What do you mean by 'you people'?" And then a whole new argument erupts over types and categories.

But the question itself deserves an answer, if only to disarm the question once and for all and render it useless as a polemical device.

One of the best answers I've seen from the Catholic women's side in recent months was given at a conference for priests in the diocese of Springfield, Massachusetts.

The speaker was Sr. Kathleen Keating, president of the Sisters of St. Joseph of Springfield and former national chairperson of the National Assembly of Women Religious.

Sister Kathleen answers the question on two levels: one at the level of ideals and general goals, and the other at the level of specific pastoral proposals. I have adapted her material for use in this week's column.

Among the broad goals are these:

1. That women will truly become coministers and copartners with priests: in parishes, on campuses, in hospitals, schools, social service agencies, and so on.

2. That there be a high degree of trust, and that this, in turn, be the basis of a fuller participation in the decision-making process for women religious and for laity, men and women alike.

3. That pastoral leadership assume a team structure, and that it operate on a consensus model.

4. That conflict be recognized as inevitable but not necessarily destructive, and that ways be developed to resolve and manage such conflict in the spirit of justice.

5. That dioceses, parishes, and other pastoral units should enter into a planning process in which women are fully involved.

Among her specific suggestions are these:

1. That women be included as special ministers of the Eucharist and as lectors and in whatever commissionings might be appropriate in the parish.

2. That women who are hired as pastoral ministers (director of religious education, for example) should codetermine their job description in consultation with the pastor and parish council. They should not simply be "assigned" to their duties.

3. That paraliturgical prayer services be held in which women can preside and/or preach.

4. That women be directly involved in correcting and revising the often sexist language used in the liturgy, in parish bulletins, in homilies, and elsewhere.

5. That parish and diocesan job openings be published and be open to qualified women as well as to qualified men. An ecclesiastical affirmative action program should guarantee the fairness of the process.

6. That women have equal access to diocesan and/or parish funds that are earmarked for ministerial training and continuing education, both degree and nondegree programs.

7. That there be frequent social gatherings and formal sessions where female and male church "professionals" can come to know one another better as persons. It is only through such contacts, Sister Kathleen suggests, that some of the ways men and women mutually threaten one another can begin to disappear.

Every diocese and parish could initiate a self-study on the basis of such goals and proposals as these. One suspects that most dioceses and parishes would find some room for improvement.

I've just exhausted my quota of understatements for the month.

The Church's Approach to Feminism
(August 16, 1985)

Less than two months before he died, Pope John XXIII issued one of the most important ecclesiastical documents of modern times, *Pacem in Terris* (Peace on Earth). What was so remarkable about this encyclical was its abidingly positive tone.

Nowhere was this positive tone more apparent than in the section at the end of part I where the pope outlined "three distinctive characteristics" of the present age: the emergence of the working classes in economic and public affairs, the new role of women in society, and the growing interdependence of nations.

Pope John XXIII did not mention these characteristics in order to condemn them, as so many previous papal documents tended to do. On the contrary, he saw each of these developments as entirely consistent with the central message of his encyclical: that respect for human dignity and human rights is a necessary condition for peace.

The fact that the pope included the women's movement on his short list, even before the publication of Betty Friedan's ground-breaking work, *The Feminine Mystique*, shows him to have been an unusually forward-looking pastoral leader.

He was not one simply to respond to developments already safely under way. He anticipated them and tried to give them shape and direction in light of the gospel.

It is "obvious to everyone," he wrote, "that women are now taking a part in public life. This is happening more rapidly perhaps in nations of Christian civilization and, more slowly but broadly, among peoples who have inherited other traditions and cultures.

"Since women are becoming ever more conscious of their human dignity," he continued, "they will not tolerate being treated as mere material instruments, but demand rights befitting a human person both in domestic and in public life."

This was an extraordinarily progressive stance for the earthly head of the Catholic Church to take. But there was a limit even to Pope John XXIII's progressivism.

Although he made it clear that women must assert their legitimate human rights at home and in society, he made no mention of the role of women in the Church. Neither did the Second Vatican Council.

It was left to the Third International Synod of Bishops, meeting in Rome some eight and a half years later, to forge the link between Church and society: "We also urge that women should have their own share of responsibility and participation in the community life of society and likewise of the Church."

We are now more than two decades beyond Pope John XXIII's *Pacem in Terris* and the publication of Betty Friedan's book, which, for many, marked the beginning of the women's liberation movement.

Feminism is an integral part of the social, economic, political, and ecclesiastical scenes, at least in the nations of the Western world, and especially in the United States. Its agenda may vary slightly from place to place and from group to group, but there are certain constants in the midst of this diversity.

Feminism, in society and in the Church alike, affirms the fundamental equality of women and men. This equality is to be recognized in law, in the marketplace, in the electoral process, in the home, and wherever else women are, or should be, active.

Feminism takes a particular form in the Catholic Church. It rejects the use of sexually exclusive language in the liturgy and in ecclesiastical documents. It insists on respect for the experience, competence, and judgment of women in ministerial positions of every kind. And, of course, it argues for equal access to all ministries, including those one enters through ordination.

Such an agenda is not supported by women alone, since there are nearly as many men who are feminists as there are women. At least one likes to think this is the case.

There is one feminist issue, however, that endangers the entire feminist agenda within the Catholic Church. That issue is abortion.

The recent convention of the National Organization for Women (NOW) in New Orleans catapulted "abortion rights" to the top of the group's agenda.

The presidential contest between Judy Goldsmith and Eleanor Smeal seemed to hinge on which candidate would press this issue more vigorously.

In a postelection interview on cable-TV, Ms. Smeal criticized Walter Mondale for concentrating too much on taxes and the deficit in last fall's campaign against President Reagan.

"Should he have made abortion the primary issue?" she was asked. "Yes," she replied, evoking an expression of utter disbelief from the interviewer.

What that political course would do for (or to) the Democratic party is not my concern here. But it would be an absolute disaster for the cause of women's rights in the Catholic Church.

Some Catholics are convinced even now that feminism and Catholicism are incompatible. They are wrong. As of today anyway.

Should support for abortion rights ever become the litmus test for feminism, even within the Catholic Church, the incompatibility argument will be difficult, if not impossible, to rebut.

A 21st Century Without Nuns

(November 24, 1989)

If current projections hold, the Catholic Church of the 21st century will be a Church without nuns, or at least without nuns as we have known them over the course of the present century.

The impact of their absence will be felt especially in two related areas: education and the social apostolate.

It is an arguable proposition that nuns have been the most significant and effective Catholic educators in this century, both in parochial schools and in parish catechetical programs.

It is also an arguable proposition that nuns have been among the most committed of Catholics in the struggle for social justice, human rights, and peace.

When it comes to the social teaching of the Catholic Church, embodied in papal encyclicals, conciliar documents, and episcopal pronouncements, many Catholics only give what Cardinal Newman once referred to as "notional assent." They accept the teachings intellectually but never make them the basis for action.

By and large, that has not been the case with Catholic sisters. They have given what Cardinal Newman called "real assent," not only accepting the teachings intellectually but also making them the basis for action.

The dedicated sisters (and one laywoman) who were raped and murdered several years ago in El Salvador are among the more dramatic examples of what "real assent" to Catholic social doctrine means. These Catholic women literally put their bodies and their lives on the line for the poor and the oppressed.

Who among the younger generations of Catholics will carry forward their work into the 21st century? Who will hand on this kind of faith in parochial schools and in parish religious education programs? In other words, who will teach subsequent generations about a faith that does justice?

Undoubtedly some of us are looking to the current students and recent graduates of our Catholic colleges and universities to fill the gap now being left by the nuns.

One hopes that our expectations are well founded. But they might not be.

Those who teach young Catholics at the college and university level today find them, for the most part, wholesome, bright, energetic, and friendly. But they are also more career-oriented than they were in the 1960s and 1970s.

Many in the current generation of students seem more interested than their predecessors in securing high-paying jobs that will make it possible for them to maintain the standard of living to which, thanks to their parents, they have grown accustomed.

Indeed, our Catholic college students, especially in the more prestigious (and expensive) institutions, come increasingly from affluent family backgrounds. Given the correlation between income and economic attitudes, these students have also moved steadily to the right on the political spectrum.

In other words, on matters pertaining to social justice, many of our Catholic college and university students tend to reflect more their own economic interests and those of their families than they do the social teachings of their Church.

Recent surveys of the student population lend support to these impressions.

A national survey of incoming college and university freshmen, conducted in 1987 by the Higher Educational Research Institute at the University of California Los Angeles (UCLA), found that college and university students are indeed more interested in personal goals than they are in social objectives.

The UCLA survey found that a full three quarters of the national sample place "becoming an authority in one's field" and "being very well-off financially" ahead of all other goals, including "influencing social values" (about 36 percent) and "promoting racial understanding" (about 29 percent).

What is most significant is the marked change that has occurred since 1967. For example, "being very well-off financially" rose from 44 percent in 1967 to 76 percent in 1987.

That our Catholic college and university students are coming from increasingly affluent homes is also borne out by the facts.

A survey conducted almost two years ago by the Student Government at the University of Notre Dame disclosed that about 40 percent of the students come from households with incomes between $50,000 and $100,000 per year, and about 22 percent come from households with incomes in excess of $100,000.

When asked whether and how much each student was borrowing per year to attend Notre Dame, over half the students replied that they were borrowing nothing at all.

That these students are moving steadily to the right on the political spectrum is also supported by the data. The same Student Government survey found that only about 16 percent of the students regarded themselves as liberal, while 26 percent considered themselves conservative. (The rest called themselves moderates.)

This shift to the right was also noted in a recent survey of Notre Dame alumni.

The editor of *Notre Dame Magazine,* reporting the results of the alumni survey in the summer 1987 issue, suggested that this shift to the right politically might be explained by the fact that "income figures show rising affluence among graduates."

Those who perceive their own economic interests to be at odds with Catholic social teachings are less likely to emphasize those teachings as they hand on the faith to the next generation.

Why Does Tradition Not Allow Ordination of Women?

(May 25, 1990)

On October 15, 1976, the Sacred Congregation for the Doctrine of the Faith published, with the approval of Pope Paul VI, a "Declaration on the Question of the Admission of Women to the Ministerial Priesthood."

Soon thereafter, this century's leading Catholic theologian, Karl Rahner, S.J., wrote a brief commentary on the document in which he argued that if the Congregation's "basic thesis is not assumed as *a priori* certain, the burden of proof evidently lies with the Declaration and not with its opponents" (*Concern for the Church,* Crossroad, p. 43).

In other words, it is not those who favor the ordination of women who have the burden of showing it to be possible. The burden is, rather, on those who claim that it is impossible.

The argument *against* the ordination of women is based on tradition and the will of Christ.

Briefly it goes something like this: Women cannot be ordained because the tradition of the Church is against it, from the earliest years to the present.

The tradition of the Church is against the ordination of women because the teaching and practice of Jesus himself is against it.

There are variations on the foregoing argument. The Eastern Orthodox churches, for example, have based their opposition on the principle of iconic representation. Only a male can adequately represent Jesus as priest.

The central argument from tradition is weak. It presumes that the Church is already in full maturity, whereas it may still be in its infancy, its period of institutional formation.

How would the year 1990 look from the vantage point of the year 19,990, for example? Would the Church of 1990 not seem very much a part of the early Church? The immediately postbiblical Church? The foundational Church even?

The argument from tradition assumes a different cast when one looks forward rather than backward across the vast landscape of history.

The argument from tradition also rests on an unhistorical reading of the New Testament. There is no biblical evidence that Jesus left us an ecclesiastical blueprint. Indeed, there is much evidence to the contrary (see, for example, Frederick Cwiekowski's *The Beginnings of the Church*).

Neither is there any evidence that Jesus explicitly forbade the ordination of women (the Pontifical Biblical Commission's report to Pope Paul VI in 1976 reached this very conclusion). Indeed, as many have hastened to point out, we also don't have any textual evidence that Jesus ordained anyone, male or female.

The argument from iconic representation also looks weak when placed alongside Paul's words in the Epistle to the Galatians that in Christ there is neither male nor female, but that we are all one in Christ Jesus (3:28).

The most interesting and revealing argument against the ordination of women is the christological one; namely, that women cannot be ordained because Christ mandated that women cannot be ordained.

Rarely does anyone ever press the questions that are raised in this appeal to the will of the Lord: Why would Jesus have made such a prohibition in the first place? What possible reason would he have had to forbid the ordination of women?

If one had the patience and the skill to peel the onion of this christological argument, one would probably uncover a particular understanding of humanity and of God: Jesus must have determined that women cannot be ordained because women are, at root, inferior to men. Women do not have the same capacity as men to approach the throne of God and to make intercession on behalf of us all.

Furthermore, since every human being is made in the image and likeness of God, and since God is masculine, women are less godly than men. Therefore, women *as women* are incapable of the priestly work of mediation between God and ourselves.

Crudely put, that seems to be the real underlying theological argument against the ordination of women. Not tradition. Not the teaching and practice of the New Testament Church. Not the teaching and practice of Jesus.

All these arguments beg the question *why*. Why does the tradition not allow for the ordination of women? Why does the teaching and practice of the New Testament Church not allow for the ordination of women? Why does the teaching and practice of Jesus not allow for the ordination of women?

The ordination-of-women question may be immediately a question about the Church and its ministries. But it is, at root, a question about the nature of God and the nature of human existence.

7

Church and Society

Introduction

On May 15, 1991, the Catholic Church celebrated the centenary of Pope Leo XIII's encyclical letter *Rerum Novarum* (On the Condition of Workers). That document is generally regarded as the first in a long line of pronouncements by popes, councils, synods, and bishops' conferences on matters of social justice, human rights, and peace. The late Protestant social ethicist Reinhold Niebuhr once noted that, in his opinion, the social teachings of the Catholic Church were Catholicism's greatest achievement in modern times.

The social teachings of the Church tend to divide the Church along different lines from its teachings in the area of sexual morality. Conservative Catholics tend to endorse the latter but resist (or ignore) the former, and progressive Catholics tend to be critical of the latter while embracing and applauding the former.

Although the Catholic Church has had very different sorts of popes over the past century, there has been a remarkable consistency in the approach each has taken toward issues of justice and peace. On a conventional spectrum of left to right, the Church's social teachings—and especially the teachings of the popes—are actually left of center.

One can perhaps understand why a pope so progressive as John XXIII would have issued two forward-looking encyclicals like *Mater et Magistra* (Mother and Teacher) in 1961 and *Pacem in Terris* (Peace on Earth) in 1963. But even so conservative a pope as John Paul II has contributed substantially to the development of Catholic social teachings, and with the same strongly progressive orientation: *Redemptor Hominis* (Redeemer of Humankind) in 1979, *Laborem Exercens* (On Human Work) in 1981, *Sollicitudo Rei Socialis* The Social Concern of the Church) in 1988, and, finally, *Centesimus Annus* (The One Hundredth Year) in 1991, on the 100th anniversary of *Rerum Novarum*.

If Catholic social teachings have any significant defect, it is their failure to apply the teachings to the Church itself. Because the Church is a sacrament, it has a missionary responsibility to practice what it preaches and teaches to others. That remains the great unfinished business of Catholic social teachings for the rest of this decade and for the beginning of the 21st century.

The Church, the Papacy, the Poor

(June 16, 1967)

It is one of the great theological and pastoral tragedies of our time that the average Christian's attitude toward the papacy and papal authority should be formed exclusively within the context of the birth-control issue.

Those on the left, who seem to have drifted off into cynicism, and those on the right, who seem to have intensified their militancy, ironically share a common "tradition" regarding the papacy. Both extremes have accepted—the one implicitly, the other explicitly—the post–Vatican I ecclesiology that exalted the pope to a kind of supertheologian. Both want the pope to speak definitively and without ambiguity on every controversial issue and to rule one position or the other out of theological order.

This attitude is reminiscent of a favorite ecclesiastical game in the 1940s and 1950s when Catholics would quote encyclicals at one another. But in the light of the theology of Vatican II and beyond, what is being fashioned today is a more critical attitude toward the papacy, a critical attitude that eschews both cynicism and militancy and an attitude that accepts the papacy for what it must be—the leading moral authority in the Church, which nevertheless shares our human condition in all things, including sin.

This change of attitude is dramatically reflected in the recent sermon (June 4) of Episcopal Bp. C. Kilmer Myers of the diocese of California (and Bp. James Pike's successor). Bishop Myers has urged Anglicans and Protestants to acclaim the pope as "the chief pastor of the Christian family, and . . . the holy father in God of the Universal Church."

"We need someone to say, as chief pastor in Christ, that the worldwide community of Christians must exert its massive power to halt war and conflict in the world. We need a chief pastor who will lead us in the fight against poverty and the powerlessness of peoples in the earth."

Perhaps the bishop was thinking of the charismatic pontificate of John XXIII, or even of Pope Paul VI's prophetic call for the end of all war in his United Nations address, or his innumerable interventions in the cause of peace in Southeast Asia, or his recent encyclical letter *Populorum Progressio,* wherein he challenged mankind in its selfishness and condemned all forms of political, economic, and cultural exploitation.

For it is precisely in proclaiming the gospel that the pope fulfills his role as chief pastor and holy father. It is not his responsibility (nor within his area of competence) to teach a particular economic philosophy or a specific biological or medical interpretation of some human problem. He proposes the gospel context within which these enterprises are to be carried out, and he does not hesitate to raise his voice when God's Kingdom is subverted.

But why should the Catholic respond with some measure of enthusiasm to the call of the pope on issues of war and peace or social justice when this same Catholic may seem cool, if not openly hostile, on other issues, such as the question of birth control? Is there an inconsistency here? Have we reverted to the pick-and-choose polemics of the 1940s and 1950s?

Inconsistency becomes a problem if one's starting point is the uncritical ecclesiology of the early 20th century: the pope is the only theologian who matters in the Church and papal encyclicals are our pipeline to absolute truth.

But it has become impossible today for many of these Catholics to support this kind of theology of the papacy. The papacy has spoken authoritatively on contraception, but the pope is "naive" about the Vietnam War. There is to be no compromise with the clear strictures of Pope Pius XI's *Casti Connubii*, but we can imagine all sorts of "factors" to ease, mitigate, and effectively destroy the force of the pope's resounding argumentation in *Populorum Progressio*.

We must leave the far right wing to resolve its own inner contradictions. My appeal in these final paragraphs is to those who have grown cynical about the papacy but who still recognize the call of the gospel in so many papal utterances and gestures. There is no problem of inconsistency here if the attitude toward the papacy is critical in the first place, and if this criticism is radically sympathetic (which is the only kind that can bear fruit in the long run).

On the birth-control issue, the pope's present disposition (if we read it correctly) does not seem to reflect an overriding consensus in the Church: neither among theologians nor, more importantly, among sensitive and serious Christian married couples (and this is a source that no theologian can ignore).

The social teachings, on the other hand, reflect the consensus of the Church insofar as it has been expressed at the Second Vatican Council: "Christ was sent by the Father 'to bring good news to the poor, to heal the contrite of heart' (Luke 4:18), 'to seek and to save what was lost' (Luke 19:10). Similarly, the Church encompasses with love all those afflicted by human infirmity and recognizes in those who are poor and who suffer, the image of its poor and suffering founder. It does all it can to relieve their need and in them it strives to serve Christ" (Constitution on the Church, par. 8).

Thus, the real foundation of the pope's authority is the gospel itself. He is subject to it, just as the entire Church is subject to it. When he proclaims the gospel as chief pastor and holy father of the Christian family, his voice finds an echo throughout the Christian community. If the proclamation is genuinely evangelical, the Holy Spirit will see to the echo; if it is not, the Holy Spirit will see to the static.

Church Must Be Bridge to Poor

(September 15, 1967)

It is becoming more fashionable nowadays to speak of the Christian community as a Servant Church. This has been common among certain Protestant and Anglican authors for the past few decades, but Catholics have only recently been influenced by their thought. The Second Vatican Council proposed, at least indirectly, a theology of the Servant Church, and Cardinal Cushing devoted his entire Advent Pastoral Letter (1966) to this theme.

The risk is that all this talk about the Servant Church might remain just talk, that we shall all be satisfied with verbal victories and isolated symbols of change.

The Servant Church is not necessarily a Church of Volkswagens rather than Cadillacs. This is a superficial approach to the problem. Indeed, there is a subtle danger inherent in this tendency to identify the Servant Church with this sort of stripping down in the area of material goods and financial resources.

What does it profit the poor and the dispossessed if a bishop wears a cigar-band ring or if the local pastor drives an old, run-down car or if the Christian community celebrates the Eucharist in a barn rather than in a tastefully appointed church? If this were all it took to refashion the Church into the Church of the Suffering Servant of God, then the task would be much easier than many people have thought.

But this is as much an illusion as the conviction of some early "liturgists" that rubrical adjustments and the demise of lace surplices would bring a new day for the Church. The genuine leaders of the liturgical movement were too well grounded in theology to be satisfied with victories of that sort. These pioneers saw that liturgical renewal demanded nothing less than a complete, radical rethinking of the theology of the Church, the sacraments, grace, redemption, and so forth.

The issues are too grave to have us get bogged down in a Cadillac-or-Volkswagen controversy. If the Church in America is to become more fully the Church of the Suffering Servant of God, it must look around itself and see where the areas of division, hostility, injustice, tension, and illness lie. For the Church finds itself in a situation of great disparity between rich and poor, white and black, educated and illiterate. There is a real vacuum of power and influence between the large, so-called moderate elements of our society and the many who live on the fringes of our vast social structure.

The hippies, for example, have opted out of the normal pattern of human behavior because they can find no room for their ideals in the rat-race pace of contemporary American life. Whatever their faults (the abdication of responsibility, for one), they have become a kind of underground champion of so many traditional Christian values: peace, charity, justice, friendship, compassion, and tranquillity, to name a few. But they feel that American society has become insensitive to these values and is callously betraying them.

The economically dispossessed are another case entirely. They are the Negro poor, the illiterate, the unemployed, the sick. They need power and money and articulate support. They need a vigorous, dedicated, and relentless lobbyist for their cause.

But the gap that exists between the hippies and the poor, on the one hand, and the large middle-class moderates, on the other, is achingly wide. If the Church wants to play the role of servant, second-hand automobiles and cigarband episcopal rings are not the path to follow. We are engaged in a massive program of self-deception if we think that this is what "suffering service" is all about.

The task of the Servant Church is more serious, more complex, and ultimately more Christian than that. The Church must now be ready to place itself at the service of these social, political, economic, and cultural outcasts. Once more the Church must preach the good news to the poor by placing its immense moral, political, and financial resources at their disposal, by becoming, in other words, the bridge between the middle-class moderates and "the other America."

The Church must be the spokesman of the highest ideals of the gospel, standing at the forefront in the struggle for peace, racial justice, and the alleviation of poverty, illiteracy, sickness, and all the evils of slumism. This means that more of the Church's time, money, and energy will be spent on the building of God's Kingdom than on the building and maintenance of her own ecclesiastical plant. This simply is not true at the present time.

As the Church moves into this new era, it can have no more profoundly evangelical model for her servant mission than the late Pope John XXIII. Even though he lived in the midst of the resplendent anachronisms of the Vatican, the light of the gospel blazed through him with uncommon force. In a real sense, Pope John was in the Vatican, but the Vatican was not in Pope John. The Servant Church, too, must somehow be *in* the world, but not *of* it.

Today's Catholics Rejecting Social Doctrine?

(October 16, 1970)

In the 1930s and 1940s the great bulk of Catholics in North America were generally sympathetic with the social doctrine of the Church. After all, this teaching was usually to their own benefit. They were the have-nots. They were the working class. They were the ones in search of rights: to a just wage, to collective bargaining, to decent housing, to equitable systems of taxation, and so forth.

Today, however, the shoe is on the other foot. Many Catholics have gone several steps up the economic ladder. Many are now the owners of various productive enterprises. Many are in positions of vast economic and social power.

Catholic social doctrine, if it is consistently applied, is no longer their friendly ally. What was for their fathers a liberating message they now declaim as a naive program designed to pamper those who will not work, who will not behave, and who will not be grateful for what they have received already.

In the two decades immediately following the Great Depression, it required no special courage for the leadership of the Church to speak out on behalf of the "the other America." Most Catholics were part of it. Economic reprisals against the Church were minimal. Little support could have been expected from the wealthy quarters in any case.

Opening ceremony for the Second Vatican Council, St. Peter's Basilica, Rome (1962–1965) [Credit: Catholic News Service].

(*Top*) Pope John XXIII addressing the first session of the Second Vatican Council, 1962. (*Right*) Pope Paul VI giving his "*Urbi et Orbi*" blessing from St. Peter's balcony, 1977 [Credit: Catholic News Service].

(*Top*) Pope John Paul I,
Rome, August 1978. He
died a month later. (*Left*)
Pope John Paul II, the first
non-Italian pope in four
and one-half centuries,
elected in 1978 [Credit:
Catholic News Service].

Sacred Heart Parish, Notre Dame, Indiana, September 1991. (*Opposite page, top*) Distribution of Communion under both species. (*Opposite page, bottom*) Meeting of the parish council. (*This page, top*) Rite of Enrollment, Rite of Christian Initiation of Adults (RCIA). (*This page, bottom*) Lector at Sunday Eucharist [Credit: Brother Martinus, C.S.C.].

(*Clockwise from top left*) Cardinal Richard J. Cushing, Archbishop of Boston (1944–1970). Cardinal John J. O'Connor, Archbishop of New York since 1984. Yves Congar, O.P., one of the Church's leading theologians and a major influence at the Second Vatican Council [Credit: Catholic News Service]. John Courtney Murray, S.J., chief architect of Vatican II's Declaration on Religious Freedom (d. 1967) [Credit: National Catholic Reporter].

(*Clockwise from top left*) Sister Theresa Kane at the National Shrine of the Immaculate Conception in Washington during Pope John Paul II's first official visit to the United States, October 1979. Cardinal Joseph Ratzinger, Prefect of the Congregation for the Doctrine of the Faith [Credit: Catholic News Service]. Theodore M. Hesburgh, C.S.C., President of the University of Notre Dame (1952–1987), and one of the most influential Catholics of the 20th century. Mario M. Cuomo, governor of New York, delivering his address on the Church and politics with special reference to abortion, at the University of Notre Dame, September 1984 [Credit: Bruce Harlan, University of Notre Dame].

(*Clockwise from top left*) Father Charles Curran addressing a press conference concerning Vatican efforts to discipline him, August 1986. Pedro Arrupe, S.J., Superior General of the Society of Jesus (1965–1983; d. 1991). Father Hans Kung, professor at Tübingen University in Germany and the first major Catholic theologian to be disciplined by Pope John Paul II in 1979. Archbishop Raymond Hunthausen, of Seattle, addressing the National Conference of Catholic Charities, 1982. Hunthausen served in Seattle from 1975 until his retirement in 1991 [Credit: Catholic News Service].

Nowadays, however, it is regarded as unusual and newsworthy if a Catholic bishop can be identified as a vigorous spokesman for the poor and for minority groups. It is a matter of some special attention, for example, when such leaders are promoted within the Church's hierarchical structure.

Why? Because now there is some real economic risk when the Church's pastoral leadership assumes the role of lobbyist for the poor and the disenfranchised. The so-called silent majority is as heavily Catholic as it is Protestant, and the sources of real wealth are as likely to be controlled by Catholics as by non-Catholics.

Catholic universities and colleges have already been stung by the financial backlash of their more economically secure alumni. Undoubtedly there are pastoral leaders who, without cynical calculation, are now reluctant to address themselves too boldly to current political, social, and economic issues that may tend to alienate further this new group of self-reliant, propertied, and financially solvent American Catholics.

As the ecclesiastical leadership emerges, as it eventually must, from this relatively recent posture of tactful moderation, there is one particular item in traditional Catholic social doctrine that will have to be exploited; namely, the responsibility of sharing our superfluous goods with those in greater need than ourselves.

This will not be a popular teaching with Catholics whose prosperous condition far exceeds that of their own parents. They will not want to be reminded of a teaching that has been part of both the biblical and patristic tradition of Christianity, and that has been reaffirmed in the social encyclicals of popes Leo XIII and Pius XI and in the Pastoral Constitution on the Church in the Modern World of the Second Vatican Council.

And yet the great disparity between rich and poor that now exists in the world at large, and even in the North American sector thereof (see, for example, Michael Harrington's influential work, *The Other America*, Macmillan, 1962), throws this teaching on superfluous goods into a whole new, acutely relevant, light.

"Furthermore, a person's superfluous income, that is, income which he does not need to sustain life fittingly and with dignity, is not left wholly to his own free determination," Pope Pius XI wrote in his encyclical *Quadragesimo Anno*. "Rather the Sacred Scriptures and the Fathers of the Church constantly declare in the most explicit language that the rich are bound by a very grave precept to practice alms giving, beneficence, and munificence."

Vatican II is even more specific and (because it is written some 34 years later) more up-to-date in its application. Indeed, the Second Vatican Council makes an even stronger argument. We are obliged to come to the assistance of the needy not only out of our superfluous goods but even at the cost of some sacrifice and inconvenience (Pastoral Constitution, n. 69).

Man must regard what he has and what he owns "not merely as his own but also as common property in the sense that they should accrue to the benefit of not only himself but of others. . . . Since there are so many people in this world afflicted with hunger, this sacred council urges all, both individuals and governments, to remember the saying of the Fathers: 'Feed the man dying of hunger, because if you have not fed him you have killed him.' "

As the social doctrine of the Church resurfaces with new force in our time, we shall see that the real crisis of faith for many Catholics will not come over issues such as the Real Presence in the Eucharist, the infallibility of the pope, the meaning of Original Sin, or the place of the Blessed Virgin in spiritual life. The confrontation will come when the Church renews its call upon all its members to bring alive the gospel of Jesus Christ through the unflinching and uncompromising exercise of social justice.

The Bridge of Social Doctrine, Part I

(January 26, 1973)

Just before Christmas the bishops of Boston, Worcester, Springfield, Fall River; Manchester, New Hampshire; Burlington, Vermont; and Portland, Maine, issued a remarkably straightforward criticism of the renewed bombing of North Vietnam.

Their collective willingness to take such a stand illustrates a point I made several months ago in this column; namely, that, as a group, many of our bishops have been far more consistent in their theological and pastoral views than their conservative-to-traditionalist counterparts among the ranks of the laity, religious, and clergy.

The bishops recognize that social doctrine is as much a part of the Church's official teaching as are her pronouncements on the Eucharist or the divinity of Jesus.

A Catholic, in their view, cannot pick and choose among papal and conciliar statements. If the pope is to be supported on *Humanae Vitae,* so is he to be supported on *Populorum Progressio.* If his occasional expressions of distress concerning doctrinal and catechetical diversity merit a reverent hearing, so, too, should we heed his words of alarm about the intensification of military operations in Indochina.

And this leads to a second point to which I have referred in earlier essays: namely, that if we are sincerely looking for a bridge of reconciliation between moderates of the left and moderates of the right in the Catholic Church today, we need not look beyond the Church's social doctrine.

Catholics who differ on the best way to select bishops can nevertheless agree with Vatican II that "the arms race is an utterly treacherous trap for humanity," and they can raise their voices together against spiraling military budgets and against the inordinate influence of militarism in political decision making.

Catholics who differ on appropriate styles of papal leadership can nevertheless agree with the constant emphasis of papal teaching, from the days of Leo XIII to Paul VI, that the gospel requires governments as well as individuals to meet the economic needs of the poor, the sick, the disabled, and the disadvantaged, and that such obligations are to be borne in large measure by those who are favored with more of this world's goods. And so these Catholics can raise their voices together in support of effective programs on behalf of the needy and for tax reforms that can insure a fair distribution of financial burdens to meet such needs.

Catholics who differ on the question of ordaining women to the priesthood can nevertheless agree with Pope John XXIII and the Second Vatican Council that women have too long been the objects of economic, cultural, social, political, and even religious discrimination.

These Catholics, too, can raise their voices as one in defense of the rights of women at every level of social life, and indeed in defense of the rights of all others—blacks, chicanos, Indians—who have heretofore often lacked able and effective lobbyists on their behalf.

Catholics who differ on the kind of authority parish councils ought to have can nevertheless agree with the American Catholic bishops that young men should have the right conscientiously to oppose particular wars and refuse to serve in them, and then to be granted amnesty at war's end.

And so these Catholics can raise their voices together in opposition to office-holders and office-seekers who cheaply prey upon both the patriotism and the prejudices of their constituents, simplifying issues to the point of blatant distortion. Catholics can embrace the politically unpopular course, working unstintingly for these twin causes of selective conscientious objection and amnesty for those who could not, in conscience, serve.

I should predict that if moderates of left and right in the Catholic Church were to make her social teachings their common agenda of unfinished business, our present divisions would narrow; positively, because our common effort for peace and social justice would help us understand and respect our separate views on other important issues; and, negatively, because the extremists, who are now one of the principal causes of the polarization afflicting the Church, would be isolated.

The Bridge of Social Doctrine, Part II

(February 2, 1973)

In last week's column I argued that if moderates of left and right in the Catholic Church were to make her social teachings their common agenda of unfinished business, our present divisions would narrow.

I offered two reasons: positively, because our common effort for peace and social justice would help us understand and respect our separate views on other important issues; and, negatively, because the extremists, who are now one of the principal causes of the polarization afflicting the Church, would be isolated.

The first reason is unoriginal. It is a corollary of one given by the Second Vatican Council in its Decree on Ecumenism; namely, that through cooperation on matters of peace and social justice, "all believers in Christ are able to learn easily how they can understand each other better and esteem each other more, and how the road to the unity of Christians may be made smooth" (n. 12).

If cooperation in the struggle for justice and peace can bring Christians of varying denominations together, then it can surely bring Christians of the same denomination together.

Moderately conservative and moderately progressive Catholics ought to take the conciliar advice to heart. They should "work together in the use of every possible means to relieve the afflictions of our times, such as famine and natural disasters, illiteracy and poverty, lack of housing, and the unequal distribution of wealth."

All mankind, of course, is summoned to this kind of joint effort, but "the strongest claims are laid on Christians, since they have been sealed with the name of Christ." Furthermore, such collaboration "vividly expresses that bond which already unites [us], and it sets in clearer relief the features of Christ the Servant."

The second reason is original, and admittedly more controversial. I have argued that our renewed collaboration in the implementing of Catholic social doctrine will also have the effect of isolating the extremists. Such isolation would, in turn, reverse the trend toward polarization, since the extremists are largely responsible for this polarization in the first place.

The extremists of the left are convinced that the Catholic Church is institutionally bankrupt, that it has nothing more to say or to contribute to contemporary society, and that its leadership and rank and file alike are insincere in their acceptance of the gospel, which proclaims a Kingdom of "justice, love, and peace" (*Gaudium et Spes,* n. 39).

An unmistakably vigorous and determined effort to apply Catholic social doctrine, without fear of the inevitable protests and threats of financial reprisals, would substantially undermine the radical left's standard polemic against their own Church.

The extremists of the left chastise the Church for not practicing what she preaches; the extremists of the right chastise the Church when she does practice what she preaches. Indeed, they wish she wouldn't preach it at all.

Simply stated, the Catholic far right does not accept the social doctrine of the Catholic Church. They see socialism behind every move to aid the poor or to restore balance to our system of taxation, and they see communism behind every revolutionary insurgency and every struggle to curb military operations or to reduce the stockpiling of weapons.

In the meantime, however, the extreme right ostentatiously parades its loyalty to the pope, its unswerving fidelity to Catholic doctrine, its unity "for the faith." Indeed, it acts as if it alone believes in, or cares about, the divinity of Jesus, his Real Presence in the Eucharist, or the mystery of the Church.

Heretofore, moderate Catholics, including those in positions of pastoral leadership, have not pressed the issue of inconsistency, but it is long past the time that they did so.

Catholics of the far right are selectively loyal, selectively orthodox, indeed selectively Catholic. A renewed commitment to peace and social justice, under the standard of *Mater et Magistra, Pacem in Terris, Populorum Progressio, Gaudium et Spes,* "Justice in the World" (Third International Synod of Bishops), and the assorted statements of our national hierarchies would have at least the indirect effect of exposing the hypocrisy of the far right and of minimizing their often intimidating impact on contemporary Catholic thought and action.

The Pope and Social Justice

(October 26, 1979)

There are Catholics who sincerely believe that criticism, not to say rejection, of any papal teaching is inconsistent with Catholic faith itself.

From them, 95 percent agreement with the pope is not enough. They call that Catholicism à la carte.

Catholicism, they insist, has to be taken whole. There is a fixed menu and a fixed price. It's all or nothing.

Let's affirm that hypothesis for the sake of argument. Good and loyal Catholics are those who accept everything the Church's supreme teacher asks them to accept. To question, to hold back, to dissent is never justified.

This means that when the pope restates the traditional teachings on birth control, ordination of women, clerical celibacy, divorce-and-remarriage, there is no way a faithful Catholic can oppose him or urge him to reconsider in light of theological and pastoral developments.

But this would also mean that when the pope restates the Catholic Church's traditional teachings on social justice and human rights, there is no way a faithful Catholic can oppose him or urge him to reconsider in light of political and economic developments.

At Yankee Stadium, for example, Pope John Paul II focused our attention on "those who are most in distress, those who are extremely poor, those suffering from all the physical, mental and moral ills that afflict humanity, including hunger, neglect, unemployment and despair.

"There are many poor people of this sort around the world," he declared. "There are many in your own midst."

But we in the United States are rich and pampered. Our life-style is "easy," he said. We are immersed in consumerism, a passion for possessions.

"We must find a simple way of living. For it is not right that the standard of living of the rich countries should seek to maintain itself by draining off a great part of the reserves of energy and raw materials that are meant to serve the whole of humanity," he insisted.

"Christ demands an openness that is more than benign attention, more than token actions of half-hearted efforts that leave the poor as destitute as before or even more so.

"We cannot stand idly by," the pope continued, "enjoying our own riches and freedom, if, in any place, the Lazarus of the 20th century stands at our doors. . . . Riches and freedom create a special obligation."

And that special obligation requires that we give not only of our surplus but of our substance.

At New York's Battery Park he carried the same theme forward. He appealed to all "who love freedom and justice to give a chance to all in need, to the poor and the powerless. Break the hopeless cycle of poverty and ignorance that are still the lot of too many of our brothers and sisters; the hopeless cycle of prejudices that linger on despite enormous progress toward effective equality in education and employment; the cycle of despair in which are imprisoned all those that lack decent food, shelter or employment."

And in his talk to the American bishops in Chicago, he commended them not only for their reaffirmation of traditional moral teachings relating to sexuality and marriage but also for their teachings on human rights and social justice.

And he reminded the bishops that, as "shepherds of the flock," they must give a special example in their own lives so that "the people really find in us the kindness, simplicity of life and universal charity that they expect."

I suggest that there are many Catholics who applauded the reaffirmation of the birth-control teaching, the prohibition on women's ordination and on a married clergy, and the hard line on divorce who have conveniently filtered out his even more emphatic pronouncements on social justice and human rights.

These are the Catholics who worry more about taxes and inflation than they do about poverty. They gladly support a Proposition 13 regardless of its impact on the poor. They urge their representatives in Congress to hold the line on spending and do not object when the cuts come on the social programs and not on defense appropriations.

These are the Catholics who are warmed by the tough political rhetoric of a John Connally, a Ronald Reagan, or anyone else who is comfortably right-of-center on the spectrum.

How many announced and unannounced candidates for president of the United States are using the same kind of language as Pope John Paul II did during his recent visit?

The one or two who do are considered throwbacks to the 1960s, as if concern for the poor were now hopelessly out of date in view of the more urgent need of protecting the high standard of living of the middle and upper-middle classes.

When Catholics of some financial standing begin giving not only of their surplus but of their substance, and when all Church leaders move out of their grand episcopal residences along the Main Lines of the nation, then the appeal of across-the-board loyalty to the Holy Father will have some persuasive power behind it.

It's easy, after all, to support the pope when his words don't touch our lives or threaten our status. But the real test is to follow him, as we must follow the Lord, even when it hurts.

Twenty Years of Social Teaching

(August 7, 1981)

It has been just over 20 years since Pope John XXIII, on May 15, 1961, issued his encyclical letter *Mater et Magistra* (Mother and Teacher).

Those were different days from our own, to be sure. The Second Vatican Council had not yet begun. John F. Kennedy was beginning his term as president of the United States. Betty Friedan's *Feminine Mystique* was still two years from publication, and so consciousness raising and concern about sexist language and the equal rights amendment were not yet on anyone's mind.

The Catholic community was different, too. In those days it was the conservative who was likely to finesse papal teaching, not the progressive. *Mater et Magistra* was greeted from the former quarter with the rejoinder "Mater, si; magistra, no!"

In that encyclical letter, Pope John XXIII reaffirmed a cardinal principle of Catholic social doctrine: No one has an absolute right to private property. We are all stewards of what we possess.

"Our predecessors have always taught," the pope declared, "that in the right of private property there is rooted a social responsibility."

The Church's social doctrine, he also insisted, "cannot be separated from her traditional teaching regarding human life." It is, as Pope John Paul II would say in his own 1979 encyclical *Redemptor Hominis,* part of the content of the gospel that the Church proclaims.

Pope John XXIII's last encyclical, *Pacem in Terris,* widened the social doctrine to include an explicit concern for human rights. If peace is the work of justice, so justice is a matter of rights.

No society can be at peace, the pope declared, if it is not well ordered. And no society can enjoy any measure of order unless the rights of every member are respected as "universal, inviolable, and inalienable."

Some rights, of course, are conditioned by social responsibility. Among these, he said, is the right to private property.

The three distinctive characteristics of our age, he continued, are the increasing demands of workers for economic justice, the growing interdependence among nations, and the increased participation of women in public life.

Long before the women's movement shifted into high gear, Pope John XXIII was acknowledging that "since women are becoming ever more conscious of their human dignity, they will not tolerate being treated as mere material instruments, but demand rights befitting a human person both in domestic and in public life."

In 1965 the Second Vatican Council underscored the importance of social doctrine by issuing an unprecedented Pastoral Constitution on the Church in the Modern World (*Gaudium et Spes*). Here again, the Church officially taught that it has a duty to speak and act on behalf of justice, rights, and peace, and it reminded us that "one of the more serious errors of our age" is the tendency to separate our religious faith from our work in the temporal order.

Two years later Pope Paul VI issued his encyclical *Populorum Progressio* (On the Development of Peoples), declaring that the Church has the right and duty not only to proclaim the message of justice but to help oppressed people "grasp their serious problem in all its dimensions." The Church can never simply "let well enough alone."

He reaffirmed the traditional principle that we do not have absolute title to our possessions. And this is true not only of individuals but of nations as well. "We must repeat once more that the superfluous wealth of rich countries should be placed at the service of poor nations."

The parable of the rich man and Lazarus, the beggar, is regularly appealed to in the official teachings, as it was by Pope John Paul II in his homily at Yankee Stadium in 1979. It shall go hard with those who close their eyes, their ears, their hearts, and their wallets to the plight of the poor.

In May of 1971 Pope Paul VI circulated an apostolic letter ("A Call to Action") on the occasion of the 80th anniversary of Pope Leo XIII's *Rerum Novarum,* and in November of the same year the Third International Synod of Bishops issued its "Justice in the World," in which it taught that "action on behalf of justice" is "a constitutive dimension of the preaching of the Gospel" and of the mission of the Church. (Pope Paul VI would make the same point in his apostolic exhortation on evangelization in 1975).

Furthermore, the Church itself "is bound to give witness to justice," because the Church must recognize "that anyone who ventures to speak to people about justice must first be just in their eyes."

Pope John Paul II's own vigorous pronouncements on social justice and human rights are entirely consistent with this whole developing body of Catholic social doctrine.

Unfortunately, that doctrine remains, for too many today, one of the Church's best-kept secrets.

Examining Latest Encyclical

(November 6, 1981)

Pope John Paul II's third encyclical letter is out, and it is a very sophisticated piece of work indeed.

I know that my regular readers will take this as a genuine compliment and not as an expression of fawning praise that some Catholics feel they must lather upon anything the pope says or does.

The encyclical is so good, in fact, that it will probably be studiously ignored by those Catholics who normally manifest an almost inordinate attachment to everything the Holy Father writes.

This encyclical, *Laborem Exercens,* is a sustained critique of both traditional capitalism and Marxism.

On the surface, it seems like a relatively innocuous document. It argues that work is important to human identity and growth, and that everyone should look upon his or her work in a highly positive way. So, too, must the Church. End of homily.

But *Laborem Exercens* says much more than that. It offers a kind of Marxist critique of economic life in a way that transcends Marxism.

In other words, it accepts some basic Marxist assumptions about the world (i.e., that evil is systemic and institutionalized) but reinterprets those assumptions in light of the gospel. It then turns around and criticizes Marxism itself in light of those reinterpreted principles.

Laborem Exercens does not give us the usual moral pabulum about business's obligation to pay fair wages and the workers' obligation to do an honest day's work for an honest day's pay.

Nor does it accept Marxism's simplistic diagnosis of the world's problems as essentially a question of class struggle: the haves against the have-nots.

The class question, Pope John Paul II insists, has yielded center stage to the world question. The world, he acknowledged, is a "sphere of inequality and injustice." Our efforts to build justice on earth cannot ignore the existence of unjust structures. They must be examined and transformed.

So it is no longer a question of labor-management in the old, naive sense of the employer on one side of the bargaining table and the worker on the other.

Indeed, there are more than "direct employers." There are also the unseen, "indirect employers," for instance, the multinational corporations.

The multinational corporation wants to sell its products with as much profit as possible. This means that it needs to obtain the raw materials (often from poorer countries) at the cheapest possible rate. And this means, in turn, that the workers in those poorer countries have to be paid according to the lowest possible wage scale.

Is the local company for which the worker toils his only employer? Or is there not also an indirect employer, who has perhaps the more decisive role in setting wages and working conditions?

Catholic conservatives in the United States will be silently appalled by the central and subsidiary arguments of this encyclical.

The pope declares, for example, that capital and labor are not equal. Labor has priority over capital. Capital, in the strict sense, is "only a collection of things." Labor alone can give them shape and meaning.

The pope also repeats that basic principle of Catholic social doctrine that the right of private property is subject to the demands of the common good. Property rights are never absolute. Goods are meant for everyone.

The only legitimate title to their use is "that they should serve labor, and thus, by serving labor, that they should make possible the achievement of the first principle of this order, namely, the universal destination of goods and the right to common use of them."

For this reason, one cannot rule out the socialization of certain means of production. But the pope's critique remains always evenhanded. He reminds us that the mere socialization of property is no solution in itself if what replaces the private owners is a new managerial class that dictates to the workers in the same way as the old capitalists dictated to them.

Contrary to one prevailing opinion in Washington, D.C., Pope John Paul II insists that people are entitled to such supports as unemployment benefits, not as a matter of charity but as a matter of justice.

Medical benefits, too, must be available to workers, at low cost or even free of charge. So, too, with pensions, insurance, and a working environment that is safe.

The pope speaks as well of the workers' natural right to unionize, and to strike. These rights are not to set workers against others but to advance the cause of social justice and to build community.

Finally, those who emigrate from one country to another to find work are not to be treated as second-class citizens in their new home. Emigration must in no way become "an opportunity for financial or social exploitation."

This is not the kind of document for which the American Enterprise Institute will want to hold a symposium.

Pope's New Encyclical Far-reaching
(March 18, 1988)

Pope John Paul II's new encyclical, "The Social Concern of the Church" (*Sollicitudo Rei Socialis*), will not be welcomed by the following Catholics:

1. Those who have persuaded themselves that the pope doesn't agree with the U.S. Catholic bishops' pastoral letters on peace and the economy, because he is actually far more conservative than the bishops on these matters.

2. Those who view the world as divided between good and evil, with the United States and its allies on the side of good and the Soviet Union and its allies on the side of evil ("The Evil Empire").

3. Those who see no moral problem at all with our individual and national habits of consumption. ("We earned it. We can spend it any way we want.")

4. Those who believe that Catholic social teachings have no religious content or significance.

5. Those who have loudly insisted (especially during the controversy over Father Curran) that unquestioning loyalty to the pope and his teachings is *the* mark of a true Catholic.

Regarding the first and second groups: This encyclical is actually to the left of the U.S. bishops' pastorals on peace and the economy.

The bishops, for example, never placed the so-called Free World on par with the Soviet bloc, as the pope does.

You find that hard to believe? Read the text. And then, by way of confirmation, sample some of the strongly negative reviews the encyclical has received already from the political right.

New York Times columnist William Safire, an unabashed conservative hawk, even accused the pope of relativism because John Paul II morally equates the West's greed with the East's power lust and then blames both sides for the plight of the Third World.

"If words have meaning," Safire declared, "that is now the official world view of the Vatican. I think it is wrongheaded."

This new encyclical is also to left of the U.S. bishops' pastoral on the economy. Pope John Paul II is much harder on capitalism, with its "all-consuming desire for profit," than are the bishops.

The encyclical says that our capitalistic system, just as surely as the Marxist system, has its own forms of propaganda and indoctrination. And these are buttressed by military power, with an inherent tendency toward imperialism and neocolonialism.

Regarding the third group of Catholics: The pope directly challenges our rapacious accumulation of goods and services, made possible by what he calls a "superdevelopment" that is fostered by science and technology, including the computer sciences.

"This superdevelopment," the encyclical asserts, "which consists in an excessive availability of every kind of material goods for the benefit of certain social groups, easily makes people slaves of 'possession' and of immediate gratification, with no other horizon than the multiplication or continual replacement of the things already owned with others still better."

Regarding the fourth group of Catholics: Pope John Paul II makes very clear that Catholic social teachings, meaning those teachings concerned with economic justice, human rights, and peace, have to do with the gospel and with the Christian life.

He calls Catholic social doctrine

the accurate formulation of the results of a careful reflection on the complex realities of human existence, in society and in the international order, in the light of faith and of the Church's tradition.

Its main aim is to interpret these realities, determining their conformity with or divergence from the lines of the Gospel teaching on humanity and its vocation which is at once earthly and transcendent; its aim is thus to guide Christian behavior. It therefore belongs to the field, not of ideology, but of theology and particularly of moral theology.

Regarding the fifth group of Catholics: When Pope Paul VI's encyclical *Populorum Progressio* appeared in 1967, the *Wall Street Journal* derided it as "warmed-over Marxism."

The point is that politically and economically conservative people, including Catholics, do not like Catholic social teachings. Those teachings are a direct threat to their self-esteem and net worth alike.

And so they dismiss the teachings as "political" or "naive" or "Marxist" or "papal *obiter dicta*" (William F. Buckley, Jr.'s expression).

But such Catholics cannot have it both ways. They cannot continue to insist, on the one hand, that the test of Catholic orthodoxy is unquestioning acceptance of the teachings of the pope, and then, on the other hand, ignore or even oppose papal teachings on economics and the world order.

If you can ignore or oppose the pope there, why can't you also ignore or oppose him in vitro fertilization or on contraception?

There's more to this new encyclical than first meets the eye.

Encyclical Challenges Liberals, Conservatives
(March 25, 1988)

Two well-known conservatives have sharply criticized Pope John Paul II's new social encyclical, *Sollicitudo Rei Socialis.*

New York Times columnist William Safire accused the pope of moral relativism because the encyclical equates the East and West blocs by calling them both "imperfect and in need of radical correction," and by adopting "a critical attitude towards both liberal capitalism and Marxist collectivism" (the quotes are taken directly from the encyclical).

"In sum," Safire complained, "the West's greed is the moral equivalent of the East's power lust, and both are guilty of impoverishing the innocent and exploited third world. If words have meaning, that is now the official world view of the Vatican. I think it is wrongheaded."

William F. Buckley, Jr., was no less displeased with the pope's latest encyclical. In a syndicated column entitled "Papal Misfire," Buckley suggested that the encyclical was so bad that it would take scholars and friends of the Church "uncounted hours" of study before finding "a little gold in all that alloy."

Like Safire, Buckley found the pope's equation of East and West blocs "so mystifyingly anti-historical as to jeopardize the credibility of any thought accompanying it."

He was no less sympathetic with the pope's traditional concern for the world's poor. "On the matter of helping the poor," Buckley wrote, "one must ruefully conclude that the pope is adamantly unaware of the great 20th-century lessons of economic emancipation.

"The raging disease in Catholic social thought," he continued, "is the inattention given to the problem of production."

Like many liberal Catholics, Buckley wondered aloud if perhaps the pope's Polish background and experience might explain his magisterial lapse. He noted that "for 30 years [the pope] lived in a culture in which capitalism was denounced in demonic accents."

"The pope," he concluded, "is going to make a lot of enemies of exactly the kind he does not need."

I think both Safire and Buckley have read the encyclical correctly. They have good reason to be unhappy about it.

The encyclical is directly opposed to conservative and neoconservative economics and geopolitical theory, of the sort that one finds in the writings not only of Safire and Buckley but also of those who are at least as much concerned with intra-Church debates.

I have in mind, by way of examples, Richard John Neuhaus (author of *The Catholic Moment*), George Weigel (author of *Tranquillitas Ordinis*), and Michael Novak, of the American Enterprise Institute and a widely published author and columnist.

Such writers, however, do not enjoy the same freedom as Safire and Buckley in criticizing the encyclical and its author, Pope John Paul II. Safire, after all, is a Jew, and Buckley, although a Catholic, rarely allows himself to be drawn very deeply into ecclesiastical discussions. His horizons and interests are much wider.

But for Catholics like Novak and Weigel, and even for a Lutheran kibitzer like Neuhaus, there is more at stake here. For them Pope John Paul II is central to a neoconservative redefinition of Catholicism.

This pope, they say, is realistic, not utopian. He knows that "the first component of justice" is freedom and that "freedom is key to being a person" (Neuhaus, *The Catholic Moment,* Harper & Row, 1987, pp. 166, 286).

"It is hardly sufficient to count the number of times that John Paul criticizes the East and the number of times he criticizes the West," Pastor Neuhaus has written.

"One must attend to the substance of his argument regarding freedom and unfreedom in order to see that this Pope discriminates very nicely. He is hardly evenhanded; nor, be it quickly added, should he be" (*The Catholic Moment,* p. 169).

Tell that to Safire and Buckley.

It was not entirely surprising, therefore, that Michael Novak, in a column in the *Washington Times,* would have made every effort to put this new encyclical in the best possible light. Surely the paragraphs on the East-West conflict were disappointing (the pope was "unguarded," according to Novak), but "a close reading of the text" undercuts the assertion that the pope believes in a moral equivalence.

And while the pope's criticisms of liberal capitalism are in the nature of a "caricature," the pope does defend "the right of economic initiative."

With this encyclical Pope John Paul II has clearly confounded many of his supporters, and he is in danger of making "a lot of enemies of exactly the kind he does not need" (Buckley).

The pope is a great man, but he is also a complex man. Which means that he is proving to be as much a problem for the conservative and neoconservative Catholic as he is for liberals, progressives, and moderates.

That's the way it ought to be. Our religious leaders should challenge us all, including even those who cheer them the loudest.

A Matter of Justice, Not Charity

(May 13, 1988)

I appeared several weeks ago on William F. Buckley's television program, "Firing Line," along with Michael Novak, of the American Enterprise Institute in Washington, D.C.

The topic under discussion was Pope John Paul II's new encyclical, *Sollicitudo Rei Socialis,* (The Social Concern of the Church).

Toward the end of the hour-long program I emphasized that Catholic social doctrine teaches that when we as individuals or as nations come to the economic assistance of the poor, we do so as a matter of justice and not as a matter of charity alone. In other words, the poor of the world actually have a right to our so-called superfluous wealth.

Needless to say, the point did not go uncontested by my two politically conservative colleagues on "Firing Line." It also preoccupied several of those who wrote to me from around the country following the telecast.

The reaction only confirms what most of those involved in the Church's social ministry already know: Many Catholics are simply unaware of the Church's official social teachings. And those who are aware (however vaguely) resist the moral conclusions of those teachings.

When most Catholics were at the lower end of the economic scale back in the 1930s and 1940s, Catholic social teaching (for example, on the just wage and the right to form unions) was transmitted through Catholic labor schools, Catholic magazines like *Social Order,* and the like.

Today most (non-Hispanic) Catholics are firmly situated in the middle class, and many others have made it into the upper-middle class and even into the ranks of the superrich.

Catholic social teachings, on the other hand, are typically concerned with the left-out, with those at or beyond the economic margins of society. Alas, the burden of supporting such people falls upon the middle class, the upper-middle class, and the superrich. That means on many millions of Catholics.

Whereas Catholic social doctrine once supported the economic aspirations of the great majority of Catholics themselves, Catholic social doctrine now makes severe demands on their children and grandchildren.

The incentive to learn Catholic social teachings, much less apply them, is, to say the least, diminished.

Some politically conservative Catholics try to circumvent the problem by stressing the episcopal origin of the teachings. Although not usually engrossed in theological debates, these Catholics follow with great interest the current controversy over the teaching authority of national episcopal conferences.

They side with Cardinal Ratzinger's position because they think it will absolve them of any obligation to abide by their bishops' recent pastoral letter on the U.S. economy, for example.

The fact is, however, that some of the teachings they find most objectionable are rooted in papal and conciliar authority and ultimately in Sacred Scripture.

The Second Vatican Council's Pastoral Constitution on the Church in the Modern World declared that our "lawful possessions" are not merely our own but are also "common property in the sense that they should accrue to the benefit . . . of others."

"The Fathers and Doctors of the Church held this view, teaching that men are obliged to come to the relief of the poor, and to do so not merely out of their superfluous goods. If a person is in extreme necessity, he has the right to take from the riches of others what he himself needs. . . . According to their ability, let all individuals and governments undertake a genuine sharing of their goods" (n. 69).

Pope Paul VI's 1967 encyclical *Populorum Progressio* made the same point, insisting that "private property does not constitute for anyone an absolute and unconditioned right. No one is justified in keeping for his exclusive use what he does not need, when others lack necessities" (par. 23).

Pope Paul VI extended this principle to nations as well: "We must repeat once more that the superfluous wealth of rich countries should be placed at the service of poor nations" (par. 49).

Pope John Paul II has also been emphatic on this social principle, in his famous homily at Yankee Stadium, New York, in October 1979, and in his three major social encyclicals, *Redemptor Hominis* (1979), *Laborem Exercens* (1981), and especially *Sollicitudo Rei Socialis* (1988).

"We cannot stand idly by," he said at Yankee Stadium, "enjoying our own riches and freedom, if, in any place, the Lazarus of the 20th century stands at our doors."

"It is necessary to state once more the characteristic principle of Christian social doctrine: the goods of this world are originally meant for all" (*Sollicitudo Rei Socialis,* par. 42).

This is where the rock of the gospel meets the hard place of material attachments. Understandably, many of us don't want to be anywhere in the vicinity when they make contact.

Social Teaching as Applied to the Church
(June 2, 1989)

There is a standard line people often use, "Nothing is certain except death and taxes." I'd add to those, "anniversary celebrations."

May 15, 1991, will mark the 100th anniversary of Pope Leo XIII's encyclical letter *Rerum Novarum* (On the Condition of Workers).

It is a document generally acknowledged as the first in a long line of major Catholic teachings on the so-called social question, the most recent of which is Pope John Paul II's *Sollicitudo Rei Socialis*.

One can safely predict that throughout the year 1991 ecclesiastical and academic institutions alike will sponsor numerous special lectures, conferences, symposia, and workshops, and individual scholars, journalists, and church ministers will generate a thick stack of articles and books on the evolution of official Catholic teaching concerning economic and social justice, human rights, and peace.

Those of a more liberal or progressive orientation will applaud the wisdom of the teaching as expressed in papal encyclicals, council documents, synodal statements, and national episcopal pronouncements, and wonder, with some measure of impatience, when those teachings will at long last be fully implemented in the realms of government and business.

Others of a more conservative or neoconservative orientation will offer selective praise, singling out those aspects of the teaching that conform with their own social, political, and economic interests, while ignoring or explaining away those elements that challenge those interests.

Still others will seek to identify areas in the teaching that require further development. This third group may have the most to contribute to the forward movement of Catholic social doctrine.

I should suggest, two years in advance of all these anniversary events, that the most pressing need for development is in the forging of a stronger link between the world and the Church.

Specifically, Catholic social teaching must be applied to the government and business of the Church itself as well as to the world of government and business outside the Church.

In almost 100 years of official Catholic teaching on the social question, only two documents (by my count) have made an explicit connection between the practice of justice outside the Church and the practice of justice inside the Church.

They are the Third International Synod of Bishops' *Iustitia in Mundo* ("Justice in the World"), issued in 1971, and the U.S. bishops' pastoral letter, "Economic Justice for All: Catholic Social Teaching and the U.S. Economy," issued in 1986. The latter document is directly dependent upon the former.

Chapter III of the synodal document, "Justice in the World," is devoted entirely to the practice of justice inside the Church.

"While the Church is bound to give witness to justice," the synod declared, "it recognizes that anyone who ventures to speak to people about justice must first be just in their eyes. Hence we must undertake an examination of the modes of acting and of the possessions and life style found within the Church itself.

"Within the Church rights must be preserved. No one should be deprived of his or her ordinary rights because he or she is associated with the Church in one way or another."

Fifteen years later the U.S. Catholic bishops made the same connection, but even more explicitly and in a more detailed fashion.

"On the parish and diocesan level, through its agencies and institutions, the church employs many people; it has investments; it has extensive properties for worship and mission. *All the moral principles that govern the just operation of any economic endeavor apply to the church and its agencies and institutions; indeed the church should be exemplary.*"

At that point in the text, the bishops cite the synodal document of 1971. In the remainder of the section, they apply the principle to wages and benefits for Church employees, the right of Church workers to bargain collectively and to form labor unions, the use of Church property, ecclesiastical investment policies, and the like.

But as remarkable as these two documents are in this regard, they stand alone in a long and growing body of teachings related to justice.

The deficiency is not a minor one. As Nat Hentoff points out in his otherwise sympathetic profile of New York's Card. John J. O'Connor, when the Church's internal practices conflict with its external pronouncements, a credibility problem arises.

"[Cardinal O'Connor] does not seem to understand that a Church seen as hostile to nearly all independent theological thinking within will not be trusted as a source of independent thinkers able to deal with the social concerns of the Church" (*John Cardinal O'Connor*, Scribners, 1988, p. 7).

The Church must practice what it preaches because it is sacramental in nature. What the Church does inside must be consistent with what the Church asks others to do outside.

8
Church and Politics

Introduction

In the pre–Vatican II period, the Catholic Church's involvement in politics tended to be focused on issues like government aid to parochial schools. For the most part, Catholics were reluctant to assume too high a political profile, lest fears of Catholic power be revived. When they did intervene, it was on safe issues like anticommunism and support for the military (à la Card. Francis Spellman of New York).

Today, with the Catholic community a full one-quarter of the entire U.S. population, such fears have long since subsided. Catholics and their pastoral leaders experience complete freedom to speak out on public policy issues and otherwise to influence the shaping of legislative and executive actions.

Since 1980 no issue has so galvanized the energies of the Catholic Church (and other church bodies as well) as abortion. In 1984 there was open combat between Card. John J. O'Connor of New York, on the one hand, and New York's Gov. Mario M. Cuomo and U.S. Rep. Geraldine Ferraro, the Democratic vice-presidential candidate, on the other. Later in the decade, there was even talk of excommunicating Catholic politicians for not toeing the anti-abortion line drawn by conservative prelates.

Most of the columns in this chapter have to do with the abortion issue and with several of the personalities who have been so directly engaged with it: Cardinal O'Connor and Governor Cuomo, in particular.

But there are other issues treated here as well: the relationship of the Catholic Church to the U.S. constitutional system, the role of priests in political office (the case of Fr. Robert Drinan, S.J.), the activism of Pope John Paul II in Poland and elsewhere around the world.

If there is any thread running through the columns on abortion, it is the insistence that our approach to the so-called life issues should be consistent. If we are against abortion, we should also be against war and capital punishment as well—and vice versa.

But the Catholic community seems no closer to that consistent ethic of life today than it was back in 1973 when the *Roe v. Wade* decision of the U.S. Supreme Court changed the shape of the moral and political battlefields.

Our Reaction to the Abortion Decision

(March 2, 1973)

The public reaction of some Catholic leaders to the recent Supreme Court decision on abortion is not going to make it any easier to persuade people to take ecclesiastical authority seriously, now and in the future.

The argument is being made, with some vigor, that abortion is always wrong because it involves the direct taking of innocent human life. When an interviewer presses the issue and asks if there might not be a legitimate difference of opinion among people of goodwill, the answer is shot back, "No, of course not. Abortion involves killing innocent life, and it is wrong."

In other words, the Church can brook no compromise on this matter. She must use whatever resources she has to fight this battle, even in the political arena alongside those who want to see a constitutional amendment drafted and passed to overturn the court's verdict.

And yet only a few years ago we Catholics were able to uncover any number of mitigating factors to justify the bombing of North Vietnam and other parts of Indochina.

Here, too, there was a direct killing of innocent human life, for bombing kills women, children, and noncombatants just as surely as a rifle fired at point-blank range. But, of course, people—reasonable people, we might assume—differed on its moral quality.

Some spoke about treaty commitments. Other about the need to stop the communists before they reached San Francisco. Others about the defense of a nation (or at least a portion thereof) that is the victim of unjust aggression. Others about the need for maintaining the honor of the United States.

The moral absolutist won't hear of these rationalizations. He insists that killing is killing, and it is always evil. Therefore, no war can ever be legitimated.

Even the less-than-absolutistic moralist is impatient with rationalizations of that sort. He, too, agrees that killing is killing, and it is evil most of the time. Therefore, before a war (and its several constituent acts) can be legitimated, it must not only pass the test of closest moral scrutiny; it must get a grade of nearly 100 percent.

Before a war can be called "just," it must satisfy beyond all reasonable doubt the following conditions:

1. It must be a war of self-defense against a clear act of grave injustice.

2. Every peaceful means of settling the dispute must have been exhausted; in other words, the war must be the last resort.

3. There must be a due proportion between the gravity of the injustice and the damage the war would do (the principle of the lesser evil).

4. There must be a reasonable hope of success.

We have to remember, too, that these principles were formulated in a preatomic age. Where there is a danger of nuclear warfare, the conditions assume a greater stringency, particularly the third.

The United States' involvement in the Vietnam War was at least dubiously moral in terms of the third and fourth conditions. And now, in the aftermath of the cease-fire, reasonable people can still wonder about the extent of our "success" and about the proportion between the damage to human life and property, on the one hand, and the gravity of such "negotiable" injustices.

The point is simply this: Reasonable people took positions on both sides of the war debate. Most Church leaders maintained a discreet, prudent silence during the greater part of the war years. Many insisted that they didn't have access to all of the facts and that some antecedent trust must be placed in the wisdom and moral judgment of our political leaders.

Today, however, some of these same Church leaders, heretofore exceedingly tolerant about accepting mitigating circumstances as a justification for the war, are now insisting that there is simply one side to the abortion question. Innocent human life is being destroyed, and that is always wrong.

Our pro-abortion political leaders, who include governors, legislators, and Supreme Court justices, are not to be granted the same kind of antecedent trust that was once placed in the governmental managers of the war effort.

Make no mistake about it, I agree with the position of the Catholic leadership on the abortion issue and have already publicly expressed that support. But the anti-abortion cause is not being helped very much by spokesmen who now protest their concern for innocent human life but who were once so silent, even apologetical, about our recent, morally dubious, military excursions.

Abortion: The Liberal's Achilles Heel

(May 23, 1975)

Norman St. John-Stevas is a British Catholic layman and a longtime member of Parliament. Watching and listening to him on William F. Buckley's "Firing Line" program last month was an intellectual pleasure.

The subject was abortion. The guests were Margot Hentoff, a writer (the wife of critic Nat Hentoff), and Fr. Joseph O'Rourke, formerly of the Society of Jesus, who was expelled from the order last year for religious disobedience, a matter brought to a head by his baptizing of the Morreale infant in Marlboro, Massachusetts.

Although Mrs. Hentoff showed some promise in the early stages of the conversation, she quickly lost points when she indulged in a typecasting of pro-abortion forces, but especially when she introduced some curious thinking of her own on such a life-and-death matter as suicide.

Father O'Rourke, on the other hand, never seemed to get started. He displayed an affable, but theologically flaccid, moral posture. He had neither a precise nor wide-ranging control over the issues involved, nor did he seem to discern the point of Mr. St. John-Stevas's occasional thrusts in his direction.

I winced at his glancing invocation of the late John Courtney Murray's name. The implication that Murray's views on liberty and justice might somehow cover a woman's "absolute right" to an abortion is thoroughly insupportable.

Indeed, while Father O'Rourke professed a general overriding concern about social and economic factors that sometimes make abortion a compelling option, it was St. John-Stevas, the anti-abortion spokesman, who manifested what seemed to be the firmer and more politically specific commitment to social justice.

There was nothing more disheartening about the O'Rourke performance than his use of that antiseptic euphemism "products of abortion" to identify the aborted fetus.

Without endorsing Mrs. Hentoff's carelessly sweeping antiliberal remarks, I should nonetheless agree that the abortion issue is the Achilles heel of many liberals, Catholics and non-Catholics alike.

Too many liberals seem positively intimidated by certain feminists on their left. The liberal wonders if he or she will appear unsympathetic with the radicals' charges of oppression and their demands for liberation. Ordinarily it is very illiberal indeed to be on the other side of issues of that sort.

Women's liberation is, to be sure, an issue that generally divides liberals from conservatives. In its main lines that movement is both sound and just.

But the women's movement has not escaped the polarization process that eventually fragmented both the black and the student movements of earlier years. Inevitably the ideologues carry the cause further and further to the left until they effectively isolate themselves from the original philosophy and spirit of the movement itself.

Radical feminism is thoroughly antimale and anti-Christian. It is so antimale that it opposes the very institution of marriage on the grounds that marriage is intrinsically and therefore inevitably oppressive of the female partner.

It is anti-Christian because it is convinced that Christianity is primarily, if not exclusively, responsible for the rationalization of women's inferior social, cultural, economic, political, and psychological status.

Abortion tends to focus both negative components. Against the male, the radical feminist asserts the absolute right over her own body, independent of tampering and control by male legislators.

And against the Church, the radical feminist insists that its defense of the rights of the unborn is a surreptitious prolongation of its historic antifeminist bias.

To be against abortion in all but the most extreme cases (and St. John-Stevas would allow for these, as would some Catholic moralists today) is not to be inconsistent with one's liberal principles.

It is, on the contrary, to be entirely consistent with the historic liberal commitment to the defense of those who cannot readily defend themselves: the poor, the retarded, the elderly, the sick, the inarticulate, the dispossessed, the refugee, and, indeed, the unborn fetus.

The lucid, temperate reasonableness of Norman St. John-Stevas should serve as a model for all opponents of abortion on demand. The cause would be far better served if he were.

Church Observance of Bicentennial

(January 9, 1976)

This year's celebration of the U.S. Bicentennial raises questions not only for American Christians but for Christians everywhere. At issue is the fundamental relationship between the Church and the nation of which she is a part.

The Bicentennial has provoked extreme reactions at both ends of the political spectrum.

The far right tends to exalt the nation to the point where dialogue on its possible failings is reduced to "Love it or leave it!"

And the far left is so saturated with self-contempt that it can tolerate no word of national benediction, however modest or restrained.

The official Roman Catholic participation in the U.S. Bicentennial observance seems to have rendered people skeptical on both sides of the spectrum.

Some have complained that the bishops have given full rein to the sell-America-short crowd, replete with unbridled adulation of the Third World.

Others have worried about the bishops' historic tendency to play the patriotic tune, in season and out of season. "My nation, right or wrong," and all that.

At the risk of sounding safely statesmanlike, I should suggest that neither criticism is entirely justified.

Our worry, rather, ought to focus on the kind of critique the Catholic Church offers in this bicentennial year, not whether the critique is positive or negative, but whether the critique is theological or purely pragmatic.

In other words, the nation is not to be praised simply because it provides freedom of religious expression. It is to be praised because it prizes freedom itself as a necessary condition for human life.

A Church that insists upon her own freedom to function within a given society cannot make her advocacy of freedom credible if she is not herself an unstinting promoter of freedom within her own household.

Neither is the nation to be praised simply because it places itself somehow "under God" or proclaims its "trust" in the deity on its coins. The nation is to be praised because it is founded on a principle that makes God's work possible: liberty and justice for all.

A Church that presumes to hold a nation to account in its struggle for social justice cannot make her watchmanship credible if she is not herself a practitioner of justice toward her own membership.

Neither is the nation to be condemned simply because it encourages a form of capitalism that oftentimes accentuates rather than diminishes the gap between rich and poor. It is to be condemned when it refuses to acknowledge the tendency and to take the constitutional means to do something about it.

Even Latin American liberation theologians receive free flights between continents and are paid respectable honoraria for their lectures—a form of incipient capitalism, to be sure. And self-appointed religious pied pipers preach the simplicity of Christ while grabbing the financial rewards with both hands.

Neither is the nation to be condemned simply for engaging in warfare, as ugly and as inhumane as modern weaponry happens to be. It is to be condemned when it silences or oppresses the voices of dissent and when it refuses to respect the consciences of those who cannot abide by the military designs of the moment.

The Church herself has to ask about the kind of force (not physical any longer, but psychic and economic) she is tempted to employ now and again to discourage dissidence and to undermine her historic devotion to the principle of freedom of conscience.

The Church can dissipate her critical function within a nation by falling into one of two extremes: praising its government and ethos beyond all reasonable limits and becoming thereby a highly predictable ally in every situation; or condemning a nation's government and ethos beyond all reasonable limits and becoming thereby a predictable scold, easily written off and marginalized.

The Church is herself a part of the nation she criticizes. It is never entirely we against they, but "us."

But the Church is also in a very real sense "over against" the nation of which she is a part. She is the corporate presence of Jesus Christ, whose mission it is to hold high the lamp of faith and to measure the nation (and herself) against the standard of his gospel and the coming Kingdom of God.

If the Bicentennial observance in the United States provokes some deeper thinking about this fundamental relationship between Church and nation, it will have served the mission of the Church more surely than it could ever have foreseen or intended.

Abortion and the 1976 Political Scene
(April 23, 1976)

Early last month, Robert N. Lynch, former director of the National Committee for a Human Life Amendment, published an article on the politics of abortion in the Jesuit weekly *America*.

The implication of Lynch's argument is that the anti-abortion view deserves a stronger advocacy than it is getting.

This year, as never before since the 1973 Supreme Court decision, television and the press have focused on the abortion issue and particularly on its political implications.

But according to Lynch, an opportunity for clarifying the terms of the debate and for correcting some obvious excesses in abortion legislation has been lost.

He attributes the failure of the anti-abortion movement to three factors.

First, there has been total disagreement among anti-abortion groups regarding the kind of political solution that must be sought.

There are sharp differences in the way in which amendment language is formulated. The largest pro-life group, for example, is committed by its own statutes to an amendment formulation drawn up in 1974 that leaves little or no room for negotiation with the Congress.

The states' rights approach is now so anathema to some pro-life organizations that two former legal "darlings" of the movement—Prof. John Noonan, Jr., of the University of California, and Prof. David Louisell of Stanford—are no longer held in esteem. On the contrary.

Most of the American bishops prefer a more flexible position, "refusing to close the door on any legislative proposal that would in effect restore some measure of protection to the unborn." Herein the bishops are following the principle of "the lesser of two evils."

Within the past few weeks that majority position has received unpublicized Vatican endorsement.

Second, the anti-abortion movement is not securing the support it needs, and should have been able to expect, from the general Catholic population—laity, religious, and clergy alike.

Most Catholics, according to available surveys, favor some kind of abortion possibility if the circumstances are sufficiently extreme, as in the case of rape.

"On the other hand," Lynch reminds us, "almost all Catholics . . . are turned off by the availability of abortion at the present time, and they would favor some legal correction of the situation."

Why, then, are so many Catholics apathetic about the issue? Lynch suggests that many view it as a conservative, even a politically partisan, cause. They don't want to be part of a crusade headed by Ronald Reagan.

And many parish priests are put off by some anti-abortion advocates. "Today's pro-lifer is the same person who yesterday was beating the rectory door down on the sex education program in the parish school."

We've reached such a point of malaise, Lynch observes, that there are now even some bishops who "stand ready to lay the subject to rest." It just seems so much like a no-win issue.

Third, the pro-life movement has been unable to "get their organizational wits together." There are six national organizations, "each with a different form of amendment, each with a different political plan, each refusing generally to communicate or work with the other."

The National Right to Life Committee, for example, has what Lynch calls "an organizational structure worthy of the late Rube Goldberg."

The article's conclusion is sobering: The abortion issue could have exercised "a radical effect" on this year's political campaign, but now it is highly unlikely.

We can see, some several weeks after Lynch first composed his essay, that his prediction is already being fulfilled.

After an initial flurry of discussion in Iowa and a few other early primaries, the issue has moved ingloriously to the back burner.

It deserves a better airing than that. And that brings us back full circle to the three reasons for our failure.

"Catholic and American"

(July 2, 1976)

Only 15 or 20 years ago some people wondered if it was really possible to be both American and Catholic at the same time.

Although the discussion reached a climax in the 1960 presidential campaign, the argument transcended that election.

The debate had engaged the attention and energies of some of the best-known religious spokesmen in the 1950s. On the Roman Catholic side: John Courtney Murray and Gustave Weigel, distinguished Jesuit theologians; John Cogley and Daniel Callahan, editors of *Commonweal*; Jacques Maritain, Thomist philosopher; and others.

On the Protestant and Jewish sides: polemicist Paul Blanshard; Methodist Bp. G. Bromley Oxnam, of Protestants and Other Americans United for the Separation of Church and State; Norman Vincent Peale, of positive-thinking fame; Leo Pfeffer, of the American Jewish Congress; social ethicist Reinhold Niebuhr; and others.

Our ecumenical sensibilities would be offended if some of the rhetoric of that discussion were reproduced today.

Catholicism did not often escape attack. Portrayed as the enemy of liberty, its tightly controlled school system, its censorship of books, and its support of Franco Spain were cited as cases in point.

"By far the most important issue between the Catholic Church and modern democracy or democratic and pluralistic nations concerns education," Reinhold Niebuhr wrote in the August 1962 issue of *The Atlantic*.

"The issue is posed," he continued, "by the insistence of the Church that the educational enterprise should include religious instruction and by its assumption that the only religious instruction valid for the faithful should be under its auspices and control."

In a 1958 collection entitled *Religion in America*, Leo Pfeffer expressed the same concern. Arguing for a broad interpretation of the 1947 Supreme Court decision in the Everson parochial school bus case, he insisted that "neither government financing of religious education nor religious instruction in the public schools is permissible."

Times have not only changed. They've changed rapidly.

Nowadays fewer and fewer Americans perceive the Catholic Church as the archenemy of liberty. Indeed, many see it as an institution wherein liberty runs wild.

Aid to parochial schools is still a controversial issue, but now there are non-Catholic Americans who worry as much about the disappearance of a competing private educational system as they do about violations of constitutional propriety.

This spring Lutheran sociologist Peter Berger appeared before the annual convention of the National Catholic Education Association to speak a word in support of parochial schools.

Franco's recent death revived none of the old animosities. No one, on either side, wanted to replay the bitter exchanges of the 1930s, 1940s, and 1950s. In later years Franco had become almost as severe a problem to the Vatican as he appeared to have been in earlier days for American liberals.

Even though the spirit of censorship may not have expired completely within the bosom of bureaucratic Catholicism, it has abandoned the Index of Forbidden Books and adopted a far more tolerant attitude to dissent within its own ranks than ever before.

Madalyn Murray O'Hair may still make occasional anti-Catholic noises— sufficient to get her a spot on a TV talk show now and again—but she is essentially an anachronism by present theological and pastoral standards.

Today the National Conference of Catholic Bishops sponsors an ambitious celebration of the nation's Bicentennial, entitling the project "Liberty and Justice for All."

And some of the most vigorous voices in defense of human, civil, and political rights are now to be found inside rather than outside the Catholic Church, much to the consternation of some of the Church's official leadership.

The question, Can one be Catholic and American at the same time? ought still be asked. But now in a different way, and with different results.

Putting Pro-Life Politics in Perspective
(February 22, 1980)

The abortion issue continues to challenge conservatives and progressives alike. The recent criticism leveled against the Administrative Board of the United States Catholic Conference on the part of the Life Amendment Political Action Committee serves only to underscore the point.

The Washington-based group, directed by a Catholic and probably composed mostly of Catholics, protested the USCC committee's renewed warning against one-issue politics.

Catholics should examine the positions of candidates on the full range of issues, and not on abortion alone. These other issues include arms control and disarmament, capital punishment, the economy, education, family life, food and agricultural policy, health care, housing, human rights, and mass media and the public interest.

The executive director of the Life Amendment group argued in rebuttal that "the strength of the pro-life movement is our ability to deliver votes. Our strength is to retain single-issue politics."

According to assorted press reports and interviews with various pro-life figures, many in the pro-life movement are actively supporting the presidential candidacy of Ronald Reagan.

I am not about to suggest that a "good Catholic" cannot vote for Ronald Reagan, only that a "good Catholic" ought to be concerned about the clear discrepancy between most of Governor Reagan's positions on national and international issues and the positions of the National Conference of Catholic Bishops (not to say, in some instances, of Pope John Paul II himself).

If our hypothetical "good Catholic" comes back and says, "The bishops can be wrong, you know," my more liberal friends will say, "Well, finally, you're beginning to see things our way! Now, look, I don't want to hear any more of this talk about fidelity to the magisterium when the shoe is on the other foot, OK?"

There is at least the hint of inconsistency on the part of many right-of-center Catholics when it comes to politics. They seem to forget that the Catholic Church also has an official social doctrine, and that this doctrine, too, deserves the "religious assent of soul, of will and of mind" that the Second Vatican Council spoke of in its Dogmatic Constitution on the Church (n. 25).

The power and commendable defense of unborn human life is less credible, and less effective as well, when it is not accompanied by a similarly vigorous and unequivocal concern for life at other stages of development.

Racists are not pro-life. They are anti-life. People who are indifferent to the poor are not pro-life. People who automatically urge military retaliation for such provocations as the taking of American hostages in Iran are not pro-life. They are anti-life.

People who mock those who are concerned about discrimination based on sex are not pro-life. They are anti-life. People who couldn't care less if military expenditures cancel out expenditures for social needs are not pro-life. They are anti-life. People who don't even see the moral implications of consumerism are not pro-life. They are anti-life.

"For it is not right," Pope John Paul II declared at Yankee Stadium last October, "that the standard of living of the rich countries should seek to maintain itself by draining off a great part of the reserves of energy and raw materials that are meant to serve the whole of humanity."

When we hear the favorite candidate(s) of the anti-abortion activists speaking that way, their support for such politicians will at least have the ring of consistency.

And when progressives begin recognizing abortion as a pro-life, not a pro-choice, issue, then some measure of consistency will be restored to their cause as well.

The U.S. Catholic bishops have exactly the right approach. They are for *all* pro-life issues. They want a candidate's position on every issue taken into account when morally sensitive Catholics close the polling booth curtain behind them.

Implications of the Drinan Case
(May 30, 1980)

There are several implications of the Vatican directive that forced Massachusetts U.S. Rep. Robert Drinan, S.J., to withdraw from elective politics. None of them is positive.

First, there is the inference that a vocation to the ordained priesthood and involvement in elective politics are inherently contradictory. This is neither theologically nor doctrinally the case.

The priesthood itself has taken many forms over the centuries. Indeed, there are no Christian "priests" as such in the New Testament, except Jesus Christ.

The earliest disciples still recognized the Jewish priesthood as valid. The Jerusalem Christians, for example, kept up their daily attendance at the Temple (Acts of the Apostles 2:46).

The closest approximation in the primitive Church to our modern notion of "priest" was the "presbyter." But presbyters did not always preside over the Eucharist in these earliest years.

We simply do not know how certain individuals came to preside and whether it came to be a permanent or regular function for those persons.

As anyone familiar with Catholic biblical scholarship knows, there was a remarkable diversity of structure and form in the New Testament churches. The most that can be said is that those who presided did so with the consent of the local church and that this consent was tantamount, but not always equivalent, to ordination.

With the spread of the Church in the postbiblical period, parishes were created outside the major Christian centers, and the presbyters (our present-day priests) were given pastoral care over them.

By the Middle Ages, of course, the Catholic priesthood from the papacy on down had made frequent excursions into politics, to say the least. That story is well known, and space prevents even a summary.

Let it only be said here that there is ample precedent for priests in politics, if one demands precedents.

One may, on the other hand, argue that such involvement was, and is, imprudent or that it diminishes the effectiveness of the priest in other ministerial roles. That may be so. But the argument against political activity by priests cannot be made on the basis of principle or dogma. That is my point.

A second implication of the Vatican directive is that it tends to reflect and to promote an exceedingly centralized concept of Church at the expense of the theological principles of subsidiarity and collegiality.

Subsidiarity requires that nothing should be done at a higher level than can be done as well, if not better, at a lower level. Decisions, in other words, should be made as closely as possible to the point where they will have their impact.

Collegiality requires that the pastoral leadership of local churches (diocesan, regional, or national, depending upon the case) should make decisions in light of local circumstances, experiences, traditions, and cultures, with the proviso always that such decisions be taken in consultation with the representatives of the universal Church.

But just as one can go too far in the direction of local initiative at the expense of the universal Church, so, too, can one go too far in the direction of the universal Church at the expense of the local churches, which are, in the words of Vatican II, the People of God in their own place (Dogmatic Constitution on the Church, n. 26).

The Vatican directive that so immediately affected Father Drinan should not have been rendered on a universal basis. The United States situation is very much unlike South America, for example, where it is a question not of priestly involvement in elective politics only but in violent revolutionary activity as well.

Nor can the political party system in the United States be compared with some European models, where such parties have often functioned as vehicles of anticlericalism, on the one hand, or of clericalism, on the other.

Which leads, then, to a third implication. The Vatican directive inevitably raises anew some of the old anti-Catholic fears and charges about the threat of Vatican interference in U.S. political life. At the very least, the Vatican should have inserted a "grandfather" clause in this particular directive, specifically exempting those priests like Father Drinan who are already serving in office and forbidding instead any new entrances into the partisan political forum.

Fourth, Father Drinan's work as a congressman was outstanding for his activities on behalf of social justice, human rights, and nuclear disarmament. Those Catholics who have become increasingly motivated to engage in these important social ministries will now be discouraged and demoralized because so symbolic a figure as Father Drinan has been removed from one of the world's most influential agencies for reform, the U.S. Congress.

One thing is clear, of course. In accepting the directive with such docility and with such a strong reaffirmation of his priesthood and his commitment to the Society of Jesus, Father Drinan has effectively pulled the rug from under the feet of those who have vilified him for years and have characterized him in such an un-Christian manner.

Bob Drinan acted in the end as he is and always was: a priest of complete integrity and a Catholic Christian of unchallengeable commitment and dedication to the gospel and the mission of the Church.

Priests in the Political Arena

(October 10, 1980)

The controversy over priests in politics did not end with the Father Drinan case.

In Boston last month Card. Humberto Medeiros stunned many people with his strongly worded attack on legislators who support government funding for abortions.

Three things were significant about the statement:

1. The cardinal insisted that not only are the lawmakers guilty of sin but also "those who promote, defend and elect" them.

2. The pronouncement was released in the last few days of two congressional primary campaigns, both involving candidates whose stand on funding for abortions is at odds with the cardinal's.

3. The statement referred to no other moral issue as a standard upon which to judge candidates, even though the National Conference of Catholic Bishops has warned U.S. Catholics about "one-issue politics."

In effect, Cardinal Medeiros was telling his flock that it would be sinful to vote for Barney Frank to succeed Fr. Robert Drinan in the Fourth Congressional District of Massachusetts or to reelect Congressman Shannon in the Fifth District. (Both candidates won, in spite of His Eminence's opposition.)

Meanwhile, the Catholic bishops of West Germany also issued a pastoral letter, two weeks before the October 5 parliamentary elections, criticizing aspects of Chanc. Helmut Schmidt's policies in terms remarkably similar to those used by Schmidt's political opponents.

The West German bishops expressed concern about the national debt, governmental interference in the daily lives of ordinary citizens, and the lowering of moral standards on divorce and abortion.

Although the bishops did not go so far as Cardinal Medeiros to suggest that pro-Schmidt voters would be accumulating material for confession, their intervention was so closely linked with an impending election that its partisan political character could not be denied or discounted.

Chancellor Schmidt, a Lutheran, was understandably annoyed. The bishops should use their pulpits for pastoral work, he complained, and not for politics.

His justice minister, Hans-Jochen Vogel, a Catholic, expressed surprise that the letter had not mentioned other moral issues such as foreign aid, the relationship between rich and poor nations, or what he described as a growing antagonism toward foreigners in West Germany.

Whatever one's attitude toward the *content* of the two episcopal declarations—Cardinal Medeiros's or the West German hierarchy's—the *fact* that they were even issued shows that the question, "Should priests be involved in politics? is really moot."

Priests *are* involved in politics as a matter of course. It is not a question of *whether* but of *how*.

Those Catholic liberals who may have resented Cardinal Medeiros's initiative during the recent congressional campaigns in Massachusetts should make clear that they disagreed with the position he took, not that they rejected his right to speak out.

How can we deny one priest the right, in the name of moral principle, to intervene in the political order while supporting the right of another priest, such as Fr. Drinan himself, or of a group of priests, such as the Brazilian bishops, to do exactly the same thing? If politically liberal priests have the right to act, so, too, do politically conservative priests.

The same test of consistency, however, must also be applied to Catholic conservatives.

One cannot deny a Father Drinan his seat in the U.S. House of Representatives on the grounds that it is somehow unpriestly for such a person to be engaged in partisan, elective politics while affirming the right of a more conservative priest to work as a full-time employee of the Republican National Committee during a presidential campaign or of another to issue a public declaration on behalf of candidates for Congress.

It is no rebuttal to say that speaking on behalf of the unborn is so overriding a moral issue that the political considerations are simply insignificant.

War, and the preparation for war, is a moral issue. A society's treatment of its poor is a moral issue. The right of workers to organize is a moral issue. Discrimination based on race or sex is a moral issue.

If priests are not to be engaged in the political arena, as a matter of principle, then let that principle apply to all priests, whatever the moral issue.

But if there is to be a wide range of exceptions based on the priests' office (a bishop, a cardinal, or a pope rather than a "simple priest") or based on the moral issue (abortion rather than militarism), then the principle is lost.

Again, the point is moot. Priests, from Pope John Paul II on down, are and always have been involved in the political order in some way or other. Our constant hope should be that their involvement will reflect credit on the Church and, more fundamentally, that it should evidently be inspired by the gospel of Jesus Christ.

Controversies over Pope in Poland

(July 22, 1983)

No sooner had Pope John Paul II returned from his triumphant visit to Poland when a storm of controversy erupted over what he may have bargained away in his second private meeting with General Jaruzelski. Did he cut a deal or not with the head of the Communist Polish government?

The sudden and unprecedented resignation of the deputy editor of *L'Osservatore Romano* fueled growing speculation that the Holy Father, however reluctantly, had come to regard labor leader and national hero Lech Walesa as an expendable public figure.

For the greater good of Poland, Walesa would have to step out of the political limelight and Solidarity could never be revived as an independent labor union.

In return, General Jaruzelski and his Soviet monitors would lift martial law by September, if not even by late July, and the Vatican would be allowed to establish a development bank in Poland to help support the nation's troubled agricultural economy. Perhaps a new labor union, under the direct control of the Catholic Church, would replace Solidarity.

As of this writing, the facts are still not clear. Cardinal Glemp, primate of Poland, suggested on his recent trip to Rome that things were "still developing," especially with regard to Lech Walesa's future.

Was deputy editor ·Fr. Virgilio Levi fired from *L'Osservatore Romano* because he disclosed the truth about the deal the pope had made with the Polish government? Or was he fired because he had engaged in irresponsible speculation?

Anyone who knows anything at all about *L'Osservatore Romano* knows that it operates under the closest supervision of the Holy Father and his aides. Idle speculation is not its style.

The Vatican paper deals in facts that are deemed appropriate to print and in interpretations of fact that are deemed appropriate to express. Editorial writers do not strike out on a course at variance with the Holy See's. They understand this when they take the job and as long as they hope to keep it.

Why, then, did Father Levi break the rules? Why did he publish a front-page editorial bidding Lech Walesa a grateful farewell, referring to him as a kind of sacrificial lamb?

Was it because, as some have charged, the Vatican establishment is internally divided over recent papal initiatives in Poland? Was the editorial intended as a shot across the papal bow, warning him that some of his highest-ranking church officials are acutely unhappy about his alleged accommodation with the Polish government?

Was the *New York Times* columnist William Safire right when he charged last month that Walesa was sacked because that was the only way the Catholic Church could get the concessions it wanted from the government?

If Lech Walesa had been a more controllable person, Safire continued, then he wouldn't have to be sacrificed. But Walesa is, as the *L'Osservatore* editorialist acknowledged, one of those "uncomfortable people" whose courage can distress great institutions—the Church as well as the State.

"Archbishops and editors will accept discipline; labor leaders may not," Safire wrote, "which may be why the Pope seeks to make himself the exclusive symbol of Polish freedom."

With unpleasant speculation like this in the air, other voices sought to downplay the whole episode. We were assured by one prominent churchman who had accompanied the Holy Father on his trip that the matter about the church bank had already been in the works before the pope arrived in Poland (but, significantly, not already formally approved). A direct question about the future status of Walesa was carefully deflected.

Only time will tell what really transpired in that second meeting between Pope John Paul II and General Jaruzelski, called at the pope's request just before he completed his whirlwind tour of his homeland.

Only time will tell what impact their negotiations will have on the Solidarity movement, on Lech Walesa, on Poland, and on other client states of the Soviet Union.

If a deal was made that is prejudicial to Solidarity and to Walesa, only time will tell what reaction there will be, not only from Walesa himself but from the more radical Solidarity leaders who remain underground.

Two things are clear even now, however. First, from the moment the Holy Father landed in Poland until the moment he emerged from his second meeting with Jaruzelski, he stirred not only his own compatriots but millions of others inside and outside the Catholic Church.

His defense of human rights, his courageous support of the Solidarity movement, his outspoken criticism of the government—all gave hope for the future of freedom around the world, and not only for Poland.

Second, the pope's activities in Poland—before, during, and after his second meeting with Jaruzelski—were as much political as they were religious.

Is it really so improper to suggest that he may have undercut his own restrictive policy regarding priests and nuns in politics? Apparently there are many Vatican prelates who think so. And perhaps a few politically involved priests and nuns as well.

Governor Cuomo at Notre Dame, Part I
(October 19, 1984)

Gov. Mario Cuomo's paper "Religious Belief and Public Morality: A Catholic Governor's Perspective," given at the University of Notre Dame on September 13, raised to a much higher level the whole discussion of religion and politics. It sets a standard for everyone else who wishes to enter the debate.

Formulas will no longer suffice, whether they come from the left ("I'm personally against abortion, but I cannot impose my views on others") or from the right ("Abortion is murder, therefore it must legally be treated as murder").

Those on the left will have to indicate in some greater detail, as Governor Cuomo has, why they find abortion morally reprehensible, and then they will have to demonstrate, as Governor Cuomo has, that they are at least aware of the various options open to anyone who shares their moral position.

Those on the right will have to show that they have at least tried to understand why so many of their fellow Christians, not to say fellow Catholics, disagree with them on their moral and political evaluations of the issue. Calling them all murderers or baby killers is, again, a formula (and an ugly one indeed), not an answer.

Even more, they will have to indicate precisely, exactly what Catholic doctrine and universal moral principles require the Catholic governor or the Catholic legislator or the Catholic judge to do about abortion.

It may be clear, as I think it is, that both Catholic doctrine and universal moral principles mark abortion as an "unspeakable" crime (Vatican II, Pastoral Constitution on the Church in the Modern World, n. 51), but it is not at all clear that either Catholic doctrine or universal moral principles point to specific legislative, executive, and judicial courses to follow in a pluralistic society—or in any society, for that matter.

We are left, then, with the age-old challenge of applying our moral and religious convictions in the real world of personal, social, national, and international existence. And this is where Governor Cuomo's paper begins.

First, he makes it clear that he doesn't pretend to have all the answers. He hopes his effort will inspire others to do better than he has done.

Second, he stoutly defends the right and even the duty of bishops to identify and address the moral dimension of public issues.

He does not deny them their constitutional right to participate fully in the political process, to the point of endorsing candidates and parties, but he suggests that it would not be wise. The point is moot, of course, since the bishops have imposed upon themselves a rule forbidding such involvement.

He is concerned, third, with the rights of all citizens, including Catholics, to be free from coercion in the realm of religious conviction and practice.

At the same time, however, he wants to protect the right of all citizens, including religious people, to argue for the translation of their moral and even religious convictions into public policy, that is, to make a given conviction into "an article of our universal public morality."

To do so, of course, they will have to convince others that their values are "desirable even apart from their specific religious base or content." This would apply also to abortion.

Fourth, it may not always be prudent to exercise this right. We have to ask ourselves if our efforts will prove more harmful to the body politic than the evil we are trying to eradicate. It is the community that must decide; therefore, it is the community that must be persuaded and then convinced.

Fifth, contrary to misinterpretations by some of his critics, Governor Cuomo does distinguish between "public morality" and "values derived from religious belief." The latter cannot become part of the former "unless they are shared by the pluralistic community at large, by consensus."

In any case, "all religiously based values don't have an *a priori* place in our public morality."

Sixth, abortion is not only a Catholic issue, nor even a religious issue. It is a life issue that would confront us even if there were no God. One's convictions about abortion are grounded not only on one's fidelity to the teaching of the Church but on fidelity to conscience.

Governor Cuomo himself opposes abortion on moral grounds, and not just because he is a Catholic. "A fetus," he said, "is different from an appendix or a set of tonsils. At the very least . . . the full potential of human life is indisputably there. That . . . by itself should demand respect, caution, indeed . . . reverence."

The difficult question emerges when one moves from moral evaluation to political judgment. What exactly does one do about abortion in the public forum?

Governor Cuomo at Notre Dame, Part II

(October 26, 1984)

The difficult question regarding abortion is political, not ethical. I say this without denying the fact that there are Catholics who disagree with their Church's official teaching.

Theological opinion, however, has not been divided on this issue, nor has theological discussion of it been marked by dissent, as in the previous case of birth control.

With abortion one finds almost all of the Catholic participants—bishops, theologians, and office-holders alike—united in moral opposition but divided on political strategy.

What does one do about abortion? As Governor Cuomo insisted in his September 13 address at the University of Notre Dame, nowhere does the Catholic Church set down an "inflexible moral principle which determines what our *political* conduct should be."

The Church, for example, does not argue for a change in the civil law regarding divorce or birth control, even though its moral teaching has not changed.

Some critics have taken Governor Cuomo to task for introducing these two issues. These critics argue that divorce and birth control are not comparable to abortion because abortion involves the destruction of an innocent human life.

But Governor Cuomo's intent was not to establish a moral parity among these three issues. There is none, to be sure.

Rather, birth control and divorce are pertinent to the abortion controversy only because they highlight the role of political judgment alongside moral judgment. These two kinds of judgment are closely related, but they are not the same.

Even though Catholic teachings on birth control and divorce have not changed, the pastoral leadership of the Catholic Church in the United States realizes it would be practically impossible and even constitutionally inappropriate to press for restrictive legislation. The bishops are not unmindful of the political history of these issues in overwhelmingly Catholic countries like Italy and Ireland.

The bishops believe, on the other hand, that there is a sufficient measure of agreement on the abortion issue in the nation at large to justify a serious effort at some form of legislative control, if not outright abolition.

But that's precisely the question: some form of legislative control or outright abolition?

Those whom Governor Cuomo described as moral fundamentalists will accept only an all-or-nothing solution. But that cannot pass. And even if it were to pass, it could not be enforced. "Prohibition revisited," he said.

A constitutional amendment banning all abortions, he argued, would allow us to ignore the many causes of abortion instead of addressing them. The Hatch Amendment, on the other hand, would give us "a checkerboard of permissive and restrictive jurisdictions."

Abortions would continue.

Neither would a denial of Medicaid funding succeed. It would not prevent the rich and the middle class from having abortions, nor would it stop the poor. It would only impose financial burdens on them.

Here is where the main brunt of criticism against Governor Cuomo's Notre Dame address has been directed. Why should citizens who feel moral outrage about the practice of abortion be compelled to spend their tax dollars in support of it?

Some have not been persuaded by the governor's argument that the withholding of Medicaid funds would, in effect, violate a woman's constitutional right to abortion.

But that argument is legal, not moral. Many of those who wish to challenge the governor's position mix the two spheres. In a straight fight between the moralist and the lawyer, the moralist will probably lose.

The moral argument, however, deserves to be pressed independently of the legal argument. In the case of civil rights, for example, individuals and groups fought the battle on moral grounds until the legal barriers fell away.

Governor Cuomo's counterargument is that no law will stop abortions because abortion is our failure, not the government's.

The most effective form of opposition to abortion, he says, is the power of our own example as Catholics and our readiness as taxpaying citizens to provide funds and help to women so that they can bring their pregnancies to term. This means working for a legislative bill of rights for mothers and children, as the bishops have already proposed.

Meanwhile the United States is 16th among the nations of the world in its infant mortality rate. Thousands of infants die each year because of inadequate medical care, and others are physically and mentally stunted because of improper nutrition. There is plenty of work for all of us to do—lifetimes of it.

Governor Cuomo at Notre Dame, Part III

(November 2, 1984)

Although many have been as favorably impressed with Gov. Mario Cuomo's September 13 lecture at the University of Notre Dame as I am, there have been two basic criticisms of his paper, "Religious Belief and Public Morality: A Catholic Governor's Perspective."

First, it is said, the governor seems to make abortion a Catholic and/or religious issue, when it is in fact an issue of life and of human rights.

Second, he seems to think that since there is no consensus in society in favor of a constitutional or legislative ban on abortion, we should not try to achieve any ban at this time. This would be to impose our beliefs on others and to invite back the days of Prohibition.

Did he or did he not make abortion a Catholic issue? Was his argument reducible to the formula "I'm personally against abortion, but I cannot impose my Catholic beliefs on others"?

The answer is no to both questions, but impressions to the contrary cannot simply be dismissed.

Although the governor does clearly distinguish between "public morality" and "values derived from religious belief," and although he does insist that we would have to confront abortion as a life issue even if there were no God, so many of his references are indeed to official Catholic teaching on abortion and to his role as a Catholic public official.

He refers, for example, to "our ability—our realistic, political ability—to translate our Catholic morality into civil law, a law not for the believers who don't need it but for the disbelievers who reject it."

He speaks parenthetically in the next paragraph of "our private observance of Catholic morality" regarding abortion, and then toward the end of his address he argues that "approval or rejection of legal restrictions on abortion should not be the exclusive litmus test of Catholic loyalty."

One has to keep in mind, however, the nature of the invitation he received. He was asked to "reflect on the relationship between faith and politics," on his "own personal journey as a Catholic in the pre– and post–Vatican II Church and [his] abiding effort to make [his] political activity a faithful expression of [his] religious convictions."

Therefore, it was neither surprising nor inappropriate for him to have emphasized the Catholic dimension of the abortion issue, particularly at the University of Notre Dame.

But given the developments that intervened between the extending of the original invitation in mid-June and the actual delivery of the lecture on September 13, it might have been helpful if the paper stressed more than it did the broader nature of the issue.

Surely the abortion controversy has special significance for Catholics and for the Catholic politician, but it is not a Catholic issue as such, nor is the nub of the problem the danger of imposing Catholic morality on non-Catholics.

The second point of criticism is more serious and more complicated. Whether the public official is Catholic or not, what should he or she try to do about abortion at the executive, legislative, and judicial levels?

Is it enough to say that while abortion is morally wrong, there is no realistic alternative to obeying *Roe v. Wade,* even to the point of accepting Medicaid funding of abortions without protest?

The governor's response is twofold. First, those who oppose abortion must set the example for the rest of society. The bishops have to convince Catholics not to have abortions. Second, all of us should get behind legislation such as a bill of rights for mothers and children to make the option of abortion less compelling.

But is there anything else we can do? Is it not possible, for example, to work for legislation that restricts rather than bans abortion?

Every survey shows that most Americans oppose abortion on demand. At the same time, most Americans, including most Catholics, want the law to allow abortions in the case of rape and incest or where the life of the mother is in danger.

Such exceptions are against Catholic teaching, but this approach offers a more realistic political course than does the effort to achieve a total ban. And it would also eliminate most of the abortions being performed today.

Civil rights advocates of the 1940s and 1950s, to be sure, weren't paralyzed by the argument that "separate but equal" was the law of the land, but neither were they caught in the moral fundamentalists' trap of "all or nothing."

In the meantime, Governor Cuomo's expressed hope seems within reach; namely, that his Notre Dame address "will provoke other efforts . . . that will help all of us understand our differences and perhaps even discover some basic agreement."

Argument Reveals Inconsistency on Procurers of Abortion
(November 18, 1988)

In a recent letter to the *New York Times* (October 23), Dr. J. C. Willke, president of the National Right to Life Committee, took exception to an editorial that had criticized Vice-President Bush's stand on abortion.

In his first debate with Governor Dukakis, the vice-president was asked whether he favored criminal punishment of a woman who has an abortion. It was one question for which the vice-president was obviously unprepared.

He conceded that "of course there's got to be some penalties to enforce the law," but he admitted that he hadn't "sorted out" what they should be or on whom they should be imposed. Governor Dukakis charged that Mr. Bush was "prepared to brand a woman a criminal for making this decision."

The damage-control squad, under the direction of the vice-president's campaign manager, James Baker, went to work immediately. The next morning Mr. Baker told a press conference that Mr. Bush "would not wish to see a woman labeled as a criminal, notwithstanding his view in favor of right to life."

"Frankly," the campaign manager continued, "he thinks that a woman in a situation like that would be more properly considered an additional victim, perhaps the second victim. That she would need help and love and not punishment."

Mr. Baker reported that the vice-president would favor some punishment of the person performing the abortion, but he did not indicate what penalty Mr. Bush had in mind.

The *Times* editorial of September 29 suggested that Mr. Bush's position would not "satisfy pro-lifers who want sinners behind bars."

Dr. Willke challenged that interpretation. The *Times,* he charged, hadn't done its "homework."

He noted that during the first 200 years of this nation's history, when abortion was illegal, not a single woman who had an abortion was put in jail or even indicted.

"But the 'hit man' was," he declared. "Abortionists were charged, convicted and sent to prison."

"I have no doubt," Dr. Willke continued, "that's the way it will be again. I don't know of a single pro-life leader who would punish the mother."

I find that position astonishing. On what moral or ethical grounds does Dr. Willke exempt a woman who procures an abortion from personal responsibility for her action?

The Catholic Church certainly does not. Its newly revised Code of Canon Law is clear and straightforward on the point: "A person who procures a completed abortion incurs an automatic excommunication" (canon 1398).

Mr. Bush regards the woman as an innocent "second victim," and apparently Dr. Willke buys that line.

Is she somehow forced to hand over her unborn child to the abortionist's deadly instruments? Is she dragged kicking and screaming into the clinic?

On the contrary, she sometimes has to fight her way through noisy lines of anti-abortion demonstrators.

Will our "bleeding heart" right-to-lifers also regard as innocent "second victims" those 10,000 women in China and France who have already procured abortions via the new RU 486 abortion pill?

Who is the morally culpable party in a pill-induced abortion? Do we send only the druggist to the slammer?

The fact of the matter is that those in the pro-life movement have always characterized abortion as murder, plain and simple.

The problem is they're not really serious about the language they put on their signs at anti-Cuomo or anti-Dukakis or anti-Ferraro rallies. They don't really believe that abortion is murder in the very same moral sense that a robbery-killing on the street is murder.

They want that street killer to go to jail. Even be executed. But the woman who has an abortion? Nothing. She gets off scot-free.

And what about the physician? How many years in prison would be appropriate for such a murderer? They don't want to say. They haven't "sorted it out" yet.

And what about the nurses? Or the taxi driver who provides transportation to the clinic? They're all accomplices to murder, aren't they? What criminal penalty do they deserve? The pro-lifers don't even talk about them.

And neither do they talk about the father of the aborted fetus. Why aren't they eager to put him behind bars? He's hardly an innocent bystander, after all.

It's time to go back to square one. What is abortion? Is it murder or is it something other than murder?

If it's murder, then let's treat it like murder—all along the moral and legal line.

If we're not prepared to do that (and the evidence is that not even the pro-lifers are), then let's start cleaning up our language—and our political posters.

9

Ecumenism

Introduction

Before the Second Vatican Council it was generally assumed that the Catholic Church was the "one, true Church of Christ." All other Christian bodies (never called churches) were regarded as schismatic (as in the case of the Orthodox) or heretical (as in the case of the Protestants).

The Second Vatican Council officially changed that popular view. The Body of Christ is larger than the Catholic Church alone. It includes Orthodox, Oriental Christians, Anglicans, and Protestants as well. Indeed, the council deliberately struck the copulative verb *is* from article 8 of its Dogmatic Constitution on the Church and replaced it with the verb *subsists in*. Thus, the Church of Christ "subsists in" the Catholic Church, but it is not simply identical with it (as the verb *is* would have declared).

From this general principle that the Body of Christ includes more than the Catholic Church, there followed a series of practical postconciliar developments: joint prayer, ecumenical theological education, bilateral consultations and dialogues, collaboration in social ministry, and many instances of unofficially sanctioned intercommunion.

Many observers have complained in recent years about a certain state of "drift" in the ecumenical movement, especially in the West. Not much progress has been achieved beyond what had already been won in the late 1960s and early 1970s. Under Pope John Paul II the ecumenical agenda seems to have been changed: from a focus on Catholic–Protestant/Anglican relations in North America and Western Europe to a new focus on Catholic-Orthodox relations in Central and Eastern Europe. I touch upon that development in my column of September 2, 1983.

Other ecumenically related issues treated in this chapter include the resurgence of fundamentalism, even within the Catholic Church (the column of May 1, 1987) and the age-old question of convert making (the column of August 10, 1990).

The columns highlight the still-unfinished state of the ecumenical movement today, at least at the official level. Timidity and inaction have replaced the boldness and energy of the early postconciliar years. At the unofficial level, however, the Church is far ahead of its pastoral leaders.

News of Ecumenism's Death Is Premature

(July 23, 1971)

There are some people in the Church today who would be inclined to say that the ecumenical movement is just about dead. It is not that ecumenism has failed; it has succeeded too well.

The ecumenical movement succeeded so well in bringing such mutual respect and understanding to the Christian Church that the representatives of the various churches and denominations no longer consciously look upon the other as "the other" at all.

It is now simply taken for granted that Christian theology must be ecumenical and that seminary education ought to occur, where possible, in ecumenical clusters, such as we have already in Boston, Chicago, San Francisco, and Dubuque.

I should suggest that the various bulletins announcing either the death or the terminal condition of ecumenism are premature in character. There are still several major issues dividing the churches, although considerable progress has already been achieved on several fronts (see, for example, the remarkable joint studies produced by the Catholic-Lutheran dialogue committee on the Eucharist and the ordained ministry).

Separated Christians have not yet resolved the delicate problem of intercommunion. Catholics have been especially reluctant and cautious on this question, but we have been positively liberal in comparison with the Orthodox tradition.

We are still a long way from the mutual recognition of one another's ordained ministry, and this issue is, in turn, related to the deeper problem of doctrinal pluralism. While it is true that the differences between and/or among some churches are more theological than doctrinal (i.e., they differ not so much on the understanding of Christian faith as on the expression of the understanding), there are still too many Christians whose attitude toward the historic formulations of faith is simply too casual.

Catholics and other High Church communities are not about to admit that the Christian movement started yesterday and that, for the sake of harmony, we can conveniently set aside the potentially divisive testimonies not only of the ecumenical councils and Fathers of the Church but even of the Bible itself.

While the problem of full ecumenical unity may appear insuperable, the good results achieved at various local levels provide some hope for the future. Indeed, one of the most constructive and promising ecumenical developments in the Church today is the Plan of Union proposed by the Consultation on Church Union.

The document was formally drafted at St. Louis on March 13, 1970, by representatives of the nine member churches: the African Methodist Episcopal Church, the African Methodist Episcopal Zion Church, the Christian Church (Disciples of Christ), the Christian Methodist Episcopal Church, the Episcopal Church, the Presbyterian Church in the United States, the United Church of

Christ, the United Methodist Church, and the United Presbyterian Church in the U.S.A.

So much of the COCU Plan of Union is faithful to the Catholic principles of ecumenism proposed and approved at Vatican II in its Decree on Ecumenism. In fact, the plan cites the decree in reminding its own member churches that "there can be no ecumenism worthy of the name without a change of heart."

The plan recognizes that the united church must be at once catholic, evangelical, and reformed. It must be catholic in the sense that it is in continuity with earlier generations of Christians, that it is open to all genuine values in the world, and that it represents a rich diversity, meaning unity without uniformity. It must preserve distinctiveness without sacrificing universality.

The church must be evangelical in the sense that it must acknowledge Jesus Christ as the beginning, the middle, and the end of its faith, its proclamation, its celebration, and its mission.

And the church must be reformed in the sense that it must ever be prepared to subject all of its traditions and practices to the judgment and correction of the Holy Spirit.

The Plan of Union is not without its faults. There are items in it that have already elicited criticism from Catholic theologians (particularly its sometimes ambiguous presentation on ordained ministry). But this is what the framers of the document want and seek.

Updating Views on Protestants

(June 23, 1972)

In the earliest days of renewal and reform, teachers, writers, lecturers, and Church officials made great efforts to show the connection between the new and the old. This had the effect of diminishing the sense of fear that the changes, and predictions of change, were creating in the minds and hearts of many Catholics.

In most instances, the effort to maintain continuity with the past was both pedagogically sound and theologically responsible. Many of the changes could be regarded legitimately as a logical development of previous views.

This was not always the case, however. Some changes in the Catholic Church's self-understanding were achieved through leaps rather than through measured steps. The matter of ecumenism is the chief example.

In the years immediately preceding the council, we Catholics identified the Body of Christ with the Catholic Church alone (Pope Pius XII, *Humani Generis,* n. 44). Protestants were outside the Church because they separated themselves from the authority of the pope (Pope Pius XII, *Mystici Corporis,* nn. 23 and 43).

Indeed, we often accused Protestants of recognizing no authority at all, save their own private judgment, which, we were quick to remind ourselves, could easily lead them into error (*New Baltimore Catechism,* no. 3, Father Connell's edition, 1949, p. 88).

Protestants could not participate in true Christian sanctity, even our sophisticated Latin textbooks insisted, because they denied human freedom and held that we are justified by faith alone without works of charity (see the tract on the Church in *Sacrae Theologiae Summa* [the so-called Spanish Summa], vol. 1, 1962 edition, pp. 943ff.).

In the worship of God, such groups are "guided more by sentiment and personal conviction than by the objective truths given to the world by Our Lord." Their founders "were not saints and generally were not holy and edifying men," and their communities "have not given saints to the world."

Their truths are "but fragments of the doctrines of the Catholic Church" and their holiness "is due to the means that the sects have salvaged from Catholic worship" (Father Connell edition, p. 90).

There are many Catholics who have forgotten or were never aware of this "common teaching" regarding the Christian worth of Protestants and other non-Catholics. That is why, I should suggest, they do not fully appreciate the extraordinary advances gained at Vatican II.

On the other hand, there are still too many Catholics who refuse to admit that the council did, in fact, leap beyond these earlier views on the nature and composition of the Body of Christ.

There are some few newspapers, magazines, and newsletters operating under ostensibly Catholic sponsorship that discuss the ecumenical question as if the Decree on Ecumenism and related theological developments never even happened. Moreover, they sharply criticize any Catholic spokesman who speaks at all sympathetically of a given Protestant point of view.

Indeed, for some of these commentators the worst charge they feel they can level against a fellow Catholic is that his or her position is reductively "Protestant."

How can they understand the council's (and Pope Paul VI's!) acknowledgment that "men of both sides were to blame" for the Reformation (Decree on Ecumenism, n. 3)?

How can they understand the council's insistence that "all those justified by faith through baptism are incorporated into Christ [and] therefore have a right to be honored by the title of Christian and are properly regarded as brothers in the Lord by the sons of the Catholic Church" (n. 3)?

How can they understand the council's reminder that "the most significant elements or endowments which together go to build up and give life to the Church herself" can and do exist outside the Catholic Church: "the written word of God; the life of grace; faith, hope, and charity, along with other interior gifts of the Holy Spirit and visible elements" (n. 3)?

How can they understand the council's admission that whatever the Spirit might produce outside the Catholic Church can contribute to our Church's own edification (n. 4)?

How can they understand the council's view that while there must be unity in essentials, there is ample room for flexibility and pluralism "in the various forms of spiritual life and discipline, in the variety of liturgical rites, and even in the theological elaborations of revealed truth" (n. 4)?

How can they understand the council's radical justification for intercommunion, albeit under highly controlled circumstances, and its insistence that ecumenical dialogue be undertaken in such a way that "each can deal with the other on an equal footing" (nn. 8 and 9)?

There is indeed a theory-and-practice gap in the Catholic Church. The question all of us face, particularly those in some position of influence and authority, is whether we take the theory seriously enough to amend the practice.

Ecumenical Conversations Produce Agreements on Some Major Issues

(June 30, 1972)

Since 1965 Catholic theologians and pastoral leaders have been in dialogue with their counterparts in the various other Christian churches: Anglican, Orthodox, Lutheran, Presbyterian, Baptist, Methodist, Disciples of Christ, and so forth.

Several of these bilateral conversations, as they are called, have produced consensus statements on topics of central ecumenical importance. While these statements are often restrained and measured in tone, they cannot obscure the major changes that have occurred in the pastoral and theological atmosphere since Vatican II.

On one controversial issue after another, the participants were able to outline significant areas of common understanding, even theological and doctrinal unity. Myths and caricatures collapsed in thundering sequence.

Contrary to the view of many Catholics that we and the various non-Catholic Christians are hopelessly divided on the question of the Eucharist, three of the dialogue groups (Anglican-Catholic, Orthodox-Catholic, and Lutheran-Catholic) claimed to have arrived at substantial agreement on the sacrificial nature of the Eucharist and on the Real Presence of Christ.

On these two issues, the Lutheran-Catholic statement concluded, "The progress has been immense. Despite all remaining differences in the ways we speak and think of the eucharistic sacrifice and our Lord's presence in his supper, we are no longer able to regard ourselves as divided in the one holy catholic and apostolic faith on these two points."

There is also significant agreement among the various groups (including now even the Disciples of Christ–Catholic) that the doctrine and celebration of the Eucharist, to be meaningful, must be understood in the context of the doctrine and life of the whole Church, as People of God, Body of Christ, and Temple of the Holy Spirit.

Contrary to the view of many Catholics that we are also hopelessly divided on the question of the ordained ministry, three of the dialogue groups (Anglican-Catholic, Lutheran-Catholic, and Reformed Presbyterian–Catholic) achieved remarkable agreement on several key points.

First, all three agreed that the special or representative ministry can be properly understood only within the context of the general ministry of the whole Church, and as one of the many gifts of the Holy Spirit that have been given to the Christian community.

Second, they agreed that the specifying note of the ordained ministry is the preaching of the Word and the celebration of the sacraments.

Third, all three agreed that entrance into this special ministry is by ordination. The Lutheran-Catholic group, in fact, insisted that ordination is permanent in its effect and unrepeatable.

Fourth, there is even some suggestion that we are nearing the point where a mutual recognition of ministries will be in order. Indeed, the Catholic participants in the Lutheran-Catholic dialogue stated that they found "serious defects in the arguments customarily used against the validity of the eucharistic Ministry of the Lutheran churches."

"In fact," the Catholic theologians continued, "we see no persuasive reason to deny the possibility of the Roman Catholic Church recognizing the validity of this Ministry. Accordingly, we ask the authorities of the Roman Catholic Church whether the ecumenical urgency flowing from Christ's will for unity may not dictate that the Roman Catholic Church recognize the validity of the Lutheran Ministry, and correspondingly, the presence of the body and blood of Christ in the eucharistic celebrations of the Lutheran churches."

And contrary to the views of many Catholics that we are also hopelessly divided on the question of dogma and doctrine, the most recent consensus statement emanating from a dialogue group (the Anglican-Catholic) offers a set of principles by which our historic differences might be confronted in a more constructive and conciliatory way.

The Anglican-Catholic committee insisted that the goal of ecumenical dialogue is "not to produce a statement of minimum essentials by which one Church can measure the orthodoxy of another, but to deepen, strengthen, and enrich the life of both."

The statement asserts, as a fundamental principle, that no formulation of faith can ever adequately express the mystery of God. This leads to a major practical conclusion; namely, the recognition "that Christians who are orthodox in their faith may express it in varying formulations."

The Decree on Ecumenism declared that "there can be no ecumenism worthy of the name without a change of heart" (n. 7). Change of heart means, of course, a kind of conversion. And conversion is never easy because it means, among other things, a repudiation of past sins.

We first have to admit those sins. There are still too many of us who cannot or will not.

Communicating Importance of Ecumenism Is More Than Annual January Project

(January 19, 1973)

Certain months of the year have acquired a special character in Catholic devotional life. May and October are traditionally associated with the Blessed Virgin Mary; November, with the faithful departed; and June, with the Sacred Heart.

In recent years a link has been fashioned between the ecumenical movement and the month of January, with its annual Week of Prayer for Christian Unity.

The older devotional writers used to insist that our prayerful interest in Mary, or the holy souls, or the Sacred Heart not be confined to one or another month of the year. Similar admonitions regarding Catholic concern for ecumenism in January would be equally appropriate.

Last year at this time *America* magazine published an assortment of views on the question, Where are we in ecumenism? Several of the contributors underlined major points at which serious progress has been achieved over the past decade, but many agreed that there has also been an apparent slackening of interest in the ecumenical movement. Indeed, the *America* Symposium was conceived as a direct response to that problem.

"Before we can move much further ahead," Fr. Avery Dulles wrote, "it will be necessary to make ecumenism seem important to every Christian believer and not just to a band of specialists."

How does the Church's pastoral leadership communicate this sense of importance? How does it enlighten the rank-and-file membership concerning the fruits that have already been harvested over the past seven or eight years?

Improvement in this latter area is a matter of highest priority. Most Christians, bishops and pastors included, are simply unaware of ecumenically significant advances in theology and in theological education.

In a special study committee report submitted last summer to the Catholic Theological Society of America, a group of Catholic theologians urged that "the responsible agencies of the various churches should take steps to ensure that the clergy and laity are kept informed of the theological developments taking place in the consultations [between Catholics and Christians of other communions]."

"The dialogues," the report continued, "could profitably be presented for study in episcopal seminars (which might well be ecumenical in composition), diocesan clergy conferences (to which clergy of other denominations might appropriately be invited), adult education programs, and popular literature."

The facts are, sadly, that very few episcopal seminars are convened, and they are almost never ecumenical in character. There has been a definite slowdown in diocesan clergy education programs, and where they are still active, with adequate funding and staffing, they are rarely ecumenical in range and composition.

Adult education programs have the same drawbacks. In some rare instances, such as the Institute for Continuing Education in the archdiocese of Detroit, the programs are professionally administered. Professionalism, however, costs money, but many ecclesiastical administrators apparently believe that they can secure high-quality performance and service without paying for them.

Finally, when theologians try to popularize some of this ecumenical material, for example, in diocesan newspapers, their efforts are greeted by indignant protestations of concern for "the simple faithful."

Ecumenism, like anything worth doing well, requires time, personnel, and money. But the greatest requirement of all is the change in theological perception that it demands of each Catholic and particularly those who have pastoral responsibility. Too many Catholics continue to speak and write about Protestants and other Christians as if absolutely nothing had happened since their childhood days.

The nonspecialist membership of the Church readily detects that attitude in its leadership. "If it's not really that important to them," they conclude, "why should it bother us?" Therein lies a problem of major proportions.

Issuing Statements on Ecumenical Agreements Only a Beginning

(January 18, 1974)

The recent agreement reached by an international committee of Roman Catholic and Anglican theologians on the thorny question of ordained ministry commanded headline attention in both the Catholic and the secular press. But doesn't anyone wonder what happens to such consensus statements once the journalistic dust settles?

This Anglican–Roman Catholic position paper on the ordained ministry is neither the first nor, surely, the last such achievement in the ecumenical field. In the United States alone, the ecclesiastical terrain is strewn with similar expressions of theological and pastoral convergence. The Roman Catholic–Lutheran dialogue provides the most impressive material in this regard.

One of the Catholic participants in this latest Anglican–Roman Catholic consultation cautioned the press against leaping to any premature conclusions. Anglicans and Roman Catholics have not solved their centuries-old difficulties regarding the validity of orders, the authority of the pope, and so forth.

Those who actively participated in the international discussions did, indeed, attain a remarkable degree of consensus on such matters, and particularly on the first. But what the scholars can agree to among themselves is one thing; what the respective churches can accept is quite another.

And so the casual observer is being warned not to think that Anglicans and Roman Catholics are back together again. This recent statement of agreement is only a beginning. The leadership and rank and file have yet to digest it. Only then will we be on the way to eventual reunion.

The exact same advice is offered each time an agreement of this sort is reached at the academic or highly professional level. The participants remind their churches that the agreements reached are agreements only among themselves and are in no way binding upon those who were not party to the dialogues (which means 99.99999+ percent of the membership).

Diplomatically the participants' stance is unexceptionable. They would cut a very arrogant figure, to be sure, if they were to come forward and say, with some measure of self-assurance, that the historic obstacles to union no longer exist, or at least are not serious enough to prevent reunion any longer, and that the leadership of the respective churches have no reasonable alternative to endorsing and implementing the results.

Such a posture would provoke open and public conflict between the scholarly community and the pastoral leadership, because, in almost every instance of this kind, the latter group has been out of sympathy with the findings of the former group.

The proof is in the record. The many ecumenical consultations that have been held in the United States since the council have already advanced several concrete proposals designed to reestablish unity among the various Christian churches. These proposals embrace a wide segment of contemporary ecumenical issues, such as intercommunion, the mutual recognition of ministries, the ordination of women, the formulation of doctrine, and so-called mixed marriages.

What is clear thus far is that nothing of a substantial nature has been done, on any side, to comply with the recommendations of the dialogue participants. When the journalistic dust has settled, in other words, the field of combat appears to be in exactly the same condition it was before the flurry of theological activity began.

Based on the record alone, it is clear—and I am speaking now from the Roman Catholic side—that the majority of our decision makers are not at all prepared to reconsider their own textbook understanding of apostolic succession. In the absence of such reconsideration, the proposal for a mutual recognition of ministries is simply beyond the range of possibility.

And if the majority of our decision makers persist, as they do, in their understanding of the Roman Catholic Church as "the one, true Church of Christ" (again in the traditional, early 20th-century textbook sense), intercommunion of any kind must continue to be prohibited. Only an abjuration of heresy and a full and complete acceptance of the primacy of the pope would satisfy the majority of the present leadership.

Given the present theological disposition of our Roman Catholic leadership, statements such as the recent Anglican–Roman Catholic agreement on the ordained ministry have no realistic chance of being implemented.

They attract ephemeral headlines and they give a few moderates a temporary sense of well-being. But they cannot excite people who know that the proof of the pudding is in the eating. Too many of our pudding plates are still in the refrigerator, well hidden behind towers of leftovers.

Decree on Ecumenism: 10 Years Later
(January 10, 1975)

It is 10 years since the promulgation of Vatican II's Decree on Ecumenism. We should be in a reasonably good position now to say something about the durability of the council's teaching.

Unfortunately, some readers will accept nothing less than the message that things are wonderful and getting better, while others want only to hear that things are bad and getting worse.

Those of us who feel constrained to issue a mixed report seem to fall unmourned between the cracks.

The decree defined the ecumenical movement as "those activities and enterprises which, according to various needs of the Church and opportune occasions, are initiated and organized for the fostering of unity among Christians" (n. 4).

The council listed five categories of such "activities and enterprises," and these, in turn, provide us with a kind of checklist against which to measure the progress of ecumenism over the past decade.

First, the effort to eliminate all words, judgments, and actions that are offensive and unfair to our separated brethren (the terms *heretic, left-hander,* and the like; the practice of rebaptizing converts to Catholicism when they were already validly baptized as Protestants; preventing Protestant ministers from conducting services in Catholic cemeteries or from participating in marriage ceremonies involving a Catholic and a Protestant).

On item no. 1 we seem to have made long strides. Pockets of bigotry still exist on both sides, no doubt, but they are the exception to the rule. Courtesy and respect have replaced provocation and triumphalism.

On the other hand, we may have succeeded too well. Some Roman Catholics today have gone from one extreme to another. Where they once inflated their own self-esteem at the expense of the Protestant, they now wonder if there is a point or purpose any longer to being a Roman Catholic at all.

Second, ecumenism is manifested in dialogue between competent experts from different churches. Each side explains its own teachings and hopes through conversation to gain a truer knowledge and a greater appreciation of the teaching and religious life of the other side.

Here, too, the record since 1964 has been good. There have been theological consultations at both the international and national levels. The bilaterals in the United States alone will keep historians of the ecumenical movement busy for many years to come.

Points of substantial agreement have been reached in areas that were regarded at one time as so hopelessly controverted that Catholics and Protestants could never be reconciled, short of the complete surrender of one side or the other.

On the other hand, the funding of these consultations has been cut back. Some of the dialogue groups in this country have had to postpone meetings for lack of financial resources. More seriously, many of the major theological conclusions have been ignored by the ecclesiastical decision makers (on intercommunion, the mutual recognition of ministries, and the like).

Third, Christian unity is fostered, the council reminded us, through cooperation in projects demanded by the common good.

Here the record is murky. There has been an intensification of Roman Catholic efforts in areas of social and economic concern (e.g., the Campaign for Human Development and the work of the USCC Division for Justice and Peace), but the extent of ecumenical cooperation is less clear.

In the more evident instances, Roman Catholic participation has been confined to those who are regarded as more marginal than mainstream (e.g., Bishop Gumbleton's admirable collaboration in the anti–Vietnam War movement).

Fourth, Christian unity is promoted through common prayer. Certainly there has been more and more of this since the council, and participants testify readily to its spiritually enriching possibilities.

But Catholic discipline still prohibits intercommunion, and, our politeness notwithstanding, we still cannot bring ourselves to accept the ecclesial validity of non–Roman Catholic orders.

Finally, the Decree on Ecumenism mentions the area of church renewal and reform that, if pursued "with vigor," can lead us to that restoration of unity for which we all pray.

There have, of course, been several structural improvements in the institutional life of the Roman Catholic Church (e.g., the coming into existence of parish councils as a way of implementing the nonclericalistic principle of coresponsibility), but by and large these have been relatively modest in substance and cautious in implementation.

There can be no real commitment to ecumenism without a corresponding commitment to "that continual reformation of which [the Church] always has need" (Decree on Ecumenism, n. 6).

If the ecumenical movement lags today, it is because of our abiding reluctance to embrace real, major reform.

The State of Ecumenism Today

(January 23, 1976)

The annual Week of Prayer for Christian Unity prompts this week's reflections on the state of the ecumenical movement.

I do not intend to reheat journalistic leftovers from previous winters: that we are in a "postecumenical" era or that the movement is grinding to a halt or whatever else.

Indeed, some new insights are just coming into focus this year.

1. It is becoming clearer now that the traditionalist opponent of ecumenism has found a new and powerful weapon against continued ecumenical exploration and collaboration.

It is the twin effect of the abortion and parochiaid questions.

Those who press these issues today cannot fail to know the ecumenical effect: the more we insist on a public fight against liberalized abortion laws, the more we divide the Christian community; the more vigorously we demand government assistance to Catholic schools, the wider the rift not only among Christians but even between Catholics and Jews.

The next few lines can easily be misunderstood. I am not speaking in favor of abortion, nor am I about to ridicule official Catholic lobbying efforts for financial assistance.

But it has to be more than a coincidence that some of the strongest Catholic voices on both those issues are also some of the least ecumenically sensitive members of the American hierarchy.

In recent years there have been major ecumenical advances on the deeper theological and biblical levels.

Official dialogue groups have called for more frequent intercommunion and even for the mutual recognition of ordained ministries. A recent Lutheran-Catholic consultation has begun removing centuries-old obstacles regarding the papacy question itself.

But many Catholic leaders have, over the past decade, chosen to ignore this rich body of material emerging from these various ecumenical conversations.

For these bishops, it is as if there were no Anglican–Roman Catholic dialogue on the Eucharist and on the ordained ministry or no Catholic-Lutheran dialogue on the Eucharist, the ministry, and the papacy or no Catholic-Presbyterian dialogue on the ordination of women.

Now the abortion and the parochial school aid issues have conveniently emerged, providing just enough leverage to wound the ecumenical process. I suggest that the unpleasant ecumenical effects have been foreseen, and not completely unintended.

2. There is a younger generation of Catholics now at college age who had barely reached the "age of reason" when Vatican II convened in 1962 and were no more than 9, 10, or 11 years old when the council adjourned in December of 1965.

These younger Catholics don't know what all the ecumenical fuss was all about in the first place. They're not overawed by the sight of the Catholic pope kissing the feet of an Orthodox patriarch, or of a priest and minister exchanging pulpits on a given Sunday morning.

For these younger Catholics, the alternatives are unthinkable: religious leaders not on speaking terms; one group of Christians completely closed off from another, and so forth.

On the other hand, many of these younger Catholics have little or no sense of history. They don't know what the fuss is all about not only because they are more instinctively democratic and humanistic but also because they don't know and appreciate the distinctiveness of the various Christian traditions, including their own.

Therefore, they are inclined to settle delicate ecumenical matters quickly, in one wave of the hand. There are no fundamental problems of theology and doctrine, only of human communication and public relations.

3. Finally, the so-called grass-roots Catholic remains essentially in the dark about matters ecumenical. Ecumenism remains, as Avery Dulles once suggested, too much the exclusive concern of specialists and too little the real concern of everyday Christians.

To be sure, many of the rank and file are aware of basic changes in Catholic-Protestant relations: ministers performing marriages that include a Catholic, Protestants being buried in Catholic cemeteries, priests preaching from Protestant pulpits, popes embracing archbishops of Canterbury, Catholic bishops appearing on TV in the company of Protestant bishops and chief rabbis, and so on.

But that general awareness is still untranslated into solid theological reasoning. Why these changes? How account for this new atmosphere? What is likely to happen in the future? What principles will, and should, govern later developments?

Full-time ecumenists have their work cut out for them.

Convergence of the Churches

(January 19, 1979)

Every year the Week of Prayer for Christian Unity provides an opportunity to take stock of the ecumenical movement.

As one reviews the recent consensus statements produced by the various bilateral consultations, it becomes increasingly obvious that the areas of doctrinal and theological difference are shrinking.

No matter what issue the several dialogue groups confront—papacy, ordained priesthood, the Eucharist, spirituality, the mission of the Church—points of agreement far outnumber points of disagreement.

The Anglican–Roman Catholic "Agreed Statement on the Purpose of the Church" (October 1975) reports a "remarkable convergence" on such questions as the origin and mission of the Church.

We are also agreed, the statement acknowledges, in our faith in the Lordship of Jesus, in our profession of the ancient creeds and the one baptism, in our acceptance of God's Word in Sacred Scripture, in our reverence for the Fathers and ancient councils, and in our structures of worship and episcopal succession.

In December 1977 the same Anglican–Roman Catholic consultation released a statement reviewing the progress of the dialogue from the beginning, some 13 years ago. What emerges is "a significant and substantial unity of faith between the two churches, a unity which demands visible expression and testimony now."

Indeed, Anglicans and Roman Catholics share so much in common and so profound is the measure of the unity already achieved, the consultation concludes, that the two churches can even now regard themselves in fact as "sister-churches" in the one communion that is the Church of Christ.

In 1974 the Roman Catholic–Disciples of Christ dialogue published "An Adventure in Understanding" in which the participants admitted that six years earlier when the consultation was inaugurated, neither side approached the other with a great sense of promise or excitement.

On the surface at least, the two traditions seemed to have very little in common. "But we were wrong," the declaration begins. "One thing we know. Wherever the future may lead us we can never think of one another in the same way we did in the past. . . . We know we are brothers in Christ."

The rest of the statement lists a number of points of basic agreement on such major topics as the unity of the Church, the Eucharist, the sacrament of marriage, and the ministry.

The Lutheran-Catholic dialogue has addressed itself directly to the most sensitive of ecumenical questions: papal primacy, papal infallibility, and the place of Mary in the Bible and in Christian life.

The consensus statement on the primacy (March 1974) is perhaps the most exciting because it represented the first time that one of the historic Protestant churches acknowledged the importance of the Petrine ministry as an instrument of unity in the universal Church, and the appropriateness of the pope's exercising such a ministry.

The ecumenical record, however, is not without its disappointing side. The Orthodox-Catholic dialogue has consistently produced guarded statements of relatively thin theological substance (in comparison with the Lutheran-Catholic consultation, for example). Its "Agreed Statement on the Church" (December 1974) insists that "our two traditions are not easily harmonized."

Granting the principle that no two traditions within the Body of Christ are "easily harmonized," it remains an arrestingly cautious judgment in view of the great areas of doctrinal and liturgical overlap between Catholic and Orthodox Christians, and also in the light of the extraordinary progress reached in some of the other dialogue groups.

A second reason for restraining our ecumenical enthusiasm is the continued reluctance of the Catholic Church's pastoral leadership to implement some of the more significant recommendations of the various consultations.

We still do not have officially approved intercommunion, even under the most controlled pastoral circumstances (for example, at the end of the Week of Prayer for Christian Unity).

We still have conferred no formal recognition upon the ordained ministry of any other church.

And at the so-called grass-roots level, ecumenism still does not perceptibly influence the worship, religious education, or social action of the average parish.

This is not to say that there has been a regression or that ecumenical relations, where they exist, are not in generally excellent condition. But progress is at once limited and selective.

Roman Catholics and Lutherans on Question of Infallibility
(March 2, 1979)

The long-awaited statement on the Lutheran-Catholic dialogue on papal infallibility is now in hand. It follows by almost five years the extraordinary Lutheran-Catholic declaration on the primacy.

In that earlier document, fundamental agreement was reached on such points as these:

1. The unity Christ wills for the Church must be manifest as well as spiritual.

2. A special responsibility for the unity of all Christians may be entrusted to one individual Minister, under the gospel.

3. Such a responsibility for the universal Church cannot be ruled out on the basis of the biblical evidence.

4. The bishop of Rome can in the future function in ways better adapted to meet the universal and regional needs of the Church.

This latest consensus statement from the Lutheran-Catholic dialogue, however, is not likely to have as much journalistic impact as its predecessor. The question of papal infallibility is by now a murky one, and the document, "Teaching Authority and Infallibility in the Church," reflects that.

Significantly, both sides admit they cannot readily show how and where they continue to disagree on the issue.

"We have found it increasingly difficult," the Catholic participants acknowledge, "to specify the exact point at which, in fidelity to our respective traditions, we are bound to disagree."

The Lutherans say almost the same thing. In the light of growing agreement on the centrality of the gospel and of trust in God and in the divine promises, "we often find it difficult to pinpoint exactly where or how we differ from each other on the question of infallibility."

In my judgment, those are two of the most important sentences in the whole text. Although much biblical, historical, theological, and doctrinal ground is covered in the course of a relatively lengthy statement, one is at a loss to find much of substance remaining on the field of controversy.

Both sides agree that Jesus Christ is the one Lord of the Church, that the Word of God in Sacred Scripture is normative for all proclamation and teaching, that the apostolic tradition is transmitted and interpreted in many different ways, that the Church will remain until the end of time (indefectibility), that its continuance is insured by, among other things, Ministries that attend to correct doctrine, that such Ministries might include a Ministry to the universal Church, that such a Ministry to the universal Church (obviously the papacy) is legitimately concerned with the formulation and reformulation of doctrine, and that the harmony between the teaching of the Ministers and its acceptance by the faithful constitutes a sign of the fidelity of that teaching to the gospel.

And all of this must be viewed in light of the fundamental theological principle that no human language ever succeeds in exhausting the diversity and richness of the gospel, and, therefore, no doctrinal definition can adequately address every historical or cultural situation.

The problem from the Catholic side, it seems to me, is that when we finish saying what papal infallibility is *not,* the other side (in this case the Lutherans) legitimately wonders what it is, in fact, that we were affirming in the first place.

Infallibility, we insist, is not limited to the pope, nor is it a personal prerogative of the pope. More important, infallibility is not independent of the consent of the faithful, which can never be lacking (a point made at Vatican I itself).

Infallibility does not cover all questions or even all religious questions. Nothing can be subject to an infallible declaration unless it pertains directly to the gospel.

Infallibility is not engaged unless it is clearly and unequivocally invoked. When in doubt about the infallible character of a teaching, one can be sure that it is *not* infallible.

But perhaps the most interesting negative of all is the admission that the Catholic Church doesn't even have an agreed-upon list of infallible statements.

I do not wish to suggest here that the infallibility statement falls under the category of "much ado about nothing." On the contrary, it is a sophisticated document with some very useful material on matters directly related to the infallibility question: the authority of the gospel, the indefectibility of the Church, and so on.

But when all is said and done, each side has to admit that it is no longer clear about where and how it differs from the other side.

And that, I suggest, says more about the topic than it does about the cordial state of ecumenical relations.

Ecumenism Between West and East

(September 2, 1983)

I think it a fair assumption that the vast majority of Latin-rite Catholics know practically nothing at all about their brothers and sisters of the Christian East, whether Orthodox, Oriental, or those Eastern churches in union with Rome.

The blame perhaps is not to be placed entirely on the Latins. Eastern Christian communities, even within North America, tend to cultivate their special identity and traditions in a way that does not encourage very much dialogue and interaction with others.

There are, for example, about as many Jews in the United States as there are Eastern Orthodox Christians, but the social, political, and even religious impact of the one group far exceeds that of the other.

Latin-rite Catholics tend to know much more about Jews than they do about their Eastern Christian brethren.

When the Latin-rite Catholics talk about ecumenism, they think of relations with Protestants and Anglicans, not Eastern Orthodox or Orientals.

Fortunately, that situation is changing. A major factor was the personal meeting in 1967 between Pope Paul VI and Patriarch Athenagoras in Jerusalem, where they embraced and sat side by side.

Eastern Christians, who are more sensitive to symbolic gestures than many Western Christians, were astonished by the pope's action. Here was the patriarch of the West coming to pay his respect to a revered Orthodox patriarch, on the Orthodox patriarch's own ground.

Eight years later Pope Paul VI received a mission from the patriarch of Constantinople in the Sistine Chapel. Suddenly the Holy Father knelt down before Metropolitan Melitone and kissed his feet. Taken completely by surprise, the Orthodox metropolitan tried to reciprocate, but the pope restrained him.

A few days later the patriarch of Constantinople, Dimitrios I, declared, "The Pope has proved to the Church and to the whole world that he is what he should be: a Christian bishop and above all the first bishop of Christendom, the Bishop of Rome, that is, a reconciling and unifying bridge between the Church and the world."

Pope John Paul II has continued to build bridges between East and West. He has traveled to Turkey to meet and pray with Orthodox leaders and in many public statements has repeatedly highlighted spiritual and doctrinal values that are held in common by both traditions.

It was especially evident during his recent visit to Poland that Pope John Paul II perceives a spiritual awakening in the East, even in the communist-dominated nations. He is making every effort to tap into this spiritual wellspring and to foster its growth.

But, of course, the groundwork for reconciliation between East and West had already been prepared by the Second Vatican Council. Several ecclesiological themes, so central to the Eastern traditions, were developed that put the Latin Church on a convergence course with the Eastern Orthodox and Orientals.

First, there was a renewed emphasis on the sacramentality of the Church. The Body of Christ is not simply a well-knit hierarchical organization, with carefully defined levels of authority, a Code of Canon Law, and so forth. It is, first and foremost, a mystery or sacrament, "a reality imbued with the hidden presence of God" (as Pope Paul VI had put it).

Second, the council accentuated the eschatological dimension of the Church. The Church is a community that, through the Eucharist, becomes an anticipatory experience of the Kingdom of God. We are somehow drawn up from the earth to heaven.

Third, the Church is a college of local churches. Each local church, under its bishop, is the Body of Christ in that particular place. The local church is not merely an administrative subdivision of the universal Church.

Fourth, the authority of church teachings is contingent also upon the way in which those teachings are received by the Church at large. The faith of the whole Church, rooted in the Holy Spirit, is the criterion of truth.

Fifth, the Petrine ministry is to be exercised not in a dominative fashion but in the mode of a servant. The example of Pope John XXIII and Pope Paul VI were effective cases in point for the Orthodox.

Finally, the council affirmed that Mary—so intensely revered in the East—is the Mother of the Church.

We've all noticed that Catholics and Protestants have come so much closer together since Vatican II. What we may not have noticed—the shift in relations between East and West—is just as significant a development.

"Fundamentalism"—A New Phenomenon

(May 1, 1987)

The April 11 issue of *America* presents an exceedingly important article, "The Rise of Catholic Fundamentalism," by Fr. Patrick M. Arnold, S.J., assistant professor of religious studies at St. Louis University.

The essay deserves a very wide readership—one that should include every member of the U.S. Catholic hierarchy.

Father Arnold argues that the recent outbreak of tensions between the Vatican and the Catholic Church in the United States (Curran, Hunthausen, et al.) must not be reduced to a matter of power politics or regarded simply as a replay of the ancient conflict between the desire for freedom and the need for order.

"A crisis as widespread as that facing the American church," he writes, "cannot be triggered simply by a few radical professors or powerful Vatican bureaucrats. The causes are rooted far more deeply in popular anxieties and social turmoil."

According to Father Arnold, "The single greatest force that precipitated the current crisis is related to the worldwide socioreligious phenomenon known as fundamentalism."

He is careful, however, to distinguish fundamentalism from conservatism. The latter he describes broadly as "a philosophy that values established, traditional ideas and practices, and seeks to preserve a given community's historical heritage—especially in times of cultural change."

Conservatism protects the Church from modern ideas and practices that are "merely trendy," and it defends and preserves the Church's "lived experience against purely rational or emotional changes." As such, it is a necessary and constructive force within the Church, the occasional excesses of conservatives notwithstanding.

Fundamentalism, on the other hand, is neither necessary nor constructive. Nevertheless, it is "a historically recurring tendency within Judeo-Christian-Muslim religious traditions that regularly erupts in reaction to cultural change."

Psychological studies describe fundamentalists of all traditions as "authoritarian personalities." They are individuals "who feel threatened in a world of conspiring evil forces, who think in simplistic and stereotypical terms and who are attracted to authoritarian and moralistic answers to their problems."

Religious fundamentalists include among their numbers Muslim Shiites, ultraorthodox (*haredim*) and orthodox (*hasidim*) Jews, Bible-belt Protestants, and increasingly, in the last few years, Catholic traditionalists.

Father Arnold identifies at least five unhealthy characteristics of religious fundamentalism in general and of Catholic fundamentalism in particular.

1. Fundamentalism is marked by paranoia and self-righteousness. There is always some terrible enemy "out there" (the U.S.A. is the "Great Satan" for the Muslim extremists; "secular humanism" for Protestant fundamentalists; modern technology and secularization for the Jewish *haredim;* modernism, secular humanism, and Marxism for Catholics). The fundamentalist alone is pure. The fundamentalist alone is faithful.

2. Fundamentalism is marked by fear and rage that are directed not at the perceived enemy "out there" but at coreligionists inside, including bishops, nuns, and theologians.

Father Arnold calls this perhaps "the most revealing and dangerous characteristic" of all, because it leads fundamentalists to divisive activities. They spend an inordinate amount of time and energy trying to purge people, to get them fired, to destroy their reputations and, therefore, their influence.

3. Fundamentalists are captivated by the "myth of the Golden Age." They believe in "an imaginary past edited of its own actual terrors." For Catholic fundamentalists, Catholicism achieved "its final, immutable form in the glorious decades before Vatican II."

4. Fundamentalism roots all truth in a single source: for Muslims, it is the Koran; for Jews, the Torah; for Protestants, the Bible; for Catholic fundamentalists, the pronouncements of the Roman magisterium (pope and Curia).

In principle, every teaching from the Vatican is to be obeyed absolutely. In practice, of course, these fundamentalists pick and choose. Pronouncements on sexuality, for example, are welcomed; pronouncements on social justice are ignored or "interpreted" away.

5. Fundamentalists almost always link themselves with right-wing political regimes and movements in the hope of advancing their own theocratic policies.

Thus, Pope John Paul II, who is not a fundamentalist, criticizes the Pinochet government of Chile for its "dictatorial" policies, while Protestant televangelist Jimmy Swaggart calls General Pinochet "one of the world's great freedom fighters." Fundamentalists apparently have never met a right-wing government or politician they didn't like.

Not surprisingly, Catholic fundamentalists are unenthusiastic about Catholic social teachings. These Catholics do everything they can to divert attention from those teachings by focusing instead on "dissent," violations of traditional religious rules, homosexuality, and the like.

They are not preoccupied with the central tenets of the Bible, the Creed, or defined Catholic dogmas, Father Arnold insists. On the contrary, they tend to harp on relatively subordinate issues as if they were primary.

They rarely mention Jesus Christ or the kind of moral issues that evidently most concerned him: greed, religious hypocrisy, or the misuse of authority.

"Their real concerns actually betray the theological and spiritual superficiality of the movement," Father Arnold concludes.

Different Views of "Church" Lead to Tension
(May 20, 1988)

It had, for a very long time, been taken for granted that Catholics and Protestants did not view the Church in quite the same way.

Catholics have regarded the Church as a supernatural reality, and object of faith in itself. Protestants have seen it primarily as a community, "the congregation of saints wherein the gospel is rightly preached and sacraments rightly administered."

Catholics have taught that the Church mediates salvation through sacraments, saints, and ordained ministries (pope, bishops, priests). Protestants, always wary of the ways of mediation, have looked upon the Church as simply a special place where the individual believer can gain direct access to God through the preached Word.

As ecumenical contacts between Catholics and Protestants increased in recent decades, thanks especially to Pope John XXIII and the Second Vatican Council, these simplistic contrasts had to be revised. The differences were no longer seen to be so sharp and unnuanced.

Catholics came to realize that Protestantism was more diverse and pluralistic than they had thought. There were Protestants—and there were Protestants.

And more than that: Catholics also came to the realization that they themselves were more diverse and pluralistic than they had imagined.

Not all Catholics think alike. And this isn't only a matter of individual Catholics entertaining unorthodox or idiosyncratic views.

We recognize that there are actually different schools of theology. Catholics differ not simply on this point or that but in the way they fundamentally view sacred realities, including the Church.

And this is how it has been for much of the history of the Church. St. Bonaventure's way of doing theology, for example, was not that of St. Thomas Aquinas.

Bonaventure distrusted the capacity of human reason; Aquinas celebrated it. Bonaventure, in the tradition of Augustine, emphasized the universality of sin; Aquinas stressed the universality of grace.

A similar contrast could be drawn today. There is the school of Hans Urs von Balthasar, following in Bonaventure's line, and that of the late Karl Rahner, in Aquinas's line.

The one emphasizes the discontinuity between nature and grace, between human wisdom and mystical illumination, and between human effort and divine initiative; the other, the continuity.

The current tension between the Vatican and large numbers of Catholic theologians cannot be understood apart from these divergences.

Cardinal Ratzinger is a theologian in the tradition of Bonaventure and Urs von Balthasar. Most Catholic theologians have been shaped by Aquinas and Rahner.

Their differences are especially apparent on the question of the Church and its place in the world.

There are Catholics (Cardinal Ratzinger among them) who view the nature and mission of the Church primarily, if not exclusively, through the prism of the third chapter of the council's Dogmatic Constitution on the Church, *Lumen Gentium*.

There are other Catholics (many bishops, pastors, theologians, and ministers of every kind) who view the Church primarily through the prism of the council's Pastoral Constitution on the Church in the Modern World, *Gaudium et Spes*.

Chapter III of *Lumen Gentium* is entitled, "The Hierarchical Structure of the Church." It assumes that Christ left behind an ecclesiastical blueprint by which the Church was to organize itself, complete with a pope, bishops, priests, and deacons.

It is a chapter preoccupied with questions of authority, magisterium, infallibility, and the obligation to submit and assent to official teaching. Nowhere is this more forcefully set forth than in article 25 of the Dogmatic Constitution—one of the conservative Catholic's favorite conciliar passages.

The Pastoral Constitution (*Gaudium et Spes*), by contrast, speaks of a Church in the world and in the service of the world.

The Church does not turn only to the magisterium to determine what it is that God is calling us to be and to do. The Church also reads the "signs of the times" and tries to interpret them in the light of the gospel.

Gaudium et Spes sees the world not as something racing headlong into sin and perdition but as a historical reality, enlivened by the presence of the Spirit, in process toward its final destiny, the Kingdom of God, when all the fruits of human endeavor will be transformed and brought to their full flowering.

Where the Bonaventures and the von Balthasars are skeptical of human effort and of human history, the Pastoral Constitution is affirming and hopeful. The very words *gaudium et spes* mean "joy and hope."

Embracing Catholicism for the Wrong Reasons
(August 10, 1990)

Convert making was a flourishing ministry back in the 1940s and 1950s, when it was simply taken for granted that the Catholic Church alone was the "one, true Church" of Christ and that all other Christian denominations (we wouldn't call them churches in those days) were false religions.

The principal difference between Catholics and Protestants, we assumed, was that Catholics had the truth, taught with certitude by the pope and the hierarchy, as well as the divinely guaranteed means of grace, known as the sacraments, while the Protestants had to rely upon an error-prone private interpretation of the Bible and the weak power of their own devotional fervor.

Thus, when Catholics confessed their sins to a priest and received absolution, they were certain of God's forgiveness because of the Sacrament of Penance. Protestants, on the other hand, might bruise their knees in prolonged prayer and drench their faces with tears of sorrow and still not be sure that God had forgiven them.

We look back upon that mentality not in anger or disgust but with understanding and perhaps not a little amusement. It was a different time, with a different mentality.

We Catholics followed the light as we saw it then. Today we see things differently because the light both of human experience and of scholarship has been cast more brightly and more broadly.

Thus, the Second Vatican Council's Decree on Ecumenism officially acknowledged that the separation between Catholics and Protestants at the time of the Reformation was the fault of people on both sides (n. 3).

All Christians, Protestants as well as Catholics, are united in "a certain, though imperfect, communion," because "all those justified by faith through baptism are incorporated into Christ. They therefore have a right to be honored by the title of Christian, and are properly regarded as brothers [and sisters] in the Lord by the sons [and daughters] of the Catholic Church."

Catholics and non-Catholic Christians share, in addition to baptism, "the written word of God, the life of grace, faith, hope and charity, along with other interior gifts of the Holy Spirit and visible elements."

The churches to which these non-Catholics belong "have by no means been deprived of significance and importance in the mystery of salvation." In fact, "the Spirit of Christ" uses them as "means of salvation."

Without denying that the Catholic Church itself possesses "the fullness of the means of salvation," the council's Decree on Ecumenism conceded that the

Catholic Church as well as these other non-Catholic churches is called to the path of reform and renewal (n. 6), indeed to a change of heart, or conversion (n. 7).

The council endorsed common worship and common prayer under certain circumstances (n. 8) as well as an ecumenical approach to the study of theology and doctrine (n. 10).

It also warned against putting all of the Church's teachings and disciplines on an equal footing. "When comparing doctrines, [theologians] should remember that in Catholic teaching there exists an order of 'hierarchy' of truths, since they vary in their relationship to the foundation of the Christian faith" (n. 11).

Why, then, would a non-Catholic become a Catholic today?

Not for the reason one recent letter writer shared with me. "Among the many qualities of the Church that led to my conversion [13 years ago] was its hierarchy and authority.

"Here at last, as opposed to the Protestant churches in which I was raised," he continued, "was a Church that very specifically proclaimed its beliefs, had an organization to implement and defend those beliefs, and claimed no less an authority than God Himself to be the author of those beliefs."

A perfect answer for the 1950s, but one not tenable in the 1990s.

If a non-Catholic is attracted to the Catholic Church today, it should not be because of "the morass of Protestantism's solipsism" (to use my correspondent's polemical words) or the perceived "centralized, authoritarian, hierarchical" nature of Catholicism.

Given the sacramental nature of the Church ("a reality imbued with the hidden presence of God"—Pope Paul VI), one should be attracted, first of all, to the Catholic people in whom God is present and active. One should want to become part of this particular community of Christian faith.

One should be attracted especially to the Church's Eucharist, its commitment to justice and human rights, its ministry to the poor, the elderly, and those persons with disabilities, its respect and reverence for conscience, and especially its sacramental vision of reality, by which it sees God in all things and, therefore, sees all reality—sin notwithstanding—as fundamentally good and holy.

The Catholic Church should welcome new members. Indeed, it should rejoice when others are attracted to the Catholic family, but it should never encourage them to come in for the wrong reasons.

Protestantism's deficiencies or a lust for certitude are wrong reasons.

10

Personalities

Introduction

The Catholic Church is not primarily an institution or an organization; it is people. Indeed, the council referred to the Church as the People of God.

The story of postconciliar Catholicism, therefore, is also the story of significant individuals who have left their mark on the Church and the world alike, for good or for ill.

In 1966 a well-known English theologian, Fr. Charles Davis, stunned his fellow Catholics by announcing his decision to leave the Church and to marry. The Church was moving too slowly, he felt, in implementing the mandate of the council.

One is led inescapably to the judgment that Charles Davis's action was premature. It came less than a year after the council's adjournment and almost two full years before the issuance of Pope Paul VI's birth-control encyclical, *Humanae Vitae*. Nevertheless, Davis's departure from the Church was a turning point in postconciliar Catholicism. It signaled a new spirit of criticism in the Church, a new sense of impatience with the pace of change, and a new experience of priests leaving the ministry to marry.

The other personalities treated in this chapter include John Courtney Murray, S.J., the architect of the council's Declaration on Religious Freedom and the first prominent U.S. Catholic theologian to suffer Vatican disfavor; Boston's Card. Richard Cushing, one of the great populist bishops of the pre- and postconciliar eras; Yves Congar, O.P., the century's most distinguished ecclesiologist and a leading force in shaping the council's teachings on the Church; Karl Rahner, S.J., the single most influential Catholic theologian in the postconciliar period; New York's Card. Francis Spellman, whose death in 1967 marked the end of the preconciliar era in America; Card. Joseph Ratzinger, head of the Vatican's watchdog Congregation for the Doctrine of the Faith; Theodore M. Hesburgh, C.S.C., former president of the University of Notre Dame; Archbp. Raymond Hunthausen, of Seattle, Washington, the first major U.S. bishop to feel the Vatican's lash; and Fr. Charles Curran, who lost his faculty position at The Catholic University of America for taking stands at odds with certain official teachings of the Church on matters of sexual morality.

The major personalities who are obvious by their absence are the popes of this period. They are included separately in the next chapter.

Father Davis's Decision

(December 30, 1966)

This week's essay proposes to consider some of the theological implications of Fr. Charles Davis's recent decision to leave the Catholic Church and to see how this event might be one of the "signs of the times" in this postconciliar era.

This essay is clearly not written to calm troubled waters or to reassure the shaken and the upset. Surely nothing can dilute the distressing and disheartening impact of Father Davis's decision. The Church has lost an exceptionally gifted member. We shall always remain indebted to this English theologian for his many lucid writings and lectures. They have not become any less valuable (or any less orthodox) because of his departure from the Catholic community.

Father Davis was not himself the source of creative currents in contemporary Catholic theology. His work was principally in the area of popularization, and at that he excelled. (His collections of essays, *Liturgy and Doctrine* and *Theology for Today,* are splendid samples of his work.) But he was not in the category of Karl Rahner, S.J., Yves Congar, O.P., or Edward Schillebeeckx, O.P. Father Davis was not a chief participant or a notable influence at the recent council, nor was there any "school" of theologians around him. Nevertheless, the many nonprofessional theologians (seminarians, religious, catechists, priests, et al.) who have profited from his writings and lectures must be in the thousands.

It should be pointed out, first of all, that Father Davis has broken with the institutional Church but not with the Christian faith. Sometimes we speak, perhaps too glibly, about "receiving the gift of faith" or "losing the faith," as if it were a kind of material commodity to be won or lost indiscriminately—or at the whim of God.

Faith is not an ideological thing (although its objective, intellectual aspect cannot be denied). Faith is a commitment of the whole person; it is an orientation, a fundamental way of looking at life and all history. Christian faith means that we accept Christ as the Lord of history and of our own lives, that life and history make no sense apart from him.

What must be emphasized in the light of Father Davis's decision is that Christian faith is not tied *necessarily* to membership in the Christian community. It is theologically possible, in other words, to accept the Lordship of Christ—explicitly or implicitly—without affiliating oneself with the Church. (Indeed, this is how the majority of mankind attains salvation.) And, similarly, it is theologically possible to sever one's relationship with the Church without *necessarily* surrendering one's faith. This is said without prejudice to the Catholic conviction that the fullness of Christian faith is realized and visibly expressed in that sector of the Christian community that is founded on the college of bishops with the successors of St. Peter as its head and heart.

Undoubtedly there is some change in the faith commitment of one who leaves the Church, but this change is one of specification, and not necessarily one of substance. If it were a question of substance (i.e., of the essence of faith), then we should have to conclude that the faith of non-Catholics is illusory. But Catholic theology does not teach this, and the documents of the Second Vatican Council (see the Decree on Ecumenism, in particular) actually point in the opposite direction.

The Christian faith of a Catholic differs from that of a Presbyterian, for example, in specific aspects. The Presbyterian would not agree that the fullness of Christian faith cannot be realized apart from visible communion with the college of bishops and the pope. This is an important difference, to be sure, but it does not strike at the very essence of Christian faith; it is not something, in other words, that would distinguish a Christian from a non-Christian. In point of fact, the Catholic and the Presbyterian agree in the essentials of faith: both confess that Jesus is Lord; both share a common baptism; both share a common reverence for Sacred Scripture; for both, the source and root of the Christian life is in the spirit and idealism of the gospel.

It would be more comfortable, of course, for all of us if Father Davis's decision could be dismissed as a simple, classic case of "loss of faith," something that can happen to any one of us, at any time. A more attractive alternative might be to suggest that Father Davis's motives are not theological at all, that his announced marriage is at the root of the problem. (No doubt this latter factor opens something of a credibility gap, but questioning motives and integrity is risky business.)

The departure of Father Davis is no ordinary happening in the life of the Church, and it cannot be dismissed so abruptly or so cynically. On the contrary, it might very well be a "sign of the times," which we ignore at our own peril. For we might now be entering a period in the history of the Church when this will become a more common occurrence, when Christians (from both left and right, reformers and traditionalists) will feel compelled to leave the community because it no longer reflects their own vision of the gospel.

People of a reformist temperament, such as Father Davis, will leave in protest against the lack of "concern for truth and concern for persons" in the institutional Church. Catholics on the right, such as Father DePauw, will continue to be horror-stricken at the sight and direction of the postconciliar Church, and they, too, may decide that their vocation is elsewhere. In some cases such a decision to leave the community will not be an entirely unfortunate event, for there are surely some in the Church today who do not really accept the gospel of Christ. (As St. Augustine once wrote: "Many whom God has, the Church does not have; and many whom the Church has, God does not have.")

But incidents such as that involving Father Davis will always be a source of discouragement, even for the stout of faith. Father Davis's many writings are evidence enough of his firm commitment to the Christian perspective of the Second Vatican Council, and there is nothing in his most recent work that would tend to blur this impression. If anything, he tended to be somewhat conservative in many of his views. What was it, therefore, in his own recent experiences in England (and, perhaps more important, in the experiences of the many laypeople with whom he dealt) that seemed for him and for them to obstruct, thwart, and contradict the spirit and vitality of the Church of Vatican II?

We must now be prepared to ask ourselves some sharp-edged questions and to answer them with ruthless honesty. Is the Church of Vatican II a product of rhetoric, or reality? Do we really intend that the Christian community be reformed and renewed—at every level—according to the uncompromising dictates of the gospel?

Father Davis's decision, however differently we may wish to interpret it, provides at least one clear message: the time for delay and half-hearted gestures is quickly drawing to a close. The Second Vatican Council held out many promises. The turmoil in the American civil rights movement today should serve as a sobering reminder that unfulfilled promises, liberally dressed with liberal rhetoric, will unleash forces of angry cynicism—destructive and divisive forces.

But the Church's mission is to bind wounds, to heal, to unify, to gather together. The Church must stand before men as the perennial presence of the Good Samaritan and the Suffering Servant of God. Promise and fulfillment must somehow be joined.

Cardinal Cushing Had Accurate Instincts on Theological Questions

(November 27, 1970)

A redwood fell among shrubs when Richard Cardinal Cushing died in Boston earlier this month.

Many lines, articles, and books have been written about the man these last few years. To my knowledge, he liked almost none of them. He insisted, in fact, that no one really understood him, except the late Pope John XXIII.

Cardinal Cushing was a man beyond the range of usual ideological categorization. There were party-line conservatives and party-line liberals who thought he was one of them, until he said or did something to confound and even infuriate them.

A few years ago the *National Catholic Reporter* drew up two lists of contemporary Catholics: the 10 most "knockable" and the 10 least "knockable." Cardinal Cushing was the only name to appear on both lists.

The man indeed was a supreme enigma, and any attempt to understand him or to capture the essence of his life in some neat, prepackaged formula is doomed to failure from the start.

The best we can say about him is that his instincts were right because they were Christian, and that is what must count in the longest of the long runs. He wanted to help people at all costs. On occasion, when weakened by the terrible sickness that afflicted him for so long, he contradicted his best instincts, and there are many people still living who knew him only in those unfortunate moments.

But there are others who knew him at his best: as a warmhearted Christian, a keen and compassionate mind, a source of strength and encouragement, and a loyal friend.

Richard Cardinal Cushing was fond of telling people how little theology he knew. He once said that he wasn't smart enough to lose his faith or become a heretic.

This was not a matter of false modesty on his part. So many people say such things when they are really fishing for reassuring compliments and accolades. He was acutely aware of his limitations, but he vastly underestimated his intellectual strengths.

Theologically his instincts were remarkably accurate. It has been said so many times by now, of course, but it bears repetition here: He was an ecumenist long before most of us could spell the word. He walked with Protestants, Orthodox, Anglicans, Jews, Masons, and others long before we heard of Pope John XXIII or Vatican II.

He was an antitriumphalist long before Bishop deSmedt made his famous council speech on the subject. He practiced the theology of the Servant Church long before the concept became popular among Catholics. He was collegial in outlook vis-à-vis the Church universal long before the historic debates on the question at Vatican II.

The conciliar teaching on the Jews in the Declaration on the Relationship of the Church to Non-Christian Religions did not require of him a shifting of theological or pastoral gears. He was long since ahead of that document in word and in practice.

The conciliar teaching on religious liberty in the Declaration on Religious Freedom did not call for fast and agile footwork on his part. He was long since ahead of that document, too, and it was no surprise that he should have been the one to make the case—successfully—for its passage at the council itself.

Cardinal Cushing was a man of such deep faith that theological dissent could not disturb him. Indeed, he seemed to welcome it at times. Furthermore, he respected too much the competence of others to cut short, or in any way obstruct, their work.

He was a man of openness and trust. If he erred, he preferred to err on the side of liberty rather than on the side of repression. The council's teaching was the platform and pattern of his whole life and ministry: "Let there be unity in what is necessary, freedom in what is unsettled, and charity in any case" (Pastoral Constitution on the Church in the Modern World, n. 92).

With Richard Cardinal Cushing there was, from the depths of his heart, "charity in any case." That charity, like the charity of his hero Pope John XXIII, will never die out. They have unleashed something which no man can stifle or contain. Thank God, and them, for that.

John Courtney Murray's Legacy
(July 16, 1976)

In this Bicentennial year no American Catholic theologian is more deserving of the respect and gratitude of his Church and of his peers than the late John Courtney Murray, S.J.

He addressed himself to the problem of American pluralism at a time when it was still risky to do so. Indeed, he was deliberately excluded from the list of *periti* (experts) invited to the first session of the Vatican Council in 1963.

Viewing the issue in the larger context of the relationship between church and state, he surgically dissected the traditional notions of religious liberty and political responsibility.

Against those who had been arguing that the state has an obligation to practice and enforce the one, true religion of Catholicism, Murray insisted that the public power is limited to the care of religious freedom. For Murray, the First Amendment was entirely consistent with the Catholic doctrine on the limitation of political authority.

Murray also appealed to the traditional principle of subsidiarity in his defense of voluntary associations within society. Higher groups are not to do what lower groups can do as well, if not better. Furthermore, the Church and the family are not derived from the state and therefore do no exist simply at its pleasure.

Public order, he also argued, must be subject to the common good. Law and morality can never be completely divorced. On the other hand, there cannot be a law for every vice (the old Connecticut and Massachusetts birth-control statutes were cases very much in point in Murray's time).

On the contrary, freedom and the common good usually require legislators to leave to the private sphere those vices that involve no disruption of the public order.

And yet the state is also the servant and instrument of the common good. It must promote liberty and justice for all. It must preserve the public order.

But since the state is both subject to and the servant of the common good, it cannot be the sole judge of what the common good is or is not.

Consequently there must always be consultation with the people, both through formal constitutional processes and through public opinion.

Although committed to both justice and liberty, Murray was more passionately devoted to the latter than to the former. At least that is the judgment of John A. Coleman, S.J., whose article in the March 1976 issue of *Theological Studies* provides a very helpful outline of Murray's thought and an equally sympathetic assessment of Murray's contributions.

It was Murray, after all, who had the greatest impact on the production of the Second Vatican Council's Declaration on Religious Freedom. And it was Murray who theologically and historically undermined the old thesis-hypothesis position on the issue of religious liberty (namely, that in the ideal order a Catholic state would have to suppress all non-Catholic forms of religious expression).

In his book *The Problem of Religious Freedom* (1965) he insisted that religious freedom is a necessary part of human freedom: the freedom to search for truth, the freedom of expression and dissemination of opinion, the freedom to cultivate the arts and sciences, free access to information about public events, and the freedom to develop one's talents and to grow in knowledge and culture.

His approach to the inevitable conflict between freedom and order is encapsulated in the following formula: Let there be as much freedom, both personal and social, as is possible; let there be only as much restraint and constraint, both personal and social, as may be necessary for the public order.

"Truth, justice, and love assure the stability of society," he wrote, "but freedom is the dynamism of social progress toward fuller humanity in communal living.

"Freedom," he continued, "is also the political method whereby the people achieve their highest good, which is their own unity as a people. . . . When the freedom of the people is unjustly limited, the social order itself, which is an order of freedom, is overthrown."

Although Murray did not often apply political theory to the Church itself, the implications of his thought for ecclesiology are reasonably clear.

Bicentennial tributes to the memory of John Courtney Murray are empty if they are not at the same time commitments to the human and religious freedom he so effectively defended.

Authority in Church and Karl Rahner
(April 27, 1984)

Catholics at opposite ends of the ecclesiastical spectrum tend to equate authority exclusively with office.

Those whose thinking about the Church is filtered through the prism of 19th- and early 20th-century neo-Scholastic theology assume that the only real authority in the Church is exercised by the hierarchy, and especially by the pope.

Since, for them, respect for authority is one of the hallmarks of Catholicism, any criticism of the pope and the bishops (but of the pope in particular) is always tantamount to a lapse from Catholic fidelity.

Others who see themselves as guardians of Christian authenticity and freedom and whose thinking about them is filtered through the prism of 19th- and early 20th-century liberal Protestant theology make the same equation of authority with office.

When they criticize or dissent from Church authority, it is the hierarchy they almost always have in mind. Indeed, they tend to identify "the Church" with "the hierarchy."

They seem not to have really assimilated Vatican II's teaching that the Church is the whole People of God and that the hierarchy is only a portion of the People of God.

Authority may not be easy to define, but one thing is certain; it is not linked exclusively with office.

The word *authority* is derived from the Latin *auctor* (author). Ultimately all authority is rooted in God, who is the Author of all that is.

"Let everyone obey the authorities that are over him," Paul wrote, "for there is no authority except from God, and all authority that exists is established by God" (Romans 13:1).

But such authority is of two kinds: *de jure* and *de facto*. *De jure* authority, that is, authority rooted in law, is attached to and springs from an office of one kind or another. *De facto* authority exists wherever "in fact" individuals influence the thinking and behavior of others.

Thus, a person who holds a high political office possesses *de jure* authority, but if he or she is not respected or taken seriously by the community, the office holder is without *de facto* authority.

On the other hand, a person may have the capacity to influence the thinking and behavior of hundreds, thousands, even millions of people and yet hold no official position at all. Such an individual would have enormous *de facto* authority but no *de jure* authority at all.

It should be obvious that *de facto* authority is, in the long run, more important than *de jure* authority. The ideal, to be sure, is that those who hold *de jure* authority should also possess *de facto* authority.

Which is to say that our official leaders ought to command respect, and not simply to command. People should want to follow their lead not because of what they are but because of who they are.

Since the Church is the whole People of God and since it is at the same time the Temple of the Holy Spirit, authority, that is, the capacity to influence the thinking and behavior of others, can be exercised by anyone who really lives by the Spirit and who, therefore, follows the gospel of Jesus Christ with integrity.

Such a one was Fr. Karl Rahner, S.J., the century's most important Catholic theologian, who died last month, a few weeks after his 80th birthday.

Catholics at both ends of the spectrum cannot really fathom the reality that was Karl Rahner. He was neither pope nor bishop, and yet he was surely one of the most authoritative Catholics in the entire century.

One can think of one, and possibly two, hierarchical figures who influenced the thinking and behavior of the Catholic Church over the past 100 years more than Father Rahner did. Pope John XXIII clearly holds first place, and history is likely to recognize the extraordinary achievements of Pope Paul VI more than some of his contemporaries have.

But beyond those two popes, no hierarchical figure has had a more profound effect on Catholic thought and life than the brilliant, self-effacing man of the Church, Karl Rahner, S.J.

May he rest in peace, and may distorted notions of authority rest with him.

Congar, Our Link to a Great Era
(April 12, 1985)

When two eminent Jesuit theologians, Karl Rahner and Bernard Lonergan, died last year, many assumed that the age of the theological giants had finally been closed, at least for this century.

Karl Barth, Rudolf Bultmann, Paul Tillich, Reinhold Niebuhr, Martin Buber—all are gone. It is sometimes remarked that those who remain—the Pannenbergs, the Moltmanns, the Schillebeeckxs's, the Küngs—are not of the same stature. We shall not see such giants again in our lifetimes.

The judgment may be substantially correct, but part of it is surely premature. The age of the giants may be in its final stage, but at least one imposing figure remains. He is Yves Congar, O.P.

By any reasonable standard of measurement, Father Congar is the most distinguished ecclesiologist of this century and probably since the close of the Council of Trent in the mid-16th century.

On April 13 Yves Congar celebrates his 81st birthday. Bedridden, wracked by pain, completely debilitated by illness, Father Congar's pen is as immobile now as are his limbs. But for as long as the Lord delays calling him home, we shall have a precious, living link with one of the most creative eras in the entire history of the Church.

At Vatican II no theologian's influence was greater than Congar's. And, at the same time, no theologian had suffered more in giving birth to so vast a corpus of writings: first as a prisoner of war in the 1940s, then as the object of constant surveillance and vilification by reactionary forces in the Curia, and finally on the cross of inexorable illness.

Since he began teaching and writing in 1930 he has produced some 1,500 books and articles, among them: *Divided Christendom* (1937), a groundbreaking work in ecumenism; *The Mystery of the Church* (1941); the magisterial article on "Theology" in the French-language *Dictionary of Catholic Theology* (1934); *True and False Reform in the Church* (1950), for which he was severely attacked by traditionalists; *Christ, Our Lady and the Church* (1952) *Lay People in the Church* (1957), which remains the major work on the subject; *The Mystery of the Temple* (1958); *Tradition and Traditions*, two volumes (1960, 1963)—all the way to his most recent, and undoubtedly his last, systematic effort, *I Believe in the Holy Spirit*, three volumes (1979, 1980).

It is almost impossible to exaggerate the impact Fr. Yves Congar has had on the self-understanding of the Catholic Church, on the ecumenical movement, and on Catholic ecclesiology generally. He towers above all other figures.

Congar has always been fond of saying that "everything begins with the seed." And so he never gave up, even when the sky was darkest, the thunder of criticism most deafening, and the results of his labors so seemingly meager.

In February of 1954 he was forbidden to teach and underwent an exile for several months in Jerusalem, Rome, and Cambridge, before being given a fixed assignment at Strasbourg from 1956 to 1958.

Those dark years were a time of "active patience," as Congar has described it. He did not sulk. He did not withdraw. He did not give up.

From this period came his *Christians in Dialogue, Mystery of the Temple,* and *Tradition and Traditions,* as well as many articles and conferences.

But then the council came. Vatican II was for Congar a time of spiritual and intellectual mobilization. At first, his role seemed modest, but he participated. Was it not "more true to be within and to work there than to criticize from without?" he asked.

Little by little he became more involved in the preparation of important texts, especially the Dogmatic Constitution on the Church, as well as the documents on revelation, the Church in the modern world, ecumenism, religious liberty, missions, and priesthood.

Until his illness finally made all manner of scholarly work impossible, Fr. Congar had been laboring 12 to 13 hours a day.

Last November he was given the Watson Prize for his valiant work in ecumenism. There was a celebration to mark the occasion at the Priory of St. Jacques in Paris, where he has resided these past several years.

His mood was characteristically honest and humble. He quoted Father Lacordaire: "What will remain in 100 years of what we have written? What is important is to have a life."

"I think that my life is rather mediocre," he continued. "But, too, it is not finished. I still have, at least in suffering, to unite myself to the chalice of Jesus (which is the unique chalice). . . . For the rest I really don't know."

He has come to understand that "whatever we have to tell and say, as sublime as it is, it is really not worth much unless it is accompanied by a praxis, by real action, by concrete service and love."

One hears much these days about how important it is for theologians to be saints and not just scholars. Yves Congar, O.P., is both.

Cardinal Spellman, His Minions, and Freedom

(April 18, 1986)

If Cardinal Spellman were alive today, what role would he be taking in the case of Fr. Charles Curran, professor of moral theology at The Catholic University of America?

Of course, Cardinal Spellman would have sided immediately with the Vatican, some would say. His Eminence was theologically very conservative, and at the same time fiercely loyal to the Holy See.

Correct on both counts. But he was also a staunchly patriotic American, and he had no patience with Vatican maneuverings that had even a trace of anti-Americanism.

He was also staunchly loyal to his own priests. When the apostolic delegate, Archbp. Egidio Vagnozzi, tried to suppress a new theological journal, the *Dunwoodie Review,* published at the New York archdiocesan seminary, under the supervision of Msgr. Myles Bourke, Cardinal Spellman resisted the delegate.

He resisted him again to save a new series of pamphlets on the Bible, published by the Paulist Press.

Cardinal Spellman had never demonstrated any particular penchant for progressive theological and biblical scholarship. But that wasn't the point. These were his priests, his seminary, and his seminarians.

He would have understood, and applauded, Father Curran's bishop, Matthew Clark, of Rochester, New York, for rising immediately and courageously to the defense of one of his own priests, even in a conflict with the Vatican.

Although Cardinal Spellman had shown no interest at all in the question of religious liberty in the earlier stages of the debate, it was he who led the charge at Vatican II against those forces who wanted to drop the subject from the agenda.

It was under his leadership that the U.S. Catholic bishops met at the North American College in Rome, at the beginning of the second session in September 1963, to discuss their course of action. It was a dramatic instance of collegiality in practice.

The bishops unanimously approved a memorandum, drafted by Fr. John Courtney Murray, S.J., demanding that the issue of religious liberty be considered and outlining the content of the proposed document.

The bishops then composed a letter, which Cardinal Spellman signed in the name of the hierarchy, and presented their petition to Cardinal Cicognani, the president of the Coordinating Commission of the council.

Cardinal Spellman also presented the petition personally to Pope Paul VI, who ordered that the Theological Commission consider the subject of religious liberty in its schema on ecumenism. (It eventually became a separate document.)

Had the U.S. Catholic bishops, under Cardinal Spellman, not mounted a united front against the anti–religious liberty bloc, the council might never have addressed the issue.

Indeed, the case of Father Murray himself further illuminates this unappreciated side of Cardinal Spellman.

Murray, like Curran, was a controversial theologian. In his writings on church-and-state and religious liberty, he staked out a position at variance with what was then the official teaching of the Church.

If the new Code of Canon Law had been in force in 1962, Father Murray probably would have had *his* canonical mandate withdrawn, because of his dissenting views.

But Murray was punished in other ways. He was forbidden to publish anything more on the subject and then was deliberately excluded from the list of *periti* for the first session of the council.

Enter, again, Cardinal Spellman. Although Murray had several important friends in the American hierarchy (he had been close to cardinals Mooney and Stritch, and archbishops Alter and McNicholas), no American bishop wanted to take the risk of appointing him a *peritus*.

Murray was at the time in severe disfavor with curial officials like Cardinal Ottaviani, head of the Holy Office and a predecessor of Cardinal Ratzinger.

It was Cardinal Spellman who, in the teeth of such opposition, named Murray a *peritus* for the second session.

And it was Cardinal Spellman who approved Murray's memorandum on religious liberty and who defended him later when the apostolic delegate reported Murray to his Jesuit superior for writing an article in *America* magazine in which he said that religious liberty was "*the* American issue at the Council."

In a letter to his superior, Father Murray noted that Cardinal Spellman had mentioned to him in Rome that he had read the article "and liked it."

On December 7, 1965, the council approved, by a vote of 2,308 to 70, the Declaration on Religious Freedom. John Courtney Murray's dissenting opinion became the Church's official teaching. The Holy Office, not the controversial theologian, found itself for the moment on the wrong side of orthodoxy.

There are several lessons and parallels to be drawn from all this, and Cardinal Spellman's role offers at least a few.

Cardinal Ratzinger's Talk Raises Questions

(July 11, 1986)

Cardinal Joseph Ratzinger, prefect of the Vatican Congregation for the Doctrine of the Faith, delivered a major address on April 15 at St. Michael's College, Toronto, on "The Church and the Theologian." (The full text is available in the May 8 issue of *Origins*.)

Because of the controversy currently surrounding Fr. Charles Curran, Cardinal Ratzinger's talk has more than ordinary importance. Indeed, the title of his talk is what the Curran case is all about.

Unfortunately, Cardinal Ratzinger's paper seems to raise more questions than it answers.

1. He says that it is "clear that theological teaching cannot exist unless church teaching exists."

Surely the cardinal does not mean to suggest that only Catholics can do theology. Theology is "faith seeking understanding" (St. Anselm). Protestants have "faith"; Jews have "faith"; Muslims have "faith."

Whenever individuals or communities (of whatever religious tradition) strive to achieve a greater understanding of their faith in God, they are doing theology—with or without "church teaching."

Furthermore, even *Catholic* theology existed before there was a single doctrinal formula "on the books"—indeed, centuries before there was a

"Denzinger" (a standard collection of doctrinal texts originally gathered together by a 19th-century German theologian).

"Church teaching" is an authoritative norm for theology, but it is also a *product* of theology. One could, in fact, turn Cardinal Ratzinger's statement around: "Church teaching cannot exist unless theology exists."

2. "The church is not, for theology, a demand extraneous or foreign to science, but rather the reason for its existence and the very condition for its possibility."

Again, one has to distinguish between *Catholic* theology and other kinds of theology.

But even for Catholic theology, the statement is not without ambiguity. How is Cardinal Ratzinger using the word *church* here? Does he mean "the hierarchy," or does he mean the whole People of God?

If the first, the statement is not true. If the second, the statement requires clarification.

To be sure, Catholic theology serves the community of faith by helping the community come to a greater understanding of its faith. It can never divorce itself from the life of the Church.

On the other hand, it is God, not the Church, that is "the very condition for [theology's] possibility." Theology, as St. Thomas Aquinas insisted, is a wisdom. God is its subject and its source.

In theology, "all things are treated of under the aspect of God, either because they are God Himself, or because they are ordered to God as their beginning and end" (*Summa Theologica,* I, q.1, a.7).

3. "There are those who say that the church has the pastoral task: It proclaims for the faithful, but does not teach for theologians."

Does "the church" mean "the hierarchy" here? Whatever its intended meaning, I know of no Catholic theologian who holds that official church teachings are not authoritative for every member of the Church, theologians included.

What is really at issue is the distinction between proclamation and teaching. Theologians *do* say that these two tasks, however closely related, are not the same.

Bishops are primarily *proclaimers* of the gospel. "Among the principal duties of bishops," Vatican II's Dogmatic Constitution on the Church declared, "the preaching of the gospel occupies an eminent place" (n. 25).

Bishops are teachers, too, but they have never been the only teachers in the Church. In the New Testament, bishops and teachers exercised distinct ministries (see 1 Corinthians 12:28).

When bishops do teach rather than proclaim, however, they are bound by the "rules" that apply to teaching. Teachers have to provide convincing arguments for their teaching and be open to questions, even challenges, from their "students." In that way, the teaching process itself advances knowledge and understanding.

4. "The church's main job is the care of the faith of the simple. A truly reverential awe should arise from this which becomes an internal rule of thumb for every theologian."

But who are "the simple"? Are *you* "simple"? And does the Church have no responsibility for "the care of the faith" of the educated and the intellectually gifted?

What happens if, in addressing "the simple," bishops and theologians put forward arguments that the un-simple find unconvincing or naive? Do we accuse them of "pride" and let it go at that?

And what, finally, *is* a theologian? An overdegreed catechist? If not, how precisely does a theologian differ from a catechist?

If the theologian's distinctive task is scientific and therefore critical, how can the theologian fulfill that task if the "internal rule of thumb" is always "the care of the faith of the simple"?

And who defines "the simple"?

Notre Dame's Exceptional Leader Retiring

(November 14, 1986)

The Notre Dame Board of Trustees will be announcing Fr. Theodore Hesburgh's successor on Friday, November 14—the day this column appears in many Catholic papers.

As I write these lines a few weeks in advance, I have no certain knowledge of the new president's identity, although I have a pretty good idea. But he's not the occasion of this week's essay; Father Hesburgh is.

This is no ordinary transition, because Theodore M. Hesburgh is no ordinary Catholic and no ordinary citizen, for that matter. He is a man of monumental stature, vision, and imagination.

Leadership fits him like a glove. He has an exceptional capacity to motivate people to do more than they think they can do, and an uncanny ability to make them feel as if they've accomplished even more than they have.

Unlike many others in important leadership positions, Father Ted (as he prefers to be called) knows how to say, "Great job!" He applauds achievement and gives credit where credit is due.

And he stands behind his people. When the going gets rough, he doesn't try to put distance between himself and difficult situations. He sticks by his decisions, unless and until it becomes clear he's made a mistake. And then he'll admit it, blaming no one else.

His list of friends reads like a "Who's Who" of the world. Almost every major public figure in the United States and abroad knows him, has worked with him, has consulted him professionally and sometimes even personally.

Some people think he name-drops. But that's like accusing Julia Child of talking too much about food or Johnny Carson of telling too many jokes or Pope John Paul II of saying too many prayers.

Father Hesburgh's world is populated with the mighty and the influential. His ideas and values have clout precisely because they are embraced and put into practice by people of political and intellectual substance. He's not their fan; he's their equal.

And yet, unlike the people he knows and deals with on an almost daily basis, his private world is one of extraordinary modesty and simplicity.

He himself enjoys pointing out, when people ask about his residence, that he lives over a dump. He does.

He has a pair of relatively small rooms, with a bath, in Corby Hall, where most of his fellow Holy Cross priests live. His suite is no bigger nor any more elaborate than any of the other priests'.

It's a little noisier, however, especially when the dump truck makes its early morning rounds just a couple of floors below.

When he came to Notre Dame as a student in 1934, he was given the campus laundry number 00652. More than 50 years later (35 of which have been as president), he still has the same number.

His work schedule makes his juniors wince. The lights in his office on the second floor of the Administration Building burn well into the early morning hours. How else would he answer immediately (that's "immediately") all the mail and internal memos he receives?

Indeed, he seems to have an insatiable appetite for reading material. Little escapes his gaze. And he reads with care.

He knows you can't exercise leadership without the necessary information at your fingertips. Which makes his patience and kindness toward some of his critics all the more remarkable. In almost every instance, their attacks are based on ignorance, misinformation, or outright prejudice.

There are many other things one can, and many will, say about Father Hesburgh as his final commencement nears on May 17, 1987: about his record as a fund-raiser, his status as the leading spokesman for Catholic higher education in the United States, the 14 presidential appointments he has held, the service he has rendered to four popes, his efforts on behalf of refugees and immigrants, arms control, and civil rights.

But when all is said and done, Father Hesburgh insists—as he will surely continue to insist throughout these weeks and months of accolades and profile pieces—that he is first and foremost a priest. Everything else is secondary.

Sometimes people will ask those of us who have worked closely with Father Hesburgh if he's "for real." He is, in every respect, but nowhere more than in the exercise of his priestly vocation.

He should have been a bishop, and a cardinal-archbishop by now. And yet there is no bishop, archbishop, or cardinal in the United States who is his equal in stature, in influence, or in leadership qualities.

Ted Hesburgh is one of U.S. Catholicism's proudest boasts. He symbolizes everything we have always aspired to be. In a tradition that cherishes example (sacramentality, we call it), he provides it in the most compelling forms.

His Church should be exceedingly grateful. Those of us who know and admire him certainly are.

Vatican, Archbishop Hunthausen Compromise
(June 19, 1987)

The case of Seattle's Archbp. Raymond G. Hunthausen has finally been resolved. And it has been resolved in the way that reasonable people resolve serious and contentious differences: by compromise.

Many people don't like compromises, but in this case one has to consider the alternative.

Had this matter been resolved without compromise, that is, to the complete and total satisfaction of Archbishop Hunthausen's supporters, the Vatican would have had to admit publicly that it had made a terribly serious error when it gave credence to the complaints of a tiny, irresponsible band of right-wing Catholics in Seattle.

It would have had to express profound regret for all the trouble its action had created, and it would have had to ask the forgiveness of the Catholics of Seattle for casting so negative a shadow over Archbishop Hunthausen's pastoral integrity, over the pastoral integrity of his principal pastoral associates, and over the archdiocese of Seattle as a whole.

Finally, the Vatican would have had to restore unconditionally all of Archbishop Hunthausen's episcopal faculties and at the same time reassign Bp. Donald Wuerl to some bureaucratic post far from Seattle.

There would have been no coadjutor bishop and no commitment on Archbishop Hunthausen's part to continue to try to implement the terms of Cardinal Ratzinger's highly critical letter of September 30, 1985.

Such a solution, however, was never a realistic possibility. The Vatican could never have made such a public admission of error. (Whether it should have done so is, of course, another question.)

Hunthausen supporters who would have preferred a "no-compromise" solution have to remember that "no-compromise" works two ways.

A "no-compromise" solution could also have been totally prejudicial to the archbishop.

The Vatican could have adopted Pilate's attitude when the Jews demanded that he change the inscription on Jesus' cross: "What I have written I have written."

In other words, Bishop Wuerl would remain in place, retaining full authority in five crucial pastoral areas. And if Archbishop Hunthausen didn't like it, he would have to resign.

This "no-compromise" solution, too, was never a realistic possibility. The wretched pastoral situation in Seattle would have worsened, and the morale of many clergy, religious, and active laity throughout the United States would have fallen even more sharply.

The Vatican knew that, and so the way of compromise was the only realistic alternative.

In every compromise, each side wins something and loses something. What did Archbishop Hunthausen win, and what did the Vatican win?

The archbishop has had all of his episcopal authority restored. That's a major victory for him (and a major defeat for the tiny group of right-wing Catholics who tried to bring him down).

Second, his new coadjutor, Bp. Thomas Murphy, of Great Falls, Montana, is a sympathetic man. Unlike Bishop Wuerl, whose strongly conservative reputation preceded him, he will not come to Seattle with his mind already made up against Archbishop Hunthausen.

Throughout Bishop Wuerl's stay in the archdiocese, Archbishop Hunthausen's enemies fed him a steady stream of complaints about pastoral abuses in the archdiocese.

That will stop. Bishop Murphy is not likely to encourage such communications, and those individuals who bitterly oppose Archbishop Hunthausen will know that it would be a waste of time. Bishop Murphy is not one of *The Wanderer*'s favorite bishops.

But in every compromise, you give as well as receive. Archbishop Hunthausen has conceded a great deal in accepting a coadjutor, even a good one, under these circumstances. No matter how one looks at it, the appointment is a reflection on Archbishop Hunthausen's pastoral performance.

Also, the archbishop has had to renew his public pledge that he would seek to implement the terms of the Ratzinger letter. Since the letter was so critical of the pastoral situation in Seattle, the archbishop is conceding that things have not been completely right in his archdiocese.

What did the Vatican win? It won what Archbishop Hunthausen lost.

The Vatican appointed a coadjutor bishop of its own choosing, and it secured from Archbishop Hunthausen the public promise that he would seek to implement the terms of the Ratzinger letter.

One hopes that this will be the end of the Hunthausen case and that the archdiocese of Seattle can now get back to being what it was before all this began: the Body of Christ trying, like all the rest of us, to be faithful to the gospel of Jesus Christ and to the mission of his Church.

Curran Case Ruling, a Pyrrhic Victory for CUA

(March 31, 1989)

Jud. Frederick Weisberg, of the Superior Court of the District of Columbia, decided on February 28 that Fr. Charles Curran's case against The Catholic University of America was without merit. He ruled for the defendant.

Father Curran had contended that his contract at CUA had been violated when, after a definitive declaration from the Vatican that he was no longer "suitable nor eligible" to teach Catholic theology, he was prevented from teaching in his area of competence anywhere in the university, even outside the so-called ecclesiastical faculty.

To support his complaint, Father Curran appealed to the often ambiguous history of the university's relationship with the Holy See, on the one hand, and its stated commitment to academic freedom, on the other.

Disagreeing with Father Curran's assessment of that historical record, Judge Weisberg ruled that the central question of the case came down "to what the contract says and what the parties to it intended."

He contended that neither party could have anticipated a judgment by the Holy See that was "both as broad and as definitive as the Ratzinger letter."

On the other hand, "certain things were unmistakably known and understood by the parties."

They knew, for example, that the university had a papal charter (a point contested by Father Curran's lawyers), that the archbishop of Washington, D.C., served as university chancellor, that 20 of the 40 members of the Board of Trustees had to be clerics, 16 of whom also had to be bishops, and that the faculty handbook and other documents emphasized the university's "unique relationship to the Holy See."

"No one—least of all a Catholic priest and a professor of Catholic Theology—could have contracted with CUA without understanding the University's special relationship with the Roman Catholic Church, with all of the implications and obligations flowing from that relationship." Father Curran himself acknowledged this in his testimony.

In light of this special and explicit relationship, the judge concluded that the university did not, in fact, breach its contract with Father Curran by honoring the terms of that relationship.

The Catholic University of America has won the case, but its victory may prove to be a Pyrrhic one. There is a time bomb set and ticking on page 34 of the 36-page opinion.

Having pointed out that the 1960s were "turbulent times, characterized by persistent testing of institutional limits on all forms of expression of individual freedom, including academic freedom," Judge Weisberg noted sympathetically that CUA "had to wrestle with its own ambivalence."

> On the one hand, it wanted to be recognized as a university—a Catholic university, to be sure—but a full-fledged American university nonetheless.
>
> On the other hand, it continued to place transcendent value on its unique and special relationship with the Holy See.
>
> Perhaps it can fairly be said that the University wanted it both ways; but on most issues it can also be said that the University could have it both ways.
>
> On some issues—and this case certainly presents one of them— the conflict between the University's commitment to academic

freedom and its unwavering fealty to the Holy See is direct and unavoidable.

And then comes the most significant sentence in the entire opinion: "On such issues, the University may choose for itself on which side of that conflict it wants to come down, and nothing in its contract with Professor Curran *or any other faculty member* promises that it will always come down on the side of academic freedom" (emphasis added).

In a similar crunch, therefore, *no* faculty member at CUA—inside or outside the Department of Theology—will have any legal basis on which to appeal an institutional violation of his or her academic freedom if that violation is committed as a form of compliance with a definitive declaration from the Holy See.

That could apply to a biology professor who takes a "wrong" stand on fetal tissue experimentation or a professor of film criticism who writes approvingly of *The Last Temptation of Christ* or a professor in religious education who reaches ethical conclusions similar to Father Curran's or, indeed, a professor of any subject who presumes to criticize publicly current church policies in general or the pope in particular.

Does academic freedom exist any longer at CUA? Is it an academically autonomous institution? Those are the sorts of fundamental questions that the Middle States Association of Colleges and Universities will be asking as it conducts its decennial accreditation review.

And they are the sorts of questions that every present and potential faculty member and student at CUA will have to ask as well.

Pedro Arrupe, S.J.

(March 8, 1991)

Fr. Pedro Arrupe, S.J., head of the Society of Jesus from 1965 until 1983, died last month after several years of illness and incapacitation.

Many of us outside the Society of Jesus share our brother Jesuits' keen sense of loss at his passing.

I was educated by Jesuits at the Pontifical Gregorian University in Rome; I taught with Jesuits at Boston College, a major Jesuit university; I have recruited distinguished Jesuit theologians to the Notre Dame faculty; and I count Jesuits among my closest friends.

In spite of their extraordinary record of service to the Church over the past four and a half centuries, the Jesuits have been too often the object of suspicion, criticism, and, on one tragic occasion, outright suppression.

Although the motivation for these attacks has been varied, they were often linked, as in this century, with the Society's firm and practical commitment to social justice, human rights, and enculturation.

During the Society's most recent period of testing in the early 1980s, I did what little I could through this column to offer support and encouragement.

Jesuits were accused of causing confusion among the faithful, of promoting secularizing tendencies, and of displaying too much independence from papal authority. Thus, when Father Arrupe submitted his resignation to the Holy Father in 1980, the pope declined it and refused to authorize the election of a successor. Soon thereafter, Father Arrupe suffered a temporarily paralyzing brain hemorrhage. He had chosen a highly respected American Jesuit, Fr. Vincent O'Keefe, to serve as vicar general.

Pope John Paul II overrode the choice and assumed governance of the Society by naming his own personal delegate to head the order until the election of a new general. For this task the pope selected Fr. Paolo Dezza, an 80-year-old Jesuit with a strongly conservative reputation. Father Arrupe accepted the decision without complaint, but many Jesuits were privately distressed by the Holy Father's actions. Contrary to the predictions of some critics, however, there were no public protests nor did any Jesuits leave the Society over this issue.

(It should also be noted that at Father Arrupe's funeral last month, Father O'Keefe stood right next to Father Arrupe's successor at the concelebrated Mass. In Rome, symbol is everything.)

The common expectation at the time was that Father Dezza would see his mandate as one of rooting out the alleged abuses and restoring discipline to the Society.

This did not happen: first, because most of the "abuses" had either been manufactured or inflated by forces unsympathetic with Father Arrupe's leadership; and, second, because Father Dezza did not regard himself as an avenging angel, with a mission to correct Father Arrupe's mistakes.

Much to the surprise and relief of many people inside and outside the Society of Jesus, Father Dezza accounted himself honorably as the papal delegate, consistently making a point of his own abiding respect for the ailing father general.

When, at Father Dezza's call, all of the Jesuit provincials came to Rome to discuss the concerns that had been voiced about the Society, it became clear that the accusations had not been well-founded. Indeed, the provincials provided a completely different picture of the Society from the one painted by a relatively few disgruntled Jesuits and by politically conservative critics, especially in Latin America.

Following the meeting of the provincials, the Holy Father granted permission for the election of Father Arrupe's successor. The first-ballot choice was Peter-Hans Kolvenbach, a Dutch Jesuit with extensive pastoral experience in the Middle East and, like Father Arrupe, a man committed to the Society's linkage of faith and justice.

In an address delivered in Spain in 1973, Father Arrupe insisted that the primary educational objective of the Society was to form men and women "who cannot conceive of a love of God which does not include love for the least of their neighbors" and who are "completely convinced that a love of God which does not issue in justice is a farce."

Those who knew him best, namely his brother Jesuits, have said that hope was Father Arrupe's most characteristic strength. He never forgot that the order of grace is more powerful than the order of sin. This from a man who, as a young missionary in Japan, lived through the atomic bomb attack on Hiroshima in 1945 and spent the following days nursing and burying hundreds of its victims.

The obituary in the *New York Times* noted that Father Arrupe left "no known survivors."

The *Times* was wrong. He left millions of brothers and sisters in Christ, who give thanks to God for his life and ministry among us.

Archbishop Whealon

(August 5, 1991)

It was just a few days after Christmas 1968 when I learned of the appointment of the new archbishop of Hartford.

At the time, I was on the faculty of the Pope John XXIII National Seminary in Weston, Massachusetts, and was at home in Hartford for the Christmas vacation. My former pastor at Our Lady of Victory in West Haven, Connecticut, the late Fr. Thomas McMahon, telephoned with the news.

I was stunned. John Whealon, then bishop of Erie, Pennsylvania, was one of the names a friend and I had placed on an imaginary list of bizarre possibilities to succeed Archbp. Henry J. O'Brien, who had retired.

Bishop Whealon had the reputation in Erie for being a stickler for detail. The biretta was always to be worn for Mass and the celebrant's shoes had to have laces.

It was only three years after the adjournment of the Second Vatican Council. By the standards of those days, John Whealon was an ultraconservative. We couldn't believe that anyone so far to the right would be imposed on Hartford.

But he was, and when I called my friend at The Catholic University of America, he thought I was joking. It was no joke. After so many years of quiet, compassionate, and fair-minded pastoral leadership from Archbishop O'Brien, we wondered what the archdiocese of Hartford had done to deserve this.

At first, the new archbishop came across as scholarly and aloof. I would hear reports that he was ill at ease with people, even with his clergy. But there was another side to the man that began to show itself. Bishops and staff people who worked with Archbishop Whealon at the national level found him to be a stickler for detail, to be sure, but always honest and fair.

It was the latter word—fair—that was to grow almost exponentially in significance for the archbishop's remaining years in Hartford. John Whealon *was* a fair man.

There are perhaps a few people in the archdiocese of Hartford and elsewhere who will see this article as a form of poetic license. One never says anything ill of the deceased, and so they will let it pass.

I cannot account for those instances when the archbishop may have spoken or acted in ways that others regarded as unfair. I can only account for my own experience of him.

Even though he and I were at different points on the theological spectrum, never once in our 22 years of association did a harsh or unfriendly word pass between us—or behind our respective backs, as far as I can tell.

Whenever anyone would report some remark he had made about me, it was always a positive and supportive one. He did not fully agree with my writings, including this weekly column, but he told others that he regarded them as balanced and orthodox.

Never once in those 22 years did he ever ask me to change a word, and never once did he interfere with its weekly publication in the *Catholic Transcript*.

That bothered some of the fire-eaters inside the archdiocese and beyond, but he never yielded to their pressure. And it was constant.

But so, too, was his loyalty.

The archbishop was for several years chairman of the U.S. Bishops' Committee on Doctrine. With graduate degrees in scripture and theology in hand, he enjoyed widespread respect and credibility as a traditional interpreter of the faith.

His fidelity to the scriptures he loved so much and the integrity of his theological and doctrinal views were simply above reproach.

It was all the more remarkable and humbling to me, therefore, that he should have been so consistently supportive, so steadfastly loyal—even when it meant on occasion standing firm against forces seemingly mightier than he.

Others who knew Archbishop Whealon more intimately than I or who worked with him more closely than I are in a much better position to assess him as a person, as a priest, and as a bishop.

I can only speak for myself and from my own very limited vantage point.

I admired Archbishop Whealon from afar for his simplicity of life, for his modesty, for his self-discipline, and for his perseverance, even in the face of serious illness.

But I admired him most, up close, for his loyalty and his fairness. When I told him that to his face not so many months ago, he seemed taken aback by the frankness and directness of my compliment. A truly humble man, he probably absorbed criticism more easily than praise.

In 1968 some of us had been worried about the impact of his appointment on the archdiocese of Hartford. Today we hope and pray for a successor as good as he was.

May Archbishop Whealon enjoy an honored place at the heavenly banquet table, and may his example of simplicity, loyalty, and fairness live on in the hearts of those who minister for the Church.

11

Popes

Introduction

The Second Vatican Council broadened the Church's understanding of authority, moving it progressively away from a monarchical to a more collegial concept of governance. Papal authority was placed in the larger context of episcopal authority. The pope is, after all, a bishop himself, albeit the president of the college of bishops.

For good or for ill, popes have always placed their personal stamp upon the life, mission, and structure of the Church. Inevitably they set a tone and create an atmosphere. All members of the Church are affected by their style of leadership, directly or indirectly.

The modern period is no exception to the rule. Who can deny the extraordinary influence Pope John XXIII had on 20th-century Catholicism? It was he who conceived of the idea of an ecumenical council; it was he who threw open the windows of the Church to let in some fresh air.

And it was Pope Paul VI who carried the Johannine idea to its practical realization, guiding the council in three of its four sessions. But it was also Paul VI who unwittingly divided the Church and undermined the credibility of the papal and hierarchical magisterium with the publication of his ill-fated encyclical on birth control in 1968.

Pope John Paul I, although in office for only a month, revolutionized the papacy by refusing to be crowned in accordance with a centuries-old imperial practice.

Pope John Paul II, still in office at this writing, has placed the Church on a new postconciliar course. Some would say he has reversed the council's forward thrust. Others would say that he has contained it. Others would insist that he, unlike his critics, understands the radical continuity between the pre- and postconciliar Church.

Whatever opinion one has regarding Pope John Paul II, it is almost impossible to be neutral about him. Will his agenda and spirit endure beyond his pontificate? Will his successor continue his hard-line approach to dissent and diversity in the Church? Will the Catholic Church of the 21st century be more in his image or in the image of John XXIII? Will there be a John XXIV (see my column of September 28, 1990)? Or will the Church and its papacy follow some different course entirely?

Revelation and Pope John XXIII

(November 4, 1966)

It has become something of a commonplace in catechetics and preaching that God reveals himself in and through history. God revealed his love and mercy when he led the Chosen People out of the bondage of Egypt and into the promised land. The Exodus event was a meaningful revelation-experience for those who participated in it, and insofar as it illuminates our understanding and love of God when we hear the event recounted in the Old Testament, it can also be something of a revelation-experience for us today.

So, too, is the liturgy a revelation-event for those Christians who participate fully in the Eucharist and the other sacraments. The liturgy is especially important because it underlines the fact that revelation occurs primarily in a community, that God addresses us not simply as individuals but as his family and as his people. And the same line of reasoning may be applied to the guidance and direction of the teaching Church.

But what of the vast majority of mankind, which is non-Christian? Are these people sealed off, so to speak, from the revelation of God? Must they learn of God's love and mercy through hearsay, indirectly?

The insights of contemporary theology and the Second Vatican Council are helpful here, not only for answering the problem of the non-Christian (whom we might picture as some forlorn soul in the poverty-ridden streets of Calcutta) but also for shedding light on the problem of the "religion-less" Christian, that is, the one for whom the Bible, and the liturgy, and the teachings of the Church have no meaning.

God speaks here and now to them and to us in and through the neighbor who cares, who lives as a "man for others." The gracious neighbor gives us an insight into the nature of reality itself. To put it in a way that is both theological and philosophical: the gracious neighbor demonstrates that being itself is gracious.

Some men, in the presence of the gracious neighbor, will be drawn, by the Spirit of God, to become a member of the Body of Christ and to give explicit witness to the fact that God has so loved the world that he gave his only-begotten Son. Still others may respond differently, that is, in the manner in which the majority of mankind responds. They may catch something of the contagious spirit of the gracious neighbor and live in like manner in their relationships with others.

These, too, have accepted the gospel of Christ, even if not explicitly. But, after all, it is not the man who says, "Lord, Lord!" who will enter the Kingdom of God, but only he who actually does the will of our Father in heaven. And what is his will? That we love one another as God himself has loved us in his Son.

In the light of our reflections of the past few weeks, I would be prepared to state that one of the most dramatic and most effective revelation-events of our time occurred in the life and ministry of Pope John XXIII. It was not simply pious rhetoric on the part of Cardinal Suenens when, in eulogizing the late pope, he compared the revelatory dimension of his life with that of John the Baptist.

"And there was a man sent from God, whose name was John. He came for testimony, to bear witness to the light, that all might believe through him. He was not the light, but came to bear witness to the light" (John 1:6–8).

St. Paul, too, recognized that Christ must find concrete expression in others if he is to be understood and imitated. He had the theological boldness and daring to say, "Be imitators of me as I am of Christ" (1 Corinthians 11:1). But even Paul is far removed from us. More meaningful than Paul, for our time, is John XXIII.

Imitate John, and you shall imitate Christ. Imitate his spirit of warmth and love, his openness to all peoples, of every race, nation, religious belief and nonbelief. Imitate his concern for the humble and the neglected, for the castoffs of our society. Imitate his spirit of resignation to God's will in the face of suffering and certain death.

Imitate his concern for justice, so forcefully expressed in his encyclical letter *Mater et Magistra*. Imitate his concern for world peace, for harmony and friendship among all people, as he expressed it so memorably in *Pacem in Terris*. Imitate his concern for Christian unity and for the renewal of the Catholic Church. These are the tasks to which God is calling us, and he is calling us through his humble servant, Pope John XXIII.

Why is it that the life and ministry of Pope John XXIII struck such a responsive chord in the hearts of all mankind, believer and nonbeliever alike? Why is it that people, so long bored and unimpressed with grandiose pronouncements, suddenly took an interest in *Pacem in Terris*? Why is it that people, so long indifferent and inattentive to the large-scale and well-organized charitable enterprises of the Church, suddenly were touched by the example of the Good Shepherd visiting the sick, the orphans, and those in prison? Why is it that people, so long cynical and bitter about the problem of evil—of sickness and suffering and dying—found inspiration and hope in the sickness and suffering and dying of John XXIII?

In and through this giant of a Christian and this tower of humanity there shone forth a power and a beauty and a strength not often experienced on such a worldwide scale. Pope John XXIII was so transparently a "man for others," a gracious neighbor, a suffering servant of God—without pretension, without self-seeking, without arrogant concern for dignity and rank.

Working in and through the humble pope was the One about whom St. Paul wrote: "Though he was in the form of God, [he] did not count equality with God a thing to be grasped, but emptied himself, taking the form of a servant, being born in the likeness of men. And being found in human form he humbled himself and became obedient unto death, even death on a cross" (Philippians 2:6–8).

The contemporary theology of revelation is eminently pastoral and practical. The Christian must be ever more sensitive to the presence of God in the people and in the reality around him. But what is most important, the Christian must so open himself to the gospel of Christ and so live it without compromise that the presence of God—the gracious God in the gracious neighbor—will be unmistakably clear.

Looking Back at the Papal Election

(September 8, 1978)

Now that the papal election is over and Pope John Paul I has assumed the burdens of the Petrine ministry, it may be appropriate to look back and acknowledge our common indebtedness to those who helped us make sense of it all from beginning to end.

I, for one, am particularly grateful to Bp. S. Fidelis Cliché, whose extraordinary capacity to cut through to the heart of a problem was a constant source of amazement and admiration.

Those who followed his counsel throughout the proceedings were not at all surprised by the selection of Card. Albino Luciani, patriarch of Venice. It could not have been anyone else. The clues were ridiculously obvious.

First, Bishop Cliché assured us the new pope would be a holy man, a saint like his predecessor. All that one had to do was to scan the list of the 111 cardinal-electors and eliminate all those who were not holy.

Second, the bishop told us to ignore all signs of politicking in advance of the conclave. None of this would make any difference at all to the Holy Spirit, who was and is the one and only Elector.

In fact, what appeared on the surface to be politicking was nothing more than proximate preparation for the spiritual retreat of the conclave. Some cardinals were known to prefer cells closest to the chapel for easy access to morning prayers and Mass.

Third, we knew from the start that a compromise choice was out of the question. Bishop Cliché insisted that whoever was elected would be the best man for the job.

When the conclave was over, the same penetrating analysis of events guided us all through the thicket of wonder and surprise at the choice and the speed with which it was made.

Of course, it had to be a quick decision. It showed how united the Catholic Church is and how powerful, and indeed irresistible, is the wind of the Holy Spirit.

If the conclave had lasted several days, it would have meant that the cardinals could not readily agree on the best man, or, more to the point, that the cardinals were collectively shutting out the inspiration of the Holy Spirit.

It would have also meant that there had been some vigorous disagreements about theological and pastoral issues and about the future course of the Church.

But that would have been out of the question, too; the Church has never been less divided by controversy. Rarely in her long 2,000-year history has she been more secure in her identity and her mission.

An exceedingly brief conclave was inevitable.

And then there was the matter of all the prayers for the success of the conclave. Never before had there been so many offered up to God.

Of course, had this been an age of materialism and secularism, Bishop Cliché could not have made that observation. People pray when they believe strongly in God and the supernatural order.

We can be thankful, therefore, that at such a critical juncture in the life of the Church, the world was in such excellent spiritual form.

What I found particularly impressive about Bishop Cliché's postconclave commentary was his engaging ability to transcend the handicap of limited or nonexistent data to make sure and steady judgments about the new pope.

Although he had never met Cardinal Luciani, the bishop knew the man intimately. He described him as a person of profound spirituality, love for the priesthood, gentleness, ecumenical sensitivity, and commitment to social justice and world peace.

I'm a theologian myself, and so I found it especially reassuring to hear from Bishop Cliché that the new pope is a profound theologian.

We theologians don't usually make such judgments about one another apart from a careful reading of a colleague's principal writings. But S. Fidelis Cliché is no ordinary person.

In fact, with a gift like that, Bishop Cliché could name his own terms with the television networks. Election-night computer analyses and projections would be a thing of the past.

God willing, we shall not have another papal election for many years to come. But when it comes, as inevitably it must, I hope S. Fidelis Cliché is around to illuminate the events.

I have a feeling he will be.

The Power That Comes from God's Presence

(September 15, 1978)

The supreme pastoral ministry of Pope John Paul I has begun on a reassuringly high note.

In his first public appearances—from the front balcony of St. Peter's on the day of his election, at his apartment window the next afternoon for the traditional Sunday blessing, in his audience with the journalists, at the Mass of installation—the new pope has shown himself to be a man of warmth and humor.

Personality is not everything in a leader, to be sure. One must have insight, intelligence, judgment, and the ability to make decisions.

But such qualities are interdependent. If personality cannot supply for intelligence, intelligence without personality will not do either.

Many Catholics, whatever their views on the great issues facing the Church today, were looking forward to a new pope who would be, at the very least, a pleasant person, one obviously at ease with people, exuding confidence and hope.

It would appear, even at this early date, that the Catholic Church has been blessed with just such a pastoral leader.

But if his personality seems strongly positive, so, too, are some of his initial gestures.

He is the first pope in more than 900 years to have rejected a ceremony of coronation (in which he would have been addressed as "the father of princes and kings"). And there is far more significance to that decision than may be initially apparent.

Some commentators were content to see it as a matter of style. The new pope is a humble man, uncomfortable with pomp and circumstance.

That may be true, but the rite of coronation wasn't just another expression of papal triumphalism, much like the noble guards, the ostrich feather fans, the *sedia gestatoria,* and the silver trumpets.

The custom of papal coronation took root in the 11th century when the popes increasingly perceived themselves to be temporal as well as spiritual rulers. Indeed, there were times in the history of the Church when their temporal power seemed more important to the popes than the spiritual.

By rejecting the crown, Pope John Paul I rejected also the notion that the Church is as much a political power as a spiritual organism and that the papacy is as much an absolute monarchy as an instrument of Christian service.

If the Church has power, it is because the Church embodies the presence of God, is faithful to the gospel of Jesus Christ, and is animated by the life-giving breath of the Holy Spirit.

If the pope has power, it is because he radiates the presence of God, is a man of faith in Christ, and is open to the Spirit wherever the Spirit leads.

And in granting a special audience to representatives of the other Christian churches just before his ceremonial installation, the new pope undoubtedly wished to ratify the ecumenical initiatives of his two immediate predecessors and show himself personally committed to the apostolate of Christian unity.

The intent and substance of the gesture were not lost upon his guests in the papal library. The reaction of these other Christian leaders was uniformly favorable.

All this is not to suggest that the problems that gravely burdened the Catholic Church on August 6, the day Pope Paul VI died, drifted miraculously off into the heavens with the gray and musty gold smoke from the Sistine chimney.

John Paul's will be a very difficult ministry. There are many serious and sincere Catholics who will be looking for evidence of tough-mindedness in dealing with theological dissent and catechetical confusion.

And there are many equally serious and sincere Catholics who will be probing for signs of flexibility on birth control, obligatory celibacy, and the place of women in the pastoral leadership of the Church.

The new pope will not be able to please both sides. But neither side expects that he can.

What many on both sides prefer is that the Church's future course at least be clear. For nothing will harm the Church more than unfulfilled expectations that were unrealistic in the first place.

Different Approaches: A New Pope's Agenda
(November 3, 1978)

Ordinarily people who make predictions that come true like to trumpet their successes before the world. The mistakes we bury silently, hoping that no one will notice the freshly turned earth.

But I've been more sobered than elated by the accuracy of some judgments I made in a column published the first week of January.

"A new year brings with it the promise of something better," I began. "Who could have expected 12 months ago that, by late autumn, the president of Egypt would make an official visit to Israel in search of peace? No political situation looked more hopelessly deadlocked last January than the crisis in the Middle East."

"But something happened nonetheless," the essay continues. "Something unforeseen, unprogrammed, unanticipated. Something strikingly akin to a redemptive moment, and inbreaking of the Spirit of healing and reconciliation."

If that could happen on the political front, why not also on the ecclesiastical? "No pastoral or doctrinal issue more thoroughly complicates our quest for Christian unity than the papacy. The papal office remains the principal obstacle to Christian union."

I pointed out that two events, one expected and the other in the hands of God (barring voluntary retirement), might suddenly alter the situation and make possible new initiatives and new solutions to an apparently intractable problem.

I referred first to the consensus statement on papal infallibility from the Roman Catholic–Lutheran consultation, and second to a possible change in the papal chair itself.

As I write this column, the statement on infallibility has already been completed, but not yet widely circulated. I shall, in fact, make some fuller comment on the document in a later piece.

Meanwhile, we have just endured the trauma of two papal deaths. We have not had the one change in the papal office I thought possible, but two.

"Who could have anticipated the extraordinary transition from Pope Pius XII to Pope John XXIII?" I asked in last January's column. "When elected, Pope John's episcopal motto 'Obedientia et Pax' ('Obedience and Peace') seemed eminently appropriate to a caretaker pontiff.

"But John XXIII's ministry was as far removed from the mode of a caretaker as the present climate in the Middle East is from a year ago."

How applicable are those words to the stunningly abbreviated Petrine ministry of the late Pope John Paul. In just over a month, he touched the world as few public figures have done since John XXIII himself.

He was, as Cardinal Confalonieri noted in his funeral homily, like a meteor flashing across the sky, brilliantly illuminating it for an instant only to disappear as suddenly as it came.

And yet who can calculate the effect of those 34 days, not only on the Catholic Church, but on the whole Body of Christ and indeed on the human community at large?

If he did nothing else, Pope John Paul removed all doubt about the world's abiding readiness to respond to warmth, humor, humility, compassion, and sensitivity.

And that has always been the message of the Church as it was first the message of her Lord: that happiness comes to those who are poor in spirit, meek, merciful, devoted to peace, committed to justice, sympathetic, steadfast in faith, and the like (Matthew 5:1–12).

The problems facing the Catholic Church have not thereby vanished. The state of the Church today is not so different from its condition on that August day when Pope Paul VI was taken to the Father's right hand.

There are Catholics on one side still pressing for additional reforms, and Catholics on the other side still worried about the preservation of doctrine and discipline.

And there are relations to be worked out still with the emerging Third World and its liberation movements, with the communist nations, and with the other Christian churches as we seek together a more effective common witness to Christ and his gospel.

But there has been in the meantime a shaking of the Church that none could have reasonably predicted even a few months ago.

A new broom sweeps clean, the saying goes. It doesn't mean we have to scorn the old broom in accepting the new. But neither can we allow our attachment to the old to get in the way of the needs at hand, needs that require new instruments, new approaches, new initiatives.

"The Lord sweeps into our midst at the most unexpected hour," I concluded that January column. "He asks only that we keep our lamps burning brightly, that we rise to the sound of his knock at the door, that we probe for him in the signs of the times."

The Leadership Role of Pope John Paul II
(November 10, 1978)

By now the period of immediate reaction to the election of Pope John Paul II has passed.

The media, of course, were struck by the nationality of the new pope, the first non-Italian in more than 450 years. It made an exciting story, and legitimately so.

Others strained to detect some similarity with Pope John Paul I. They looked for the smile, the display of warmth, the light touch.

But as several of the cardinal-electors acknowledged before the conclave, there are no carbon copies of Albino Luciani.

Nevertheless, they employed the same formula in selecting his successor:

1. They looked again for a warm and friendly man with pastoral rather than curial experience.

A few cardinals argued, somewhat defensively perhaps, that bureaucratic work is also "pastoral," but they were stretching the point, not only theologically but sociologically as well.

Running a Vatican congregation is as different from presiding over a diocese as administering a federal office is from serving as governor of a state or mayor of a town.

Both are political forms of activity, but in the one case the politician answers only to the president and in the other he or she answers to a whole spectrum of competing constituencies. All kinds of practical implications follow.

2. The cardinal-electors looked again for a pastoral man with a reputation of concern for the poor and a record to back it up.

With the emergence of the Third World as an important ecclesiastical as well as political force, no social conservative could realistically count on the votes of the Latin American, Asian, and African cardinals.

The new pope had to be a man with a strong commitment to social justice and human rights.

3. The cardinals looked, finally, for a pastoral man, committed to the cause of the poor and the oppressed, who was at the same time sufficiently traditional on matters of theology and piety and yet fundamentally open-minded in his attitudes and collegial in his approach to the governance of the Church.

This excluded candidates who had been essentially unhappy about the Second Vatican Council and/or who prefer an authoritarian rather than collaborative model of leadership.

This third criterion also excluded progressive cardinal-candidates who might be "soft" on such questions as divorce-and-remarriage, ordination of women, priestly celibacy, and birth control.

The Italian cardinals who came closest to meeting these criteria failed, for one reason or another, to garner the necessary 75 votes (two thirds plus one).

Age and health, of course, were much more significant factors this time because of the suddenness of Pope John Paul I's death. Cardinal Ursi of Naples was undoubtedly sidetracked for this reason. He is 70 and has eye problems.

Cardinal Karol Wojtyla, archbishop of Kraków since 1964, was among several non-Italian possibilities who also clearly met these criteria. Once the psychological barrier was broken and many of the cardinals felt comfortable casting some of their ballots for non-Italian colleagues, it became only a matter of which non-Italian candidate would make the best pope.

Pope John Paul II is a man of extensive pastoral experience, with an uncompromising concern for the oppressed. And he can smile.

He is traditional in theology and piety and yet not inflexible in the former nor intolerant of diversity in the latter.

And as he proved himself at Vatican II and in subsequent synods of bishops in Rome, he can be a vigorous champion of collegiality, the principle of coresponsibility in the governance of the Church.

But the formula that elected Pope John Paul I and now Pope John Paul II has yet to be tested. John Paul I didn't live long enough to indicate lines of direction in policy. He was with us only for a moment, sufficiently prolonged to fix himself in our hearts and memories as an extraordinarily warm and sympathetic human being.

The question remains for the Catholic Church: Is a moderate conservative pope who can smile the kind that will provide the leadership such times as these require?

The birth-control issue is a case in point. Is it better to say nothing more about it, knowing all the while that it is a teaching widely rejected in practice by Catholics themselves? That is the moderate conservative's approach.

Or is it better to face the issue head-on and, in the interest of Catholic truth, demand obedience on the matter, or else? That is the strong conservative approach.

Or, in the interest of honesty and credibility, revoke the teaching and admit it was too absolutely formulated? That is the progressive approach.

The same kind of choices face the Church on such internal matters as diversity in catechetics, theological dissent, qualifications for ordination to the priesthood, the promulgation and enforcement of laws regulating marriage.

It was precisely such internal problems as these, not his vigorous initiatives on the foreign front, that eventually brought a measure of agony to the last years of Pope Paul VI.

What Qualities Were Cardinals Looking For?

(November 24, 1978)

The world has just been treated to two very rare occurrences: the election of the first non-Italian pope in more than 450 years and the first back-to-back conclaves since 1605 (newly elected Pope Leo XI had survived only 17 days, half the term of Pope John Paul I).

Papal elections tend to bring out the best and the worst in us.

They force us all to take stock of where we are as Church, where our principal problems lie, whether or not we can afford to continue the kind of leadership we've had in the recent past, which opportunities seem ripe for exploiting, and so forth.

But papal elections also seem to tap our darker (or should I say "rosier"?) side. They provide a field day for pieties and platitudes.

Fortunately, it got a little better, not worse, from the first to the second conclave.

There was much less talk this time about the prompting of the Holy Spirit. Not that the cardinals were about to deny the abiding influence of the Lord, but they were much less inclined in October than they were in August to try to convince the world that the Holy Spirit, and not they, would make the selection.

Perhaps it was because of the sadly abrupt end of Pope John Paul I's ministry. If we're going to give the Holy Spirit credit for electing him, do we also have to assign the Spirit the blame for taking him away so quickly?

Did it mean, for example, that the first conclave had made a terrible mistake, and that God had no alternative but to correct it, and fast?

That's precisely the kind of "reasoning" some emotionally troubled souls reached upon hearing the news of Pope John Paul I's death.

So there was much more sober Spirit-talk this time than before.

And, then, there was the holiness factor. In August it seemed that the only criterion the cardinals would be taking into account was the holiness of the candidate.

He must be a saint, just like his predecessor, they insisted. No one bothered to ask, of course, whether any of their brother cardinals failed to measure up on the holiness scale.

Which of the candidates were not holy? How can you tell one way or the other? What are the signs of sanctity?

Is it posture? Does a holy person hold himself in a certain way or walk at a certain pace?

Is it pallor? Does a holy person appear drawn, anguished, or just this side of depressed?

Is it physiognomy? Does a holy person "look" holy? Is it in the eyes, the forehead, the chin, the sheepish smile, the slightly pained frown?

This time around there was less talk about holiness and more talk about faith.

But here again, the same question. Who among the possible candidates were not men of "faith"? And how can you tell?

Is it the passion in the voice as he talks about God or Christ or the Blessed Mother?

Is it an attitude of unquestioning obedience to the teachings of the pope, of whatever kind and in whatever form?

Is it tough-mindedness toward theologians and especially toward critical theologians like Hans Küng, Edward Schillebeeckx, even Yves Congar and Karl Rahner?

Is it an understanding of the Christian message as expressed in the seminary textbooks the cardinals used when they were preparing for ordination 30, 40, or 50 years ago?

Is it a stubborn resistance to theological development?

Does "man of faith" mean someone who believes that nothing new can be added to our understanding of Jesus Christ or that nothing wrong can ever be discovered about any of our previous moral teachings, especially those relating to sexual ethics?

Or is it a sense of confidence in the direction of human history, a spirit of joy in the face of crises and setbacks?

Is it a vision of the gospel steeped in the most up-to-date biblical, historical, and theological scholarship?

I do not want this essay to be taken as a cynical piece. I do not for a moment deny that holiness and faith are indispensable criteria for the selection of church leadership.

But it is one thing to talk about holiness and faith in general. It is quite another to say precisely what you mean by each term.

Undoubtedly all of the cardinals were looking for a holy man of faith both in August and in October. But I dare say that some of them had very different notions of what "holiness" and "faith" actually mean.

It would have been healthier for the Church to have had those differences surface and exposed for constructive discussion.

As it turned out, conservatives, moderates, and progressives alike spoke as if personalities and not points of view were all that counted in the end, as if there were really no arguments about policies and directions or about priorities and opportunities.

We got generalities at the time when particulars matter.

The Pope's Second Year

(January 4, 1980)

We are only into the second year of Pope John Paul II's supreme pastoral ministry. I think that many Catholics on both sides of the liberal-conservative line are misreading the early signs.

On the right, one notices a growing aggressiveness, even belligerency. Letters of complaint to bishops, religious superiors, and ecclesiastical publications boldly demand that such-and-such a person be muzzled or that such-and-such a practice be stopped.

Sisters working in parish settings have encountered scolding "I-told-you-so" reactions from people who have never accepted the disappearance of formal religious garb.

Columnists and others with a public forum sense that theologians are now fairer game than usual, what with Hans Küng and Edward Schillebeeckx and who knows who else in the inquisitorial frying pan.

A distinguished Catholic scholar, venerable by reason of age as well as of achievement, has confided to one reporter that he sees the American Catholic Church to be even more divided in the wake of the pope's visit than it was before he came.

I suggest the reason to be that some conservative-to-traditionalist Catholics have now concluded that the pope is "one of them" and that, with the top man on their side, they can safely become more accusatory, more judgmental, more hard-line.

I think that they underestimate the depth of the pope's intelligence and humanity.

He takes a much more nuanced approach to problems and to people than they do, and when he expresses strong views, he is never harsh or mean-spirited, as they are.

On the left, one notices a growing discouragement, tending even to back-biting. They ridicule the pope's personal preferences on such issues as sisters' habits and are dismayed by his seemingly fixed positions on birth control, priestly celibacy, and the ordination of women, and now his approval of Hans Küng's censure.

Some talk about the pope as if he were an uninformed and close-minded cleric, poised to launch a new era of repression in the Church. And yet it was Paul VI, not John Paul II, under whom the investigations of Hans Küng and Edward Schillebeeckx were initiated.

I think that they, also underestimate the depth of the pope's intelligence and humanity.

The imprint of that extraordinary intelligence is obvious in his first en-cyclical, *Redemptor Hominis,* and in his remarkable speech at the United Na-tions. The former is a vigorous affirmation of human dignity, and the latter, of social justice and human rights in the service of that dignity.

An earlier work of his, *The Acting Person,* makes clear that repression has to be utterly foreign to the pope's mentality. In that book the pope defined the "acting person" as a participant in community. Community, in turn, depends upon two "authentic attitudes": "solidarity" and "opposition."

Solidarity refers to a "constant readiness to accept and realize one's share in community," a readiness to "complement the action of other members."

Opposition, on the other hand, consists of voicing disagreement without withdrawing from community. "Opposition," he wrote, "is not inconsistent with solidarity." In fact, opposition may arise precisely out of "deep concern for the common good."

Opposition of this sort is "essentially constructive," and communities must both expect and encourage it. Since the common good is dynamic, not static, it requires solidarity without repression of opposition.

Undoubtedly opposition places a strain on community, the pope acknowl-edged. But conflicts that are expressed dialogically bring to light "what is right and true in these differences." Communal life is thereby enriched.

Just as solidarity and opposition are "authentic attitudes" necessary for community, so there are also "unauthentic attitudes," namely conformism and noninvolvement.

Conformism, the pope insisted, is sterile. The conformist simply moves along with the majority and accepts whatever the majority decides. Compliance is really superficial. There is no genuine participation in community.

Noninvolvement is a form of withdrawal from community. It makes no pretense at unity even for the sake of appearances.

How are we to tell when solidarity becomes servile compliance (conform-ism), and when opposition becomes destructive rather than constructive?

"Conscience," the pope declared, "is the ultimate judge of the authenticity of human attitudes."

As a man of intellectual integrity, the pope knows that these principles apply just as much within the Church as outside it.

Those who would now tightly embrace the pope had better know what they are embracing, and those who would now reject him had better know what they are rejecting. There may be more to the man than meets the left eye or the right eye.

Papacy Exists for Unity, Not Division
(July 18, 1980)

The papacy exists for the sake of the unity of the Church. According to the Second Vatican Council's Dogmatic Constitution on the Church, the Petrine office "presides over the whole assembly of charity and protects legitimate differences, while at the same time it sees that such differences do not hinder unity but rather contribute toward it" (n. 13).

One of the unpleasant developments in recent months, however, is the tendency of some individuals and groups in the Catholic Church to make the pope an instrument of division rather than of unity.

They wave the pope's more conservative statements almost defiantly in the face of the opposition. "You see! We're going to have none of this foolishness about ordination of women or a married clergy or theological freedom that plays havoc with the truth."

Or, knowing how worried and disturbed many of their more progressive brothers and sisters are with some of the Holy Father's views, they deliberately exaggerate his virtues and inflate their rhetoric whenever speaking of his impact upon the Church and upon the world at large.

Suddenly—in spite of the pope's humility—they speak of him as if he were one of the world's leading philosophers or one of the Church's most sophisticated theological minds or one of history's most saintly figures.

One does not want to deny just praise to anyone, least of all Pope John Paul II. One need not suppress a swelling sense of pride in a man who has so obviously touched and excited millions of people all across the earth.

But when the praise is overdone, one begins to wonder about its point. Is it to honor the pope, or is it to honor oneself? Is it to declare the pope a "winner," or is it to declare oneself a "winner"?

It would be a tragedy for the Church and for the pope as well if everyone began taking all these one-sided views at face value and then concluded that the pope may not be the pope of the whole Church after all, but only the pope of its more traditional numbers.

He would become, in that instance, no longer the Holy Father of the many women who feel alienated from the life of the Church, of the thousands of priests who have resigned from the active ministry, of the divorced-and-remarried, of religious educators and other teachers for whom truth is not tied always to the official interpretations of the local bishop or a Vatican Congregation, and so forth.

One is tempted to offer some friendly advice to Pope John Paul II's most devoted admirers: Don't rub it in. The Holy Father doesn't need that kind of support. In fact, it's counterproductive to the purpose of his ministry: to heal, to reconcile, to unify.

In that regard, take a look at the address the Holy Father gave to the French bishops on June 1. He expressed concern precisely over the polarization between progressives and traditionalists.

And notice, he didn't criticize only the progressives. He also criticized the traditionalists who, he said,

> are shutting themselves up rigidly in a given period of the history of the Church, and at a given moment of theological formulation or liturgical expression which they have absolutized, without penetrating sufficiently the profound meaning, without considering history in its totality and its legitimate development, fearing new questions without admitting, in the long run, that the Holy Spirit is at work today in the Church with its pastors united around the successor of Peter.
>
> These two extreme tendencies foster not only opposition but also division, which are both deplorable and a cause of prejudice. . . . So much energy is spent on mutual suspicion and criticism. . . . It is to be hoped that both these opposing groups, whose faith and generosity are not lacking, will humbly learn along with their pastors to overcome these antagonisms . . . in order to tackle together the mission of the Church.

Pope John Paul II charged the bishops to serve as "instruments of unity" — and so must we all, and no one more certainly than the Holy Father himself. Don't make him instead an instrument of division.

Just a little friendly advice, that's all. And it may be all the more pertinent in light of the pope's recent trip to Brazil.

More Thoughts on the Pope

(June 26, 1981)

If anyone still needs proof that Pope John Paul II is one of the most remarkable "human" men ever to occupy that office, the photograph of him propped up in a narrow hospital bed in Rome should dispel all residual doubt.

Some of us are old enough to remember the papacy before John XXIII. It was inconceivable that an injured or ailing pope should allow himself to be photographed.

Indeed, like many priests and nuns of the pre–Vatican II Church, he would never even be seen eating in public. ("What do priests eat?" the anxious cook would ask if "Father" were coming to dinner.)

It was almost as if the mystique would be destroyed if the pope (or priest or nun) were suddenly perceived to be as human as the rest of us.

But here is this extraordinary man who, in less than three years, has captured the hearts and imaginations of millions of this earth's population and the respect of its leaders, showing himself to the entire global village as a dependent, vulnerable, mortal human being: bandaged and wired, drawing nourishment from tubes, and adorned only in the kind of simple white gown that is the unpretentious uniform of patients the world over.

A lesser person would have nervously asked his aides, "But what will they think if they see the Vicar of Christ like this?" The sycophant would have responded, "Of course, Holy Father, we shall tell the photographer to leave." A valuable confidant would have snapped back, "They'll think you're human like the rest of us. Is that so bad a message to give to ordinary men and women struggling to live the gospel?"

But this pope surely did not have to be coaxed. Anyone who has taken the time and trouble to read what he has written knows that the starting point for all of his reflections on the Christian life is human life itself.

The essence of the good news, he insisted in his first encyclical, is that we are all worth something. It is our humanity that has been redeemed. God created each one of us and saw that we were good.

What kind of credibility would such a message have, however, if delivered by a reserved, unsmiling, distant man, shrouded in mystery, the better to maintain the mystique of godliness?

One wonders, in fact, if that photograph of the Holy Father in Rome's Gemelli Hospital made some Catholics wince.

The pope, after all, is next to God, the most sacred of persons, they insist. Doesn't a photo like that tend to weaken the image? Can the pope really be as vulnerable to physical calamity as the rest of humankind? And if vulnerable to human weakness on the physical level, might he not also be vulnerable on other levels as well?

But, then, one doesn't readily photograph a pope making a theological mistake. It can happen, and historically it has happened. But some were brought up to believe it's impossible. Thank God, they must be thinking, such a thing *can't* be photographed and plastered all over page one.

One other thought strikes me this week as I reflect anew on this recent tragedy.

The pope's power as a symbol of Christian faith, as a source of Christian hope, and as a model of Christian love is not sufficient unto itself to change even fellow Catholics' minds and behavior on debated issues.

People can thoroughly admire him as a person even as they continue to think and act in disagreement with his views.

A case in point: Pope John Paul II had incurred the wrath of many Italians during the days immediately preceding the shooting because of his outspoken advocacy of the repeal of Italy's abortion law.

After the pope was struck down by his assailant's bullets, it was widely assumed throughout Italy and in other countries that there would be a sympathy vote for him in the hotly contested referendum.

But to the surprise and consternation of many, the voters in 97.5 percent Catholic Italy rejected the widely publicized papal view by a two-to-one margin.

Italy's controversial three-year-old law remains intact: Women over the age of 18, and minors with the consent of their parents, may have abortions during the first 90 days of pregnancy.

The teaching of the Church on abortion is clear—prophetically so. One can only deplore the holocaustic trend in society today to destroy fetal human life without proportionate reason.

So the lesson of the Italian referendum is not that the pope is wrong and the voters are right. The lesson is that personal popularity is not automatically translated into political clout.

It is a lesson especially for our brothers and sisters on the Catholic right, who think the Church is going to get back to their way because they now have a strong pope who's on their side. They are bound to be disappointed.

There are very, very few Catholics the pope can really compel to his way of thinking or penalize for acting contrary to his wishes. These are the Church's priests. But therein lies another story for another week.

In the meantime, the whole Church looks forward to the day when Pope John Paul II returns to full health and resumes his ministry of showing us all what it means to be human, so that we can more fully understand what it means to be Christian and Catholic.

Observers Compare Late Pope, Soviet Leader

(August 12, 1988)

It was inevitable. The parallel was simply too close to ignore.

Serious political observers are beginning to note remarkable similarities between Soviet leader Mikhail Gorbachev and the late Pope John XXIII.

Does it seem farfetched, if not irreverent, to draw such a comparison?

A recent article in the *Boston Globe* by Olin Robison, president of Middlebury College in Vermont and a longtime adviser to the State Department on Soviet affairs, makes a persuasive case for it.

Robison argues that the Soviet Communist party conference held in Moscow at the end of June was to Gorbachev what Vatican II was to John XXIII.

In October 1962, during the fourth year of his papacy, Pope John convened the Church's 21st ecumenical council in order to bring about an updating (*aggiornamento*) of the Catholic Church. It was the first such council to be held in 92 years.

Right from the start it became clear that the unquestioned power of the Roman Curia had been broken. The curialists tried to set and then control the agenda, but they failed.

During the opening debates various documents prepared by the Vatican bureaucrats were strongly criticized and then rejected. The outcome stunned everyone, including even the progressive bishops and their advisers. They simply didn't realize how widespread the desire for reform had become.

In June 1988, in the fourth year of *his* reign as general secretary of the Communist party of the Soviet Union, Gorbachev convened the 19th party conference in an attempt to restructure (*perestroika*) and modernize Soviet communism—what Robison calls "the most expansive secular religion of the 20th century."

"It has been 43 years since the last party conference, which in its own way [like Vatican I] also dealt with the subject of infallibility."

Pope John had announced that he was throwing open the windows to let some fresh air into the Church. In his turn, Gorbachev proclaimed a new era of openness (*glasnost*) for the Soviet Union.

Robison is quick to point out, lest anyone take offense at such comparisons, that Lenin had expected the Communist party to replace the Church in the lives of the Russian people.

It has not turned out that way, but the notion remains. And so the party conference was intended to articulate "a new vision of the Marxist-Leninist faith."

The secular religion that Gorbachev is trying to modernize is no less captive to entrenched bureaucratic interests than was the Catholic Church in Pope John's time.

As was the case with the aged pope at Vatican II, Gorbachev's primary goal at the party conference was to set and control the agenda. They were to be his ideas to which others reacted. They were to be his initiatives that others would support or resist.

Because ideology is as important in the Soviet system as doctrine is in the Catholic Church, the party conference, like the council, had a second major purpose: to make the boundaries of the faith less rigid.

"Never mind," Robison observes, "whether it works, or whether it is practical. The Soviet system cannot change in fundamental ways unless and until there is a rearticulation of Marxist-Leninist ideology to suit the moment."

Gorbachev, therefore, was very careful in his opening three-and-a-half hour speech to insist that his program for reform was firmly grounded in the true faith of Marx and Lenin.

He had to keep his conservatives in line. After all, it was their support that had been crucial in his selection as general secretary, just as the votes of conservative cardinals had been decisive in finally putting Angelo Roncalli over the top in 1958.

Although Gorbachev's lengthy agenda (like Pope John's) could not possibly have been acted upon, it didn't really matter. Just as the process had counted most for John XXIII at Vatican II, so it was the process that now counted most for Gorbachev at the party conference.

Vatican II made it impossible for the Catholic Church to go back to the old ways (as schismatic Archbp. Marcel Lefebvre came to realize). Robison suggests that Gorbachev would be fortunate if his party conference were to achieve the same result for the Soviet Union and its Communist party.

What Robison doesn't mention in his perceptive article is that the forces of reaction never give up. Even if Gorbachev prevails, there will always be resistance, as his successors will discover.

Both inside and outside the party hierarchy, some will stubbornly refuse to accept Gorbachev's program of *perestroika,* and they will use every available bureaucratic maneuver to thwart it, in spite of the 19th party conference.

Just as some Catholics, both inside and outside the hierarchy, continue to resist John XXIII's call for *aggiornamento,* in spite of the Second Vatican Council.

Take the Time to Listen to the Pope Speak

(June 1, 1990)

With his recent eight-day visit to Mexico (his second to that country since his election in 1978), Pope John Paul II continues his exhausting schedule of pilgrimages and pastoral visitations all around the world.

Each of these trips has several components: round-trip flights, airport greetings, motorcades, meetings with government officials and other dignitaries, meetings with local bishops, clergy, religious, and lay groups, visits to hospitals, orphanages, poor neighborhoods, and the like, celebration of the Eucharist in churches and in open fields and stadiums, and speeches—hundreds and hundreds of them.

For many people, absorbed in a visual culture dominated by television, a papal visit is composed only of airport ceremonies, motorcades, and outdoor Masses. Those are what make the evening news—in 30 seconds or less.

Almost never are the pope's speeches highlighted. A few of them are reported in the print media, but television, not the press, shapes the public's perception of what's important.

Without denying that what the pope *does* is of great importance, I should suggest that many Catholics miss the full significance of these papal trips because they ignore, or are simply unaware of, what the pope *says* during them.

Catholics of one type (let's call them conservative or traditional, for want of better terms) readily applaud the pope's penchant for far-flung travel.

They tingle with pride at the sight of world and national leaders bowing before the pope, and the white-robed Successor of Peter, regally erect in his glass-encased popemobile, blessing the cheering throngs of well-wishers all along the motorcade route or presiding in wind-blown vestments at a Mass attended by hundreds of thousands of people.

But these same conservative Catholics tend to pay little or no attention to what the pope says on such occasions, especially his prophetically pointed and consistently emphatic exhortations on social and economic justice.

Catholics of another type (let's call them liberal or progressive, for want of better terms) tend to be critical of Pope John Paul II's pastoral globe-hopping.

Their reasons vary: the trips are too costly or too triumphalistic or encourage a cult of personality.

To the extent that these liberal Catholics pay any attention to what the pope says during these trips, they somehow manage to notice only his predictable reaffirmations of Church teaching on birth control and abortion.

Both groups of Catholics render their judgments about papal trips on the basis of partial evidence only.

Take again, for example, the pope's recent visit to Mexico.

On May 9 in Durango John Paul II delivered himself of a devastating critique of modern capitalism, so cherished by his neoconservative admirers in the United States.

The collapse of communism in Eastern Europe, he said, does not mean that capitalism has triumphed. On the contrary, he chastised capitalism for having neglected its ethical responsibilities.

He accused capitalists of pursuing profits "at any price," at the expense of workers' rights, social justice, and the environment.

He also directly challenged the neoconservative dogma that production, not distribution, is the answer to the problem of economic imbalance in the world.

"The excessive hoarding of riches by some," the pope declared, "denies them to the majority, and thus the very wealth that is accumulated generates poverty.

"We must not forget," he said in words that could be directed at President Bush and U.S. congressional leaders as they ponder ways of reducing the federal deficit, "that often it is the poor who are forced to make sacrifices while the possessors of great riches do not show themselves ready to renounce their privileges for the good of others."

Liberal Catholics should applaud those papal words, but they either don't hear them or don't believe he means them. Conservative Catholics, on the other hand, should take those words to heart, but they close their ears to them instead.

The very next day in Chihuahua the pope preached another hard sermon, but this time about birth control and abortion.

"If the possibility of conceiving a child is artificially eliminated in the conjugal act," he said, "couples shut themselves off from God and oppose his will."

Invigorating words for conservative Catholics; off-putting words for liberal Catholics. But, again, neither side is really listening.

Their focus of attention is on the airport, the motorcade, and the mass-audience Eucharist. Conservatives like those; liberals are bothered by it all.

If only the pope could find a way to make his strongest supporters really listen to what he is saying about social and economic justice. It would be good for them because it would test their loyalty not only to him but to the gospel itself.

An Excursion into the Future with Pope John XXIV

(September 28, 1990)

VATICAN CITY—With a series of sweeping moves designed to change the course and image of the Catholic Church as it prepares to enter the 21st century and the third Christian millennium, the newly elected Pope John XXIV has firmly grasped the levers of papal power less than three days after his surprising first-ballot election.

The 64-year-old Italian pontiff has decided not to wait until his formal installation as the 264th successor of St. Peter as bishop of Rome and earthly head of the Roman Catholic Church.

A Jesuit and an accomplished biblical scholar, the new pope has announced his intention to call another ecumenical council, Vatican III, to address such subjects as traditional Catholic teaching on human sexuality, including contraception; the vocational crisis in the priesthood, with special attention to the discipline of celibacy; the place of women in the Church and the current prohibition against the ordination of women; and the present structure and powers of the Roman Curia.

In the meantime, he has abolished the college of cardinals and established a commission to propose a more broadly participatory way of electing his own successor.

He announced, at the same time, the resignation of Card. Joseph Ratzinger as prefect of the Congregation for the Doctrine of the Faith, and the suspension of all investigations of theologians by that office.

Among other actions taken by the scholarly pontiff were the abandonment of the Universal Catechism project and the proposed schema on Catholic universities, as well as the nullification of the recently promulgated loyalty oath and profession of faith.

In his first public appearance on the balcony of St. Peter's Basilica immediately following his election last Sunday, the new pope sent an unmistakably clear signal that his pontificate would take the Church in a completely different direction from that of his predecessor.

In place of the traditional white cassock worn by popes since the election of a Dominican in the Middle Ages, the new pope greeted the cheering throngs in St. Peter's Square in unadorned black garb.

His words on that occasion were also simple and direct: "I come before you as a servant in the manner of Christ and of *his* humble servant, the saintly predecessor whose name I have dared to take, Pope John XXIII of truly happy memory," he said.

"What I presume to offer before all else is hope. As the Church enters a new century and a new millennium, we must show the world what it means to be a community of understanding, of patience, of mercy, and of compassion.

"At the same time, the Church itself must remain acutely conscious of its own sinfulness and weakness. That is why I will issue no call for discipline and obedience, unless it is the discipline of the gospel, which is good news, and unless it is obedience to the reign of God, which is a reign of justice and peace.

"The faith that we proclaim," he continued, "must be a faith that does justice, especially on behalf of the poor and the powerless."

And then he revealed that his first trip outside Italy would be to El Salvador, where he will celebrate the Eucharist on the spot where six Jesuits were murdered by right-wing military forces in November 1989 and in the church where Archbp. Oscar Arnulfo Romero was assassinated while saying Mass in 1980. The pope referred to all seven as "martyrs in the cause of justice."

At a subsequent press conference, the pope fielded questions straightforwardly and with ease. He said that Vatican Council III would include laypersons as well as bishops, and at least as many women as men. Formal invitations will also be extended to representatives of other Christian churches. Unlike the practice of the previous council, however, these delegates will have the right to participate directly in the discussions and debates.

"I expect that some members of the Church who were pleased with many ecclesiastical policies during the past decade will not be comfortable with the changes I have announced since my election," he told the press.

"I want them to know that I love them all as sisters and brothers in Christ and that I have no intention or desire to hinder them in the practice of their faith as their consciences guide them.

"On the other hand," he continued, "such Catholics must show the same respect for others in the Church who are determined to move the Church forward again in the spirit of Vatican Council II, revising where necessary certain structures and disciplines in order to meet the enormous challenges of the coming century.

"But I am hopeful about the future, because the Spirit is with the Church. So long as we do not try to contain or to control the Spirit, we shall not fail. This can be, indeed, a new springtime for the Church."

There was general and sustained applause, even from many in the press section.

12

The Future of the Church:
Looking Toward the Third Christian Millennium

We're living in a time that Alvin Toffler once called "future shock," in a best-selling book of the same title. Jules Verne's late 19th-century science fiction fantasies are today's technological realities. And the developmental process continues to accelerate. So, too, in the field of politics.

Who would have guessed, as recently as the early 1980s when the Solidarity movement in Poland was outlawed and many of its leaders were in prison, that a leading Solidarity intellectual, Tadeusz Mazowiecki, would have been appointed prime minister of the Polish government and Solidarity leader Lech Walesa would have been elected president of Poland?

Indeed, who could have imagined, back in the days when Pres. Ronald Reagan referred to the Soviet Union as "the Evil Empire," that the Soviet Union itself would select a leader who would be compared with the late Pope John XXIII or that he would have generated across the face of Europe a new form of political enthusiasm known as "Gorby fever"? And who could have anticipated the break-up of the Soviet Union in 1991, preceded by the failed coup attempt of August 19 and the declarations of independence by the various republics?

"Future shock" was also generated by the political upheavals throughout the rest of Eastern Europe: in East Germany, with the dramatic opening of the Berlin Wall in November 1989, followed by the formal reunification of the two Germanys, in Czechoslovakia, Hungary, Bulgaria, Romania, and even the last Stalinist holdout, Albania. Václav Havel, imprisoned as a dissident less than a year earlier, became president of Czechoslovakia!

The phenomenon of "future shock" also applies to the Church, as it moves closer in time not only to a new century but also a new millennium. Since no event in this century has had a more profound impact on the life of the Catholic Church or even on Christianity at large than the Second Vatican Council, we cannot possibly understand these last two decades and a half of Catholic history without reference to the council, nor are we even minimally prepared for the 21st century and the beginning of the third Christian millennium.

Vatican II's Guidelines for the Future

1. The first and most basic theological principle advanced at Vatican II is that the Church is a *mystery,* or *sacrament.*

To say that the Church is a mystery means, in the words of the late Pope Paul VI, that it is "a reality imbued with the hidden presence of God." In other words, the Church is not just an organization to which we belong or that we serve. It is the corporate presence of God in Christ, with a unity created and sustained by the Holy Spirit.

A sacramental understanding of the Church has helped us to see how essential renewal and reform are to its mission and ministries. *Perestroika,* if you will. More and more, the Church has had to practice what it preaches because the Church recognizes more surely than ever before that it has a missionary obligation to manifest what it embodies. It is supposed to be a visible sign of the invisible presence of God in the world and in human history.

In the words of the document "Justice in the World," from the 1971 Synod of Bishops: "While the Church is bound to give witness to justice, it recognizes that anyone who ventures to speak to people about justice must first be just in their eyes."

I should expect that this sacramental understanding of the Church will continue to shape the life and ministries of the Catholic Church in the years to come. More and more frequently, the connection will be made between the call for justice *outside* the Church and the practice of justice *inside* the Church. Indeed, this is the great unfinished business of Catholic social teachings, which, as of May 15, 1991, have been a full century in the making.

In their pastoral message of November 1990, to mark the centenary of Pope Leo XIII's social encyclical, *Rerum Novarum,* the U.S. Catholic bishops acknowledged that Catholic social teachings must apply equally to the Church itself. "We are also called," they said, "to weave our social teaching into every dimension of Catholic life, especially worship, education, planning and evangelization. . . . We cannot celebrate a faith we do not practice. We cannot proclaim a gospel we do not live."

The bishops' 1986 pastoral letter on the U.S. economy was even stronger in its language: "*All the moral principles that govern the just operation of any economic endeavor apply to the church and its many agencies and institutions; indeed the church should be exemplary.*"

How Catholics function as Church at the parish, diocesan, regional, and national levels, in the Catholic school, or in any Catholic agency and institution, how money is spent, how ministries are distributed and exercised, what sort of environment is provided for worship and education, how pastoral leaders live—all this teaches more than all of the Church's textbooks, films, videos, and special programs together.

The principle of sacramentality is as practical a principle as Catholics shall ever be called upon to implement between now and the beginning of the 21st century—and indeed *into* the new century and the new millennium. Catholicism's mission, according to the Second Vatican Council, is to be a universal sacrament, or sign, of salvation for all the world.

Gustavo Gutiérrez made the same point in his now-classic work, *A Theology of Liberation* (Maryknoll, N.Y.: Orbis Books, 1973): "If we conceive of the Church as a sacrament of the salvation of the world," Gutiérrez insisted, "then it has all the more obligation to manifest in its visible structures the message that it bears. . . . The break with an unjust social order and the search for new ecclesial structures . . . have their basis in this ecclesiological perspective" (p. 261).

As always, it's not a question of either/or but of both/and.

2. A second major theological principle advanced by the council is embodied in its now-familiar insistence that the Church is the whole *People of God*. The Church is not only the hierarchy, the clergy, or members of religious communities. It is the whole community of the baptized. And that community is marked by a rich diversity of class, education, social status, race, ethnic background, and culture.

The People-of-God principle also highlights the plurality of charisms and ministries that have always belonged in the Church and that now are beginning to flourish anew. *Lumen Gentium* affirms that charisms are available to all the faithful, "of every rank" (n. 12). Indeed, the whole Church, and not just the ordained or religiously professed, is called to holiness (*Lumen Gentium*, chap. 5).

We find this People-of-God principle realized, with very different degrees of success, in parish councils, in base communities, in the multiplication of so-called lay ministries, and particularly in ministries associated with liturgy, education, and social justice.

The Church that enters the 21st century and the third Christian millennium will be a church in which even more of its members, women and men alike, will be ministerially involved, as they are increasingly today. But unless the Church changes its current discipline on obligatory celibacy and opens the way to the ordination of women, and unless a different kind of bishop is appointed, less ideologically rigid and more pastorally open, it will be a Church with too few ordained priests who are at the same time healthy human beings.

As always, the principle of sacramentality remains crucial. If we are truly the People of God, we must look and act like the People of God. Catholics have to practice what they preach and teach, and then preach and teach what they practice.

3. A third major conciliar theme is contained in its teaching that the mission of the Church includes *service* to human needs in the social, economic, and political orders, as well as the preaching of the Word and the celebration of the sacraments.

Better still: evangelization, that is, the preaching of the gospel, essentially includes the pursuit of justice and the transformation of the world. As Pope Paul VI put it in his Apostolic Exhortation of 1975, *Evangelii Nuntiandi* (The Evangelization of the Modern World), evangelization involves "a message especially energetic today about liberation."

This surely represents one of the most significant changes wrought by the council. The Church is seen now, more clearly than ever before, as a Servant Church, an instrument of social justice, human rights, and peace, as well as the comforter of the afflicted, the healer of the spiritually sick, the reconciler of sinners, and the like. Again, it's not a matter of either/or but of both/and. The Church is called to be both the comforter of the afflicted and the afflicter of the comfortable.

It is highly instructive that even so conservative a pope as John Paul II should continue to be so forthright, so aggressive, in fact, about the Church's social teachings. This is evident not only in his social encyclicals, especially the 1981 document *Laborem Exercens* (On Human Work), the 1988 document *Sollicitudo Rei Socialis* (The Social Concern of the Church), and the 1991 document *Centesimus Annus* (The One Hundredth Year), but also in the homilies and public addresses Pope John Paul II has given in Central and South America, in Poland, in the Philippines, in Africa, and at the United Nations.

As the Church moves into the 21st century and the third Christian millennium, one expects that its social teachings will focus with increasing frequency on a moral issue to which the pope has been especially sensitive: consumerism. Not the consumerism we in the United States may identify with Ralph Nader's movement but the consumerism criticized in Pope John Paul II's first encyclical, *Redemptor Hominis,* published in 1979, and in the U.S. Catholic bishops' 1986 pastoral letter on the economy.

Consumerism is the sin of consuming more than we need, even for comfortable living, in a world where so many have less than they need even for bare human survival. Faithful Christian discipleship challenges consumerism. We have a right to what we need, but we have an obligation in justice, and not only in charity, to share what the medieval theologians called our "superfluous goods" with others in greater, and sometimes desperate, need. As the pope reminded us in his famous sermon at Yankee Stadium in New York in October of 1979, this moral principle applies to nations as well as individuals.

"We cannot stand idly by, enjoying our own riches and freedom," the pope declared, "if, in any place, the Lazarus of the 20th century stands at our doors. In the light of the parable of Christ, riches and freedom mean a special responsibility. Riches and freedom create a special obligation."

Preaching in Edmonton, Alberta, on September 17, 1984, the pope declared that "in the light of Christ's words, this poor South will judge the rich North. And the poor people and poor nations—poor in different ways, not only lacking food, but also deprived of freedom and other human rights—will judge those people who take these goods away from them, amassing to themselves the imperialistic monopoly of economic and political supremacy at the expense of others."

"The kind of talk one heard from Pope John Paul," William F. Buckley wrote in his syndicated column soon thereafter, "is generally heard in the United Nations, and generally listened to by nobody."

"The problem now and as far back as the popes have got into big-think economic matters," Buckley continued, "is that they tend, driven no doubt by the impulses of magnanimity, always to think of distribution, never to think of production." But once again, it's not a matter of either/or but of both/and.

It goes without saying that Catholic social doctrine is not a message that is universally applauded in the Church. It meets with resistance by some and with indifference by most.

The challenge Catholics face as they approach the 21st century and the third Christian millennium is to articulate much more effectively, and then really put into practice, Catholic social teachings. Nowhere is this dual responsibility more sharply stated than in the 1971 World Synod's "Justice in the World," chapter III. On the one hand, we are reminded that "action on behalf of justice and participation in the transformation of the world" are "a constitutive dimension of the preaching of the Gospel." On the other hand, we are also reminded of the sacramental nature of that commitment to justice: "While the Church is bound to give witness to justice, it recognizes that anyone who ventures to speak to people about justice must first be just in their eyes."

Both/and, not either/or.

4. A fourth conciliar theme is expressed in the principle that the Church includes more than Catholics. The Church is the whole Body of Christ: Catholic, Eastern Orthodox, Anglican, Protestant, and Oriental Christian alike. The Church is *ecumenical*, which means, literally, that it embraces "the whole wide world."

These postconciliar years have been marked by formal ecumenical dialogues, joint prayer, collaboration in social ministry, and cooperation in theological and pastoral education.

It is now theologically improper to use the word *church* and mean only the Catholic Church, unless we make it clear that we are, in fact, limiting our reference to Catholicism.

Although newsworthy advances have been few and far between in recent years, the ecumenical movement still lives. There were ecumenical observers at the 1985 Extraordinary Synod in Rome, and they issued a generally positive statement about the synod and about their hopes for the future of ecumenism.

Perhaps the most successful of all the pope's many trips abroad was his visit to England in June of 1982, in the midst of the Falklands War between Britain and Argentina. It was an ecumenical triumph, highlighted by a joint prayer service led by the pope and the Anglican archbishop of Canterbury, Robert Runcie. Catholic-Anglican relations in Britain have never been the same since, so profound an impact did the visit make.

Ecumenism will continue to shape the course of Catholic life and mission well into the next century, in all the areas where it has already made its mark. Two major breakthroughs remain to be achieved, but I dare not predict they will occur before the year 2001.

The first will involve some official recognition of, and support for, intercommunion, on however limited a basis; and the second, some official recognition of the validity of one another's ordained ministries, at least between churches where substantial agreements have already been reached, such as Catholics and Anglicans, and Catholics and Lutherans.

But these issues infrequently touch ordinary Catholics at the parish and diocesan levels. The real challenge to ecumenism that affects Christians at the level of everyday life is that of biblical *fundamentalism,* embraced now by many thousands of Catholics and ex-Catholics.

A prominent Catholic biblical scholar once observed that the number of Catholics who have been lost to the Catholic Church because of the dissenting views of Hans Küng could hold a convention in a telephone booth, but the number lost because of biblical fundamentalism is in the hundreds of thousands.

Biblical fundamentalism may be the single most serious threat to Catholic faith in the United States and in Latin America today—greater even than Charles Curran and Leonardo Boff!

As I pointed out in chapter 3, in my column of July 26, 1985, thousands of Catholics belong to fundamentalist Bible-study groups and flock to preaching-and-healing services in convention centers and outdoor stadiums all across the United States and Latin America. And there are countless ex-Catholics in the Jehovah's Witnesses, the Assembly of God, and various Pentecostal churches.

The phenomenon warranted a front-page report in the Sunday *New York Times* of May 15, 1989. "In a huge cultural transformation that is changing the face of religion in the United States," began the report, "millions of Hispanic Americans have left the Roman Catholic Church for evangelical Protestant denominations.

"From storefront churches in urban slums to gleaming temples along suburban freeways, perhaps more than four million of the roughly 20 million Hispanic Americans now practice some form of Protestant Christianity, according to several demographic studies," the story continued.

"And the movement away from Catholicism, which traditionally claimed virtually the entire Hispanic population, has accelerated in the 1980's."

The Catholic biblical renewal, endorsed by Pope Pius XII and given new impetus by the Second Vatican Council, has had no impact at all on such Catholics' catechetical formation—and I am not limiting my remarks to Hispanic Catholics. They are equally applicable to non-Hispanic Catholics.

It is as if the biblical renewal of the 1940s, 1950s, and 1960s did not happen. Many continue to read the Bible (*when* they read it) as any uninformed Catholic might have read it 50 years ago.

But the Catholic Church's most effective response to the challenge of biblical fundamentalism will not be one of condemnation or ridicule. The Church will have to commit itself anew to the best biblical education it can provide. Everything it does must have a solid biblical foundation: courses, workshops, conferences, retreats, days of prayer, programs of spirituality, homilies, lectures, and educational publications of every kind.

"Just as the life of the Church grows through persistent participation in the Eucharistic mystery," the council declared in its Dogmatic Constitution on

Divine Revelation (n. 26), "so we may hope for a new surge of spiritual vitality from intensified veneration for God's word, which 'lasts forever.' "

The stakes are high: "For ignorance of the Scriptures is ignorance of Christ," as St. Jerome put it.

I have selected only four conciliar principles to illuminate Catholicism's path into the next century and the next millennium, but these are among the Council's most important teachings on the Church. They have guided and shaped its life during these postconciliar years and one hopes they will continue to do so into the next decade, into the next century, and into the next millennium. There are forces of reaction at work in the Church today that would like to prevent that from happening.

Cardinal Leo Jozef Suenens of Belgium, one of the great leading figures at Vatican II, once spoke of the teachings of the Second Vatican Council as seeds. They are there "like unopened buds awaiting the sun."

The council has been adjourned now since 1965 and the buds continue to open.

In the meantime, Catholics continue to affirm with the council's Pastoral Constitution on the Church in the Modern World that beneath all the changes we have experienced in the Church and in the world at large, "there are many realities which do not change and which have their ultimate foundation in Christ, who is the same yesterday and today, and forever" (*Gaudium et Spes*, n. 10).

This is the faith and the hope that Catholics will bring to the dawn of the 21st century and the third Christian millennium.

List of Columns

Chapter 3: Catholics in Conflict

Chapter 4: Ordained Ministry

Chapter 5: Laypersons in the Church

Chapter 6: Women in the Church

Chapter 7: Church and Society

Index of Names